DAWN LANGMAN undertook a mainstream speech and acting training in Australia, followed by seven years of performing and teaching at secondary and tertiary levels. Her quest for an integrated approach that includes the spiritual dimension led her to train with Maisie Jones at the London School of Speech Formation in the method developed by Rudolf and Marie Steiner. She then taught for ten years at Emerson College in Sussex. Following this, Dawn trained in Michael Chekhov's acting technique with Ted Pugh and Fern Sloan of the Actors Ensemble in New York. Returning to Australia, she founded the School of the Living Word, where for eight years she continued to research the integration of Speech Formation with Chekhov's technique. She currently teaches this methodology at the Drama Centre, Flinders University, South Australia. Dawn is the author of *The Art of Acting, The Art of Speech* (both 2014), and *Tongues of Flame, The Actor of the Future Vol. 1* and *Word Made Flesh, The Actor of the Future Vol. 2* (both 2019).

By the same author:

*The Art of Acting, Body—Soul—Spirit—Word, A Practical and Spiritual Guide*

*The Art of Speech, Body—Soul—Spirit—Word, A Practical and Spiritual Guide*

*Tongues of Flame, A Meta-Historical Approach to Drama, The Actor of the Future, Vol. 1*

*Word Made Flesh, The Actor of the Future, Vol. 2*

# BETWEEN EARTH AND HEAVEN

## *The Actor of the Future, Vol. 3*

### DAWN LANGMAN

Original artwork by Raphaela Mazzone

TEMPLE LODGE

Temple Lodge Publishing,
Hillside House, The Square
Forest Row, RH18 5ES

www.templelodge.com

Published by Temple Lodge 2021



A catalogue record for this book is available from the British Library

ISBN 978 1 912230 82 2

Cover by Morgan Creative
Typeset by Symbiosys Technologies, Visakhapatnam, India
Printed and bound by 4Edge Ltd., Essex

'…what should such fellows as I do crawling between earth and heaven?'

*Hamlet*, Act 3, scene 1

*Creative Speech transforms the human larynx into a grail cup*

*Eurythmy integrates the human ether body with the life that sustains the universe*

# Contents

# Acknowledgements

Thanks to all of you whose encouragement and belief in this unfolding work, throughout so many years, has given me the courage to continue; friends who have supported me with your enthusiasm, time and energy, your skills and honest appraisal of what was not yet working; who have become the team on which I have relied and without whom this volume and the series of books of which it is a part, would not exist.

My long time editor Clare Strahan who has faithfully read and reworked the endlessly proliferating drafts the project has required and, against all odds, made space for its demands within the commitments to your own life and creative work.

Tanya Coburn who miraculously always reappears to rescue us when needed with your editing expertise and depth of insight. Without you this volume would not have seen the light of day.

Raphaela Mazzone, whose images and illustrations have expressed what I could never have expressed in words and who responds with gracious equanimity to each tentative additional request for 'just one more'.

Diane Tatum for the sun-filled spirit of adventure of your wise eurythmic guidance.

Annika Andersdottir for the depth of your speech and eurythmic guidance.

Margot Horne for your depth of insight into all things astrological and astrosophical.

Dr Jane Gilmer, for your ongoing support and feedback and the contribution you have made to the evolution of my ideas in Chapter 8 through the opportunity to provide feedback on the manuscript of your own book 'The Alchemical Actor'.

Dr Diane Caracciolo, and Lindsay Dearlove for your depth of insight and honest feedback about style and content.

Katerina Vlachou and Clement Kouroukis for your guidance in all things Greek.

Marjolein Baars for your guidance in all things comedic.

Penelope Snowdon-Lait for your depth of insight into speech.

Neil Anderson and Renate Millonig for your support and guidance philosophical.

Rosamond Luffman for your hours of patient listening and the crystal clarity of your insights, especially in relation to Chapters 7 and 8.

Nicole Ostini and Katrina Stowe whose devotion to the practice of this methodology has helped it to evolve and allowed you to discern how to clarify the text for the practitioner.

Rosalba, for your belief in me and in my work, your steadfast support throughout the years and the opportunities you have provided for my research to continue as an artist and a teacher.

William and Patricia for your lifelong support.

# Introduction

> There are more things in heaven and earth, Horatio,
> Than are dreamt of in your philosophy.
>
> *Hamlet*, Act 1, scene 5

In this third volume of *The Actor of the Future*, as I continue to share my research into the applications of the integrated Steiner speech and Chekhov acting methodologies, ever richer pathways are revealed for actors of the future. These include processes that allow us to explore even more of Steiner's indications from the *Speech and Drama* course and to understand more deeply the impact Steiner had on Chekhov's work. The expanded vision of character-creation for actors of the future, arising from the cosmic perspective of the human being — the fruit of Steiner's spiritual-scientific work — invites us to consider how every aspect of technique (no less the tools for life than art) can be illumined by it.

Proficiency in Chekhov's basic psycho-physical techniques for actors and Steiner's art of speech formation or creative speech[*] makes it possible to integrate the two in increasingly sophisticated combinations. *The Actor of the Future 2, Word Made Flesh* explored how the integration of these two streams of work achieves its full potential when it is enriched by the practice of eurythmy. This present volume takes that integration and enrichment further. Through the processes explored, our instrument becomes ever more receptive to the infinite ways in which the supersensible dimensions of our work, grounded in precise and reliable techniques', can stream into the actor's psycho-physical experience.

It would be impossible to describe each time again the basic processes on which each exploration in this book is based. Therefore, readers will always be referred to the relevant sections in the other books within this series, which it is presumed will be on hand. The increasingly advanced ability to layer different tools results in more complexity and depth in the artistic research undertaken. However, because of the vast range of tools available and the protean nature of creativity, I have not found it possible to lead the reader on a linear path from one step to another. Nevertheless each chapter serves as a gathering point for related themes and processes. The vastness of the themes explored and the impossibility of including in these books a basic course in eurythmy, has meant that I have leapt over its preliminary steps in order to suggest the contribution that this

---

[*]See page 221 of *The Art of Speech* for a discussion of these names. In recent years the term 'creative speech' has been more wisely adopted as the English rendering of '*sprachgestaltung*' and will henceforth be used throughout these books.

art can make to actors of the future. It is hoped, however, that the glimpses offered will inspire the need in some to undertake the basic work. Nevertheless the last four chapters progress from an initial exploration of the vowels as expressions of the planetary beings, to suggest how this can enrich and deepen other themes of research for the actor of the future.

My discoveries may well be different from those of others. The experience and insight such explorations generate can only ever represent our current level of artistic evolution and will continue to evolve and change as we ourselves mature. What matters is that the tools bequeathed by Steiner and by Chekhov provide us with a speech and acting methodology that takes its place amongst the other theatre practices that claim direct experience as a valid basis for investigation of artistic questions.[*]

As in my other books, the phenomenonological foundation of this work has often meant I needed to convey a more immediate, visceral, emotional experience. Therefore readers can expect to weave between more objective prose and a 'stream of consciousness' attempt, *always in italics,* to invite them into that direct experience.

In her Preface to Steiner's *Speech and Drama* course, Marie Steiner writes:

> To understand what is offered to us in these lectures on the Arts of Speech and Drama we must be ready to affirm the cosmic spirituality that lies hidden behind the world of appearances; and if we want to go further and put into practice what we have learned, we shall find we need to have real experience of this hidden cosmic substantiality … Provided our vision is free and unclouded, we shall be able to recognise in the sounds of speech our divine teachers and to know the very breath of man as cosmic substance actively at work within him.

This 'real experience of the hidden cosmic substantiality' in all its layers and complexity lies at the heart of the processes developed in these books, based as they are on research into Steiner's *Speech and Drama* course. The integrated speech and acting methodology, deepened by the practice of eurythmy, that forms the content of these books, constitutes a spiritual, psychophysical technique that allows us to experience, as direct sensation in our instrument, the creative impulses at work within the cosmos.

This volume 3 will build towards a focus on the rich dimensions that the spiritual beings, whose activity is centred in the planetary spheres, contribute to our lives and artistry. Although brief glimpses will be given from the region of the zodiac, our investigation of the starry realm will be more central to the theme of volume 4.

Once again it must be understood that experience and knowledge of the basics of eurythmy and Creative Speech, on which so many of the processes suggested here

---

*See Appendix A: A phenomenological approach.

depend, lie outside what can be encompassed in these books. Therefore, I encourage anyone who has not experienced these basics in a living way but feels inspired by their possibilities to seek the teachers and/or trainings who provide them.[*]

The chapters that follow suggest how the skills developed so far can cross-fertilise each other and provide the basis for developing new skills. As they do so they transform our instrument into an ever more richly textured organ through which our intuitions may be sensed and realised.

---

*See Appendix F.

**Chapter 1**

# Advanced layering of Steiner/Chekhov processes

When we observe creation in the world of nature, we can become aware of archetypal principles that, if we learn to work with them, also support us as creators in the human world. We met these principles first in *The Art of Acting* through the processes designed by Chekhov to explore the sense of *ease*, *beauty*, *form* and *the whole* which he referred to as *Four Brothers*. It is time now to explore them further, particularly in relation to Creative Speech. In addition to the vocal skills we have already gained, we can learn how to consciously control our use of volume, pitch and tempo to serve these creative principles. In doing so our application of these skills will not be crass or arbitrary.

## The archetypal process of creation

In the realm of nature, creation begins when the feminine principle is fertilised by the masculine,[*] followed by a merging of their qualities within the seed. It then evolves from stage to stage through intensifying cycles, culminating in a final form. Depending on the levels of complexity involved, the culmination of each stage within a cycle may manifest as a new form or organ. For example, on the way to the mature plant we see successive forms unfolding from the seed; root, stem, leaf, flower and finally the fruit, which, in turn, contains the seed for further cycles of creation.

Intensification manifests in *space* through cycles of expansion and contraction. It manifests in *time* through change of tempo. Periods of growth in which outwardly (in space) nothing seems to happen or happens only very slowly, are followed by a quickening of tempo that culminates in a climax or explosion of the impulse that had been gathered inwardly throughout the time of outer inactivity. We see this in the sudden springtime spurt of growth that quickens and expands from the outwardly inactive buds of winter.

For all the stages in these cycles within cycles to unfold, the impulse driving the creation has to pre-exist, whether we call it the divine thought in the seed or a genetic code. Of course, human beings can construct something as we go along, without a pre-existing impulse. But for construction to become creation, the *sense of the whole* that gives

---

* The theme of masculine and feminine will be explored more fully in Chapter 7.

birth to the impulse, and the meaningful forms in which it clothes itself along the way towards completion, must at some point be intuited.

To consciously create depends on our cooperation with these principles. We learn the skills within our chosen medium that allow us to contract and gather in order to intensify, and build towards a climax that is finally released as outer form into the world. Or, in the case that it is not the final form, how not to lose the impulse but gather what has thus far been achieved, sense its place within the cycles of creation and use our skills to once again intensify and build towards the next stage of its current cycle.

In the context of our work, what enables the speaker to cooperate with this fundamental principle are the skills to control our use of *volume*, *pitch* and *tempo*. We have been working with them all along but without identifying how their qualities might serve our present purpose. We can learn this from the way they manifest in that other art in which the creative principles express themselves in sound: the art of music.

Great music demonstrates how volume, pitch and tempo work together to generate experience within our souls. We can therefore use it to develop our appreciation of their contribution when we speak. Before we learn how to consciously apply their voice and speech equivalents, it would be good to recognise how all along, even when we have been focusing on other tasks, our voice and speech unconsciously adjust, becoming louder or softer, higher or lower, faster or slower. We will begin by observing how these vocal qualities respond when we layer Steiner's fundamental *breathing styles* (declamation and recitation) with Chekhov's *qualities and sensations* and *qualities of movement*. This advanced application makes our instruments more flexible and will allow us to observe the range of tempo, pitch and volume that we have available.

## Integrating the two styles of breathing with Chekhov's qualities-of-movement*

### Exploration 1—Breathing style for declamation

Reforging gales

Through foghorns

Hails through surges

Through whirlpools

Whirlpool wails

In wavering

Wails in quavering

Waves veiling

---

* See *The Art of Speech*, pp. 100–113 and *The Art of Acting*, pp. 57–66.

Waving breathing
In freedom
Freedom winning
Kindling

*Declamation and moulding*
1.  Warm up *reforging gales*.
2.  Warm up *moulding* full-bodily with its accompanying speech exercises.
3.  Layer *reforging gales* with *moulding*.

*Declamation and floating*
Repeat steps 1–3 above, substituting *moulding* with *floating*.

*Declamation and flying*
Repeat steps 1–3 above, substituting *moulding* with *flying*.

*Declamation and radiating*
Repeat steps 1–3 above, substituting *moulding* with *radiating*.

## Exploration 2—Breathing style for recitation

In the vast unmeasured world-wide spaces
In the endless stream of time
In the depths of human soul life
In the world's great revelations
Seek the unfolding of life's great mystery

*Recitation and moulding*
1.  Warm up *in the vast*.
2.  Warm up *moulding*.
3.  Layer *in the vast* with *moulding*.

*Recitation and floating*
Repeat steps 1–3 above, substituting *floating* for moulding.

*Recitation and flying*
Repeat steps 1–3 above, substituting *flying* for moulding.

*Recitation and radiating*
Repeat steps 1–3 above, substituting *radiating* for moulding.

## *Integrating the two styles of breathing with Chekhov's qualities and sensations*

### *Exploration 3 — Reforging gales — qualities and sensations*

1. Warm up *reforging gales*.
2. Warm up a series of *qualities and sensations* e.g. sadly, joyfully, fearfully, confidently, angrily, bravely etc.
3. When your instrument is penetrated thoroughly, layer each quality in turn with *reforging gales*.

### *Exploration 4 — In the vast — qualities and sensations*

Repeat steps 1–3 above replacing *reforging gales* with *in the vast*.


If you observed how volume, pitch and tempo unconsciously adjusted in response to changing other layers of artistic choice, you can learn how to use them consciously to serve the laws of the creative process: contract and gather, intensify, expand and build to climax, then release.

Our qualities of voice depend on the interaction of muscle tensions in our mouth, throat and larynx with the tensions in chest and diaphragm that organise our breath. It is a fact of our anatomy that increase of volume, pitch and tempo all require increase of tension in our vocal instrument. However, we can only access these *necessary* tensions without *unnecessary* tension if we distribute them throughout our instrument. Chekhov's full-bodied, psychophysical approach provides the methodology for implementing this support. In *The Art of Acting* and *The Art of Speech* we laid the basis for working with the range of volume, pitch and tempo in this healthy way. Without such support we force the muscles of our throat to strain as they bear the full responsibility in isolation.

Now we can learn how to adjust these tensions consciously to craft a text.Physical analysis of sound shows that what we perceive as *volume*, *pitch* and *tempo* are continuums of wavelengths, frequencies and energies. These can all extend beyond what can be tolerated by the psycho-physical-etheric constitution we inhabit in the world of time and space. To tamper with the healthy edges of each range risks damage to our instrument. Hearing is affected when our ears are constantly subjected to excessive volume. Vocal chords develop nodules from consistent strain. Pathologies aside, we are organised so finely that we generally hear *only that portion of the spectrum of soundwaves we can process healthily*. Bombardment with wavelengths of greater or lesser amplitude (volume) or frequency (pitch) than our instrument has been designed to register and process can be harmful, as can the excessive tensions to which our speech organs are subjected when we shout too loudly, speak too quickly or produce an unnaturally low or higher pitch.

Technology is able to transport our bodies at ever greater speed and increase the decibels that make routine the violations of our healthy hearing threshold. Nevertheless the negative effects on those who are more sensitive (including animals) reveal how unconscious we can be of the consequences for our subtle bodies of excessive speed or volume. For, as Vladimir observes in *Waiting for Godot*, 'Habit is a great deadener.'

When speaking is approached in a solely mechanistic way, the need to achieve extremes of volume, pitch or tempo can tempt us to distort or manipulate the voice in ways that harm our instrument. However, to master these most physical aspects of our voice in healthy ways, we need to recognise they have their roots in levels of activity that are no less grounded in the spiritual dimension of reality that lies beyond the range of our material perception than any other aspect of our art.

The following explorations invite us to extend the spectrum of our vocal expressivity by learning to control the ability to move within our range of volume, pitch and tempo, in a healthy way. This will enable us to craft a text using the creative principle: *contract, intensify, expand* and *build to climax*, then *release*. Once again, we use *reforging gales* and *in the vast*, this time to focus on each range in turn.

## *Volume*

We aim to use volume, from maximum to minimum, to craft a text. Shouting strains the throat and sounds aggressive. Even when that is not what is intended, other nuances of soul are overpowered in more or less degree by what sounds like anger.* A louder voice does not equate to more intensity nor a softer voice to less: each end of the spectrum takes us to a threshold. At the loudest end the voice comes closest to embodying the density of matter; at the softest, it refines that density until our perception hovers at the edge of spirit once again. Our goal is to never be so loud that the volume overpowers our capacity to form our breath with the shaping forces of the consonants or to ensoul the vowels and yet, however soft, still be able to project and intensify. Until we master this capacity, undifferentiated loudness pushed out by unhealthy tension in the throat or a weak voice unable to project will remain our default settings.

It will help us to remember that strength of volume can only be achieved without undue tension in the throat if the increased necessary tension is distributed throughout our body. This can be easily achieved by the processes described in the explorations into counter tensions,† and for warming up your will centre.‡

---

* See *The Art of Speech*, pp. 150-160.
† See *The Art of Acting*, pp. 77–83.
‡ See *The Art of Acting*, pp. 140–146.

### *Volume exploration 1*

Improvise chopping up a large log of wood. Each blow makes you aware that the next one needs more strength. For this greater strength to be effective, it cannot just be generated through the arms and shoulders, but must be supported by the muscles of your whole instrument: your diaphragm (allowing you to breathe more deeply as required), your hips and thighs, your calves and ankles and the way your feet grip the earth.

Before each blow, therefore, take the time to ground yourself with the support it needs and let your voice release organically with your exertion.

As you adapt this sequence of sensations and integrate them with the volume explorations, it will become second nature when you want to speak more loudly, to ground yourself more deeply so your voice is channelled through the whole of you.

### *Volume exploration 2*

Warm up the volume and projection work on pages 150–160 of *The Art of Speech*.

### *Volume exploration 3—Reforging gales*

Let us treat *reforging gales* as an artistic text.

1. Try a simple progression. Speak the first line as softly as you can. Increase the volume with each line. Whatever degree of volume you are aiming for you must still form it out of breath, penetrated by the active consonants. In this way even a softer voice can still be the bearer of intensity. Learn to sense how each increase in volume needs correspondingly more breath and more activity to form it with the consonants. This will ensure that your voice is not just louder but penetrated with your consciousness.
2. Now make the first line your loudest and decrease the volume with each line while still intensifying your activity.

3. Explore intensifying through the range from soft-to-loud and loud-to-soft.

4. Build towards a climax with the loudest volume in the final line.

5. Try beginning with your loudest line: an explosion out of which the other lines unfold more softly but without reducing their intensity.

6. Build to the major climax at the end with a lesser one along the way.

7. Experiment with how to build intensity and climax with a softer voice. Can you achieve a climax with the softest line?

8. Experiment with changing volume to create lesser climaxes along the way towards the major one.

Observe the range of volume you are able to achieve by integrating full-bodied penetration of your instrument, increased breath and consonant activity. Trust that if you work in this healthy way your ability to speak more loudly, healthily, will strengthen. Learn to recognise the threshold between loudness achieved by straining and loudness you can manage healthily without the violation of that boundary.

### Volume—reforging gales/qualities and sensations

1. Layer the text with *qualities and sensations* e.g. sadly, joyfully, angrily, warily.

2. Repeat steps 1–8 of *volume exploration 2*.

### Volume—reforging gales/monologue to partner

1. A and B, make eye contact.

2. A, treat *reforging gales* as a monologue. Engage your partner and take them with you through the build-up of intensity towards the climax, using shifts in volume to achieve it.

3. Reverse roles.

### Volume—reforging gales/dialogue with partner

1. Treat *reforging gales* as a dialogue, A exchanging lines with B.

2. Use shifts in volume to achieve the build-up of intensity in your exchange.

3. Learn to listen so you can respond to each other's shifts in volume with your own. Use your whole range of volume, not just the extremes.

4. Layer the exchange with different *qualities and sensations*. Sometimes A and B prepare the same quality, for instance, *sadly*: sometimes each prepare a different one. For example: A, *sadly*, B, *compassionately* or *impatiently*.

When we treat 'In the vast' as an artistic text, our focus shifts from the intense outpouring of immediate sensation and emotion demanded by *reforging gales* to our quest to channel it through *clarity of thought*.

### *Exploration 4—Volume/In the vast*

Repeat all the steps of *volume explorations 3*, substituting *in the vast* for *reforging gales*.

# *Pitch*

To master the full range of our vocal pitch without distortion, we need to understand that pitch reflects our psycho-physical relationship to *gravity* and *levity*.

### *Pitch exploration 1*

1.  Warm up the gravity/levity work on pages 118–121 of *The Art of Acting*.
2.  Warm up the exercises that while they do not, of necessity, demand a higher pitch, nevertheless encourage and support the high end of your range: floating/bubbling and flying, *children chiding* on pages 62–64 of *The Art of Acting* and page 121 of *The Art of Speech*.
3.  Warm up the exercises that while they do not, of necessity, demand a lower pitch, nevertheless encourage and support the low end of your range: moulding, floating/ loppety; *judicious genial* on pages 59–60 and 122 of *The Art of Acting* and pages 40 and 122 of *The Art of Speech*.
4.  Warm up the exercises that encourage you to move from high to low and back again, e.g. *to whit twinkle* from page 124 of *The Art of Speech,* and the whole range of floating on pages 60–62 of *The Art of Acting*.

### *Pitch exploration 2*

Work with *volume explorations 1–4*, substituting *pitch* for *volume* as the means to shape the text towards a climax: as a soliloquy, a monologue in interaction with a partner, and finally a dialogue.

# *Tempo*

The healthy mastery of tempo also requires that we do not rip it from its greater context in our human instrument and our experience. Gilbert and Sullivan operas are full of entertaining choruses and arias whose comedy depends on the ability to speak/sing at a tempo that defies belief and yet can still be understood. However, such patter songs depend precisely on the separation of the will and feelings from the intellect. The genre of rap often features fast tempo driven by an unrelenting beat. This means that, unless handled by a genius, the emotional intensity out of which the words were born is flattened and the voice divested of emotion.

The path we are exploring here teaches how to work with tempo in a way that integrates our will and feeling with our clarity of thought; an integration which will be revealed in Chapter 2 to be a central feature of the modern pathway of initiation. We do not want to speak so quickly that we cannot integrate our mind and heart with what we say. Speaking with a faster tempo for artistic purposes is not the same as rushing so fast that the words become incomprehensible. Nor should speaking slowly lead to loss of dynamic or intensity.

## Pause

Pause is one of our most potent tools. It is the stillness that exists in the infinity beyond extremes of fast and slow, in which nothing happens outwardly. We can move so quickly that we are flung by the momentum beyond the threshold that has kept us in the plane of time or we can slow down to the point of total stillness. Each of these extremes result in what we call a 'pause'. This is not an empty gap when it is filled with the intensity of conscious presence and activity. We use the expression 'pregnant pause'. But a pause is only pregnant when it is filled with what has been and what is preparing to become.

### Tempo exploration 1
1. Warm up the tempo and dynamic work on pages 104–115 of *The Art of Acting*.
2. Warm up any other exercises that provide the opportunity for change and flexibility of tempo: e.g. *to whit twinkle twas … name neat norman* etc.

### Tempo exploration 2
Work with the steps explored in *volume explorations 1–4*, but substitute shifts in *tempo* and *dynamic* (including *pause*) for *volume* as the means to shape the monologues and/or build your vocal interaction with a partner.

## Combining all three skills

You have probably observed it is not possible to isolate the elements of volume, pitch and tempo. Focusing on one always activates the others. However, as you master your control of each, so will your ability to consciously combine them grow.

### Combining volume, pitch, tempo exploration 1
1. Warm up the preparations for volume, pitch and tempo (including pause).
2. Work with the steps explored in *volume explorations 1-3* but experiment with integrating volume, pitch and tempo in all their combinations as the means to shape each monologue or dialogue.

Observe that you cannot build towards a climax unless the impulse to do so was prepared from the beginning. You cannot only think of and construct it as you go along. From that very first line, the listener must feel engaged in the journey and led by your intention step by step towards the culmination.

When you are confident with all three skills then treat *reforging gales* and *in the vast* as a monologue or dialogue consisting of two beats, then three etc. In other words, when you have built to your climax at the end of each, instead of ending there, gather all that you achieved into a new beginning that builds towards a second and so on.

## *Artistic application*

The following speeches from a scene in Peter Schaffer's *Equus* which I have condensed into a monologue, provide an opportunity to integrate management of volume, pitch and tempo with a declamatory use of breath. Like *reforging gales*, Alan's language in this monologue suggests predominantly short bursts of intense emotion and sensation and requires us to control the increase of intensity through several cycles, each of which builds towards its own climax that in turn contributes to the final one.

If our application of these skills is not to sound simplistic, the impulses and energy that drive the speech must arise within the depth of Alan's character. A few layers will serve our present purpose:

- The full-bodied exploration of such *archetypes* as 'rebellious teenager', 'ecstatic worshipper', 'heroic warrior'.
- A full-bodied exploration of the stages of his ride. Begin with his run and jump onto the horse and follow the progression of verbs from 'stay', to 'walk', 'trot', 'canter', 'gallop'. Sustain the journey of sensation generated by this full-bodied action sequence while reducing outer movement to a minimum, finally to standing in one place.

Each stage of movement creates a tempo framework for your journey through each section of the text. Identify the climax of each stage and use your tools of volume, pitch and tempo to intensify, remaining in control as you build the culminating climax of the speech.

Until now, Alan has resisted the psychiatrist's attempts to understand what drove the boy to blind the horses that he loved. Under hypnosis, Alan finally relives the secret weekly midnight ritual in which he rides his horse. He runs and leaps up onto Nugget's back:

*Alan*: Hurts! … Hurts! … Knives in his skin! Little knives — all inside my legs. Stay, Equus. No one said Go! ... That's it. He's good. Equus the Godslave, Faithful and True. Into my hands he commends himself — naked in his chinkle-chankle. [He punches Nugget] Stop it! ... He wants to go so badly ... [ritually] Equus — son of Fleckwus — son of Neckwus — Walk ... Here we go. The king rides out on Equus, mightiest of horses. Only I can ride him. He lets me turn him this way and that. His neck comes out of my body. It lifts in the dark. Equus, my God–slave! ... Now the king commands you. Tonight, we ride against them all ... My foes and his ...

My foes. The Hosts of Hoover, the Hosts of Philco. The Hosts of Pifco. The House of Remington and all its tribe! ...

His foes. The Hosts of Jodhpur. The Hosts of Bowler and Gymkhana; All those who show him off for their vanity. Tie rosettes on his head for their vanity! Come on, Equus. Let's get them! ...Trot. Stea-dy! Stea-dy! Stead-y! Stead-y! Cowboys are watching! Take off their Stetsons. They know who we are. They're admiring us! Bowing low unto us! Come on now — show them! Canter! ... CANTER! [He whips Nugget.]

And Equus the Mighty rose against All!

His enemies scatter, his enemies fall!

TURN!

Trample them, trample them,

Trample them, trample them,

TURN!

TURN!

TURN!

[Shouting] WEE! ... WAA! ...WONDERFUL!...

I'm stiff! Stiff in the wind!

My mane, stiff in the wind!

My flanks! My hooves!

Mane on my legs, on my flanks, like whips!

Raw! Raw! I'm raw! Raw!

Feel me on you! On you! On you!

I want to be in you!

I want to BE you forever and ever!

Equus, I love you!

Now!

Bear me away!

Make us One Person.

[He rides Equus frantically.] One Person! One Person! One Person! One Person! [He rises up on the horse's back, and calls like a trumpet] Ha–HA! ... Ha-HA! ... Ha-HA! [The trumpet turns to great cries] HA-HA! HA-HA! HA-HA! HA-HA! HA! ... HA! ... HAAAAA! [He twists like a flame. Silence ...] AMEN!

In contrast, the following monologue from Shaw's *St Joan* allows us to apply these skills to sentences whose structures require the use of breath to weave our way through complex passages of thought—like *in the vast*. Once again, we need to find the impulse and the energy that drives the speeches in the character itself. Therefore, it would be good initially to separate the task of character-development from that of mastering the sentence structures. As we gain confidence in both, these layers will integrate. We will then be driven by impulses arising from the circumstances and the character, yet remain in control of volume, pitch and tempo in order to gather, intensify, release, gather, intensify, release, from one climax to another through the web of main and secondary clauses, till we reach the major climax at the end.

Here are some character suggestions:

- Full-bodied exploration of the *archetypes* of 'peasant', 'saint' and 'warrior' and how they interweave and integrate.
- Psychological gestures embodying her possible objectives, for example: *I want to fight for truth; I want to expose your corruption and hypocrisy.*
- *Qualities and sensations:* fearfully, courageously, trustingly, exhaustedly, resolutely.

As the work progresses the rest of the ensemble/class can create the environment of accusation in which she has to speak. This can be done very simply if each member chooses a few accusing words or phrases such as 'heretic', 'burn the witch', 'how dare you?' and finds a PG (psychological gesture) to express the accuser's objective and uses these to interject Joan's speech and interact with her.

When Joan understands that by denying the divine inspiration of her voices she has saved herself from burning at the stake but not from life imprisonment, she tears up the confession she had signed.

*Joan*: Yes: they told me you were fools and that I was not to listen to your fine words nor trust to your charity. You promised me my life but you lied. You think that life is nothing but not being stone dead. It is not the bread and water that I fear. I can live on bread: when have I asked for more? It is no hardship to drink water if the water be clean. Bread has no sorrow for me and water no affliction. But to shut me from the light of the sky and the sight of the fields and flowers; to chain my feet so that I can never again ride with the soldiers nor climb the hills; to make me breathe foul damp darkness, and keep me from everything that brings me back to the love of God when your wickedness and foolishness tempt me to hate Him; all this is worse than the furnace in the Bible that was heated seven times. I could do without my warhorse; I could drag about in a skirt; I could let the banners and the trumpets and the knights and soldiers pass me and leave me behind as they leave the other women, if only I could still hear the wind in the trees, the larks in the sunshine, the young lambs crying through the healthy frost, and the blessed, blessed church bells that send my angel voices floating to me on the wind.

But without these things I cannot live; and by your wanting to take them away from me or from any human creature, I know that your counsel is of the devil, and that mine is of God.

On page 216-219 of *The Art of Speech* we explored how to differentiate in speech between main and auxiliary/secondary phrases and clauses. Here are my suggestions for identifying main and secondary clauses in Joan's last more complex sentences and how they interweave with the intensifications that enable us to build towards a climax. If we layer the processes decribed in *The Art of Speech* with our skills in using volume, pitch and tempo it will allow us to create a clear journey through these structures before we try to integrate them with the character and situation.

## *Structure of long sentences*
### *(main structure is bold, secondary structures bracketed, progressions of numbers and letters suggest stages of intensification)*

First sentence:

But

    1. **to shut me** a) **from the light of the sky** b) **and the sight of the fields and flowers**

    2. **to chain my feet** [so that I can never again a) ride with the soldiers b) nor climb the hills]

    3. **to make me breathe foul damp darkness**

    4. **and keep from me everything that brings me back to the love of God** [when a) your wickedness b) and your foolishness tempt me to hate Him]

**all this is worse than the furnace in the Bible** [that was heated seven times].

Second sentence:

    1. **I could do without my warhorse;**

    2. **I could drag about in a skirt;**

    3. **I could let the**

        a) **banners** b) **and the trumpets** c) **and the knights** d) **and soldiers**

    i)  **pass me**

    ii)  **and leave me behind** [as they leave the other women],

*if only*

**I could still hear**

    a)  **the wind in the trees,**

    b)  **the larks in the sunshine,**

    c)  **the young lambs** [crying through the healthy frost],

    d)  **and the blessed, blessed church bells** [that send my angel voices floating to me on the wind].

## The 'Four Temperaments' and Chekhov's qualities-of-movement

As explored in *The Actor of the Future 1*, Chekhov's psycho-physical technique is but one of several attempts in the last 100 years to explore the intimate connection between soul and body in relation to performance practice. These include Meyerhold's experiments in Russia and Grotowski's later on in Poland, Eugenio Barba's at the Odin Theatre based in Denmark, and Suzuki's based on the eastern stylised tradition.[*]

It is in this larger context that Steiner's observations find their place concerning movements that grant access to the inner life of characters known to a more ancient system of psychology as the four temperaments.[1] At first glance, they may seem unrelated to Chekhov's qualities-of-movement, that we explored as a basis for these temperaments on pages 71-74 in *The Art of Acting*. Yet we will see that our capacities to *mould* and *float* and *fly* and *radiate* allow us to experience the truth of Steiner's observations and reveal their compatiblity with Chekhov's psycho-physical techniques.

## *The four temperaments*

It was not Steiner's task to provide a systematic methodology for actors but to plant seeds out of which a future methodology might grow. The examples in the *Speech and Drama* course based on his observation of the temperaments illustrate how deeply he understood the psycho-physical connection. Chekhov's methodology allows us to integrate his own comprehensive psycho-physical technique with Steiner's observations.

Our immersion in how the principles of *archetypal* and *particular* translate into full-bodied or naturalistic movement/gestures,[†] has taught us that even our tiniest

---

[*]  See *The Actor of the Future 1: Tongues of Flame*, Chapter 5.

[†]  See *The Art of Acting*, Terms of reference.

or seemingly most trivial and insignificant movements can be potentised when they embody impulses arising from our inner life. We have learned to identify and channel these more consciously by expanding them into their full-bodied counterparts. We have also learned how to move back and forth between full-bodied (level 10) and naturalistic (level 1): condensing macro gestures and dynamics into their micro counterparts and expanding them again to reveal the energies, dynamics and intentions out of which they have arisen.

## Melancholic

Steiner observed that by suppressing the natural expression of our sorrow or compassion, not allowing the muscles of our face to respond, we press the emotion deeper into our psycho-physical constitution. This arouses the sensation of the *melancholic* temperament. He suggests we can experiment like this: while we listen to a passage being read that arouses our sorrowful compassion, we slowly move our head and consciously control our facial muscles so that no expression is revealed. Gertrude's description of Ophelia's death in Act 4, scene 7 of *Hamlet* is one suggestion.

If we practise this with instrument attuned, we recognise the movement to be level 1 of a continuum we can expand to the full-bodied level 10 commitment to the quality of movement we identify as *moulding*. If we move back and forth between levels 10–1, we discover that the slow movement of the head that Steiner recommends does not take place in isolation but is the final remnant (naturalistic level 1) into which the full-bodied (level 10) *moulding* has condensed. Moving back and forth between levels 10–1 we recognise that the movement of the head described by Steiner is indeed a stage in the continuum of *moulding* as explored in *The Art of Acting*. This enables us to integrate it with the forces we require to speak and also with other layers of a character who shows a *melancholic* tendency but cannot be reduced entirely to its type.

## Phlegmatic

To experience the *phlegmatic's* body of sensation, Steiner suggests that we allow our face to sink into the level of repose that happens as we fall asleep: holding back all movement, allowing nostrils and eyelids to droop and in the upper lip, no muscular response. Described in this way, once again his instructions appear isolated from the whole human being and not able to be integrated in a complex context. But if we do the experiment with instrument attuned, we are led into the psycho-physical awareness that outer stillness is not the same as inactivity. If we pay attention to the subtle sensations that arise from relaxation of the facial muscles in repose and expand that relaxation into full-bodied movement (level 10) we find that we are *floating*. The face in repose is the level 1 counterpart of *floating*. Our imagination of the liquid element in which we float full-bodily finds expression at the micro-level in the glandular secretion which Steiner has observed. Once again our mastery of moving back and forth through the whole continuum from level 1 (where the floating sensation permeates our instrument but is hardly outwardly perceptible) to level 10, enables us to integrate it with the forces we require to speak and other layers of a character who shows phlegmatic tendencies but cannot be reduced entirely to its type.[*]

## *Sanguine*

To access the body of sensations of a *sanguine* temperament, Steiner suggests that the actor responds to a sensational announcement with vigorous, expansive movements of the face, arms and hands. Attempting the experiment with instrument attuned and expanding the movements to full-bodied level 10 results in *flying*. The level of expression first described is more like level 8–10 than level 1 (least outwardly perceptible). Once again, our mastery of moving back and forth through the whole continuum enables us to integrate the sanguine body of sensation with the forces we require to speak and other layers of a character whose tendencies are sanguine but cannot be reduced entirely to its type.

Lopakhin's announcement in Act 4 of Chekhov's *Cherry Orchard*, that he, the son of a serf, was the one who bought the cherry orchard at the auction, serves as a sensational announcement. Made to the astonished gathering, of course each character will process their response in different ways but, for the purpose of the exercise, each actor can explore what Steiner has proposed.

## *Choleric*

To access the *choleric* body of sensation, Steiner suggests we stand with soles of the feet planted firmly on the earth while we listen to a passage of abuse with all our muscles tense: especially our calves held taut, fists clenched and knitted brow. We find, as we did with the melancholic and phlegmatic temperaments, that the concentration of the energy resulting from the full-bodied gesture of restraint intensifies sensations that are not released. When we do release them into full-bodied movement level 10, we find that we are *radiating fire*. Restraining the outer movement while sustaining the intense sensation is a process we recognise by now. Once again our mastery of moving back and forth through the continuum enables us to integrate the choleric body of sensation with the forces required to speak and other layers of a character who shows choleric tendencies but cannot be reduced entirely to its type.

The speeches of Queen Margaret and York from Act 1, scene 4 of Shakespeare's *Henry VI, Part 3* provide many opportunities to hurl abuse and to be on the receiving end.

---

[*] See, *The Art of Acting*, pp. 71–74.

### Balancing the temperaments

Human beings can tranform their one-sided tendencies and bring them into balance with the less developed aspects of their nature. Such a character is Brutus in Shakespeare's *Julius Caesar*. In the last words of the play, Marc Antony describes his friend as someone in whom 'all the elements [were] so mixed ... that all the world could say, "Here was a man".' Our experiments integrating Chekhov's *qualities-of-movement* with Steiner's corresponding observations provide us with tools to explore some of the layers that compose a balanced human being.

### Balancing temperaments exploration 1

1. Identify moments in the play when Brutus displays:
    a) The melancholic's deep and serious concern.
    b) The phlegmatic's slow reaction to conflict or resistance.
    c) The mercurial enthusiasm and excited interest of the sanguine.
    d) The choleric's burning will to overcome resistance or injustice.
2. Allow each tendency to manifest and then be held in check by the other three.

Other characters providing opportunities to balance all the temperaments are Sir Thomas More in Robert Bolt's *A Man for all Seasons*; Paulina in *The Winter's Tale*, and Cordelia in *King Lear*.

# Chapter 2

# Advanced applications of the three centres and their speech placements

*Figure 1 Head centre, heart centre, will centre*

The following explorations provide opportunities to strengthen and become more flexible in weaving full-bodily and vocally between our head, heart and will functions. Our growing skills allow us to experiment in a range of artistic contexts. We begin by examining the thinking function of our soul.

## *Layering the head-centre with psychological gesture (PG)— bringing will into our thinking*

As discussed in *The Art of Speech*, there is a fundamental difference between the passive state of *having thoughts* and the activity required for us *to think*.[*] The latter requires that we direct our will, whose forces stream into our limbs through the centre in our belly, to penetrate the function that is channelled through the centre in our head. Language contains many idioms whose images express the thinking that requires the activation of our will:

- *wrestle* with an idea/problem;
- *explore* or *investigate* an idea/feeling/problem;
- *rack* our brains;
- *give birth* to an idea;
- William Blake's *mental fight*;
- this image from Gerard Manley Hopkins' sonnet:

O the mind, mind has mountains, cliffs of fall;
Frightful, sheer, no man fathomed. Hold them cheap
May who ne'er hung there.

When we explore these images full-bodily, the resulting muscular activity, integrated with the head-centre and its speech placement, generate a body of sensation that enables us to actively engage with the thought-content of a text.

### *Speech placement/centre exploration 1—Will into thinking*

1. Explore full-bodily each of the idioms above and condense your movement into a PG that embodies its objective.
2. Integrate your PG with the full-bodied movement generated through the centre in your belly.
3. Consciously direct that body of sensation through the centre in your head so you experience the *active will* that takes place in your mind.

---

* *The Art of Speech*, Chapter 2, pp. 110–112.

4. Channel it through the speech exercises for the speech placement: *see fee shielding* etc.*

5. Layer all of this into *in the vast* etc.†

### Speech placement/centre exploration 2—Will into thinking (application to text)

Apply the process to the excavation of the thought-content of a text. As always when approaching text, it is helpful to begin by rendering its content in your own words. The struggle to give birth to the thoughts ourselves forces us to activate our will. Then we can carry the sensation of that struggle back into the text, not just reciting finished thoughts but creating them anew.

1. Warm up your character choices for St Joan.

2. Layer them with steps 1–5 from *speech/centre exploration 1* and explore the thought-content of the *St Joan* monologue from Chapter 1.

3. Explore the same processes with other texts, especially Shakespeare's.

## The application of thinking, will and feeling to character development

Mastery of the full-bodied work with archetypal centres along with their accompanying speech placements gives us many tools for character enrichment and more precise deliniation. Unlikely as it is that any character would function exclusively in only one of these, we do observe that some people are predominantly thinking, will or feeling types. Others function more through two of them, and a few rare individuals achieve a conscious integration of all three. Most commonly in life, however, we observe how each may take its turn to dominate depending on the situation or the moment. *Now I am filled with feelings and emotion; now my thinking takes control; now I am moved to action.*

Remembering that the following suggestions are in no way meant to be prescriptive, we focus first on shifts of function in a single character. These choices on their own cannot constitute a character creation. It is assumed the character has already been or can still be developed according to the principles explored in *The Art of Acting*. What follows allows us to more precisely craft the different functions as they manifest throughout the character's experience.

---

* *The Art of Speech*, pp. 136–137.
† *The Art of Speech*, pp. 109–112.

### *Speech placement/centre exploration 3—thinking, will and feeling functions in a single character*

*Lady Macbeth*

1. Warm up the full-bodied work and speech exercises from pages 131–142 of *The Art of Speech*.

2. Warm up a few basic choices for her character e.g. archetypes, PGs, qualities and sensations etc.

3. Apply the suggested centres with their speech placements to the following examples:

*Will*

She dominates her husband with her will:

> But screw your courage to the sticking-place
> And we'll not fail.

She suppresses her compassion by imposing her will on herself:

> Come you spirits that tend on mortal thoughts
> Unsex me here and fill me from the crown
> To the toe top full of direst cruelty …

*Thinking*

She tries to understand her husband:

> … Yet do I fear thy nature;
> It is too full o' the milk of human kindness
> To catch the nearest way; thou wouldst be great,
> Art not without ambition, but without
> The illness should attend it; what thou wouldst highly,
> That wouldst thou holily; wouldst not play false,
> And yet wouldst wrongly win …

Later, after her dream of power has been shattered, she tries to penetrate her own experience with understanding:

> Nought's had, all's spent,
> Where our desire is got without content.

'Tis safer to be that which we destroy
Than by destruction dwell in doubtful joy.

*Feeling*
She remembers the moment of the murder, how she felt the difference between the idea
of killing and the actuality:

Yet, who would have thought the old man to have had so much blood in him?
… All the perfumes in Arabia will not sweeten this little hand. Oh, Oh, Oh!

*Hamlet*
1.  Warm up the full-bodied work and speech exercises from pages 131–142 of *The Art
    of Speech*.
2.  Warm up basic choices for his character, e.g. archetypes, PGs, qualities and sensa-
    tions etc.
3.  Apply the suggested centres with their speech placements to the following extracts:

*Thinking*
With his razor-sharp wit he deflects his own pain and the attempts by others to find
where he has hidden the body of Polonius:

Not where he eats but where he is eaten: a certain convocation of politic worms are e'en at
him. Your worm is your only emperor for diet. We fat all creatures else to fat us, and we fat
ourselves for maggots: your fat king and your lean beggar is but variable service; two dishes
but to one table: that's the end.

Any passage of extended self-reflection in his soliloquies, or as in this example:

I have heard
That guilty creatures, sitting at a play,
Have, by the very cunning of the scene
Been struck so to the soul that presently
They have proclaimed their malefactions.
For murder, though it hath no tongue, will speak
With most miraculous organ.

*Will*
At last Hamlet acts decisively by leaping into Ophelia's grave:

This is I, Hamlet the Dane.

*Feeling*
He expresses his love for Ophelia:

> I loved Ophelia: Forty thousand brothers
> Could not, with all their quantity of love,
> Make up my sum …

### Speech placement/centre exploration 4—identifying thinking, will and feeling in a single character

1. Warm up the full-bodied work and speech exercises from pages 131–142 of *The Art of Speech*.
2. Prepare basic choices for a character you are working on e.g. archetypes, PGs, qualities and sensations etc.
3. Apply the suggested centres with their speech placements to the text you are working with.

### Speech placement/centre exploration 5—identifying thinking, will and feeling types

Now we focus on characters that suggest a dominant function that acts as a fundamental layer in the structure of the character.

1. Apply steps 1–3 of *speech placement/centre exploration 4* to the following characters and texts.

The words of the three daughters of King Lear suggest the following choices:

*Thinking*
  *Regan*: We shall *think* further on it.

*Feeling*
  *Cordelia*: Alas! I cannot heave my *heart* into my mouth.

*Willing*
  *Goneril*: We must *do* something and in the heat.

Hamlet, Romeo and Fortinbras:

*Thinking*
  *Hamlet*: To be or not to be: that is the question …

*Feeling*

> *Romeo*: If I profane, with my unworthiest hand
> This holy shrine, the gentle sin is this:
> My lips, two blushing pilgrims, ready stand
> To smooth that rough touch with a tender kiss.

*Willing*

> *Fortinbras*: Go captain, from me greet the Danish king …
> Go! Bid the soldiers shoot!

None of these characters function exclusively from one centre.

Hamlet is often overwhelmed by his intense emotion and we are told throughout the play how capable of action he has been and still could be, if he were convinced of what action he should take. However, it is fundamental to his disposition that he analyse each moment with his thinking; he is tormented and paralysed by relentless, self-conscious introspection.

Likewise, though Romeo is capable of thought and action, his behaviour is determined by his strong emotions.

Fortinbras, at the end of *Hamlet*, is confronted with the bodies of the dead and forced to think about the implications of a life of violence. Yet he remains fundamentally a warrior and, as Hamlet earlier observed, is someone whose thoughts and feelings never block his will to action.

## *Integrating speech placement and centre with iambic pentameter*

Shakespeare's plays provide a template for the actor just as many great musicians claim Bach's music does for them. They stretch us beyond the earthly levels of experience in which their characters are firmly anchored, into the archetypes and supersensible realities that stream into our lives. We can take full advantage of this gift when we master the rhythm of his language and the infinite dimensions it calls forth in our souls. Integrating this with our growing mastery of speech placements and the archetypal centres allows us to express the range of experience embodied in his words. As our instrument evolves we are empowered by the strength and flexibility, the pulsing heartbeat of his lines.[*]

### *Speech placement/iambic pentameter exploration 1*

1. Stand and gently press your hands against your heart. Become aware of your heartbeat. Feel its pulse: shortlong shortlong shortlong.

---

[*] For a detailed exploration of the iambic pentameter see *The Art of Speech* pages 181-187 and page 184 for the significance in this rhythm of the number 5.

2.  Gently and as intimately as your own breath, sound the rhythm as your hands express the pulse:

$$\cup \quad — \quad \cup \quad — \quad \cup \quad — \quad \cup \quad — \quad \cup \quad —$$

boom boom/ boom boom/ boom boom /boom boom/ boom boom

3.  Step the rhythm, gathering enough breath and impulse to take you through the five feet, feeling how the pulsing of your blood provides the impulse for each line. Observe when the rhythm's living pulse degenerates into a mechanistic beat and reawaken the sensation of the flow of blood that pulses through your heart.

4.  Experiment with change of tempo: how the same rhythm (five feet in a line) can arouse a different mood or feeling when the line is fast or slow.

5.  Experiment with changing tempo. For example, begin a line slowly and increase the tempo. Or begin quickly and slow down.

6.  Speak the words as you step the line, alternating *shortlong shortlong* with *boom boom*.

## *Speech placement/iambic pentameter exploration 2—heart centre*

1.  Warm up your heart centre with its speech placement on the lips and *by miner wafer/ by boom/by vie*.

2.  Step the rhythm while you speak the following words. Keep the rhythm regular while you digest the words, feeling how the impulse of each line streams from your heart. When you are confident, speak and feel how the life flow of your blood, pulsing through your heart provides the driving impulse through each line:

> My heart brims over with my love for you,
> Your beauty woos me, soft and warm and sweet,
> My wounded heart, untrusting, dares to hope.

3.  As each line courses through you, interrupt the steady flow with your intentioned emphasis. Try each line in several different ways. You are still carried by the underlying pulse or current through the line but now the words or syllables no longer correspond exactly to the beat but carry your particular intention.

4.  While you work your way inside the words and rhythm, keep your voice as intimate as your heartbeat and your breath.

5.  As you become more confident in integrating all the layers (speech placement, centre, words, intentioned emphasis and rhythm), experiment with tempo, pitch and volume to further shape this heart-based monologue .

6. When you are ready, work with a partner and exchange each set of lines as a dialogue, playing with their combinations.

### *Speech placement/iambic pentameter exploration 3—head centre*

1. Repeat the steps of speech placement/iambic pentameter *exploration 2*, substituting the heart centre/lips placement with the head centre/teeth placement exercises *see fee/shielding/reeled far/full reeled needy*.

2. When your instrument has been prepared, explore these words, following steps 3–5 in the previous exploration:

> My intellect is razor-sharp as yours,
> My rapier wit can slice and pierce and poke,
> Dissect my syllables to make my point.

3. When you are ready, work with a partner and exchange each set of lines as a dialogue, playing with their combinations.

### *Speech placement/iambic pentameter exploration 4—centre in the belly*

1. Once again repeat the steps of *speech placement/iambic pentameter exploration 3*, this time substituting the head centre/teeth placement with the will centre/soft palate placement exercises *noon air lark anger ink/ink ringer growl/ink ringer grows shaft*.

2. When you are ready, explore these words, following steps 3–5 in *exploration 2*:

> I grab you and I grapple, grip for grip,
> I want to know my equal, strength for strength,
> A foe that neither buckles nor retreats,
> I want you under my complete control.

### *Speech placement/iambic pentameter exploration 5—partner work*

When you are ready, work with a partner to exchange each set of lines as a dialogue, experimenting with their combinations.

1. A and B, warm up with the heart centre and its speech placement.

2. Make contact and approach each other; use the lines from *iambic pentameter exploration 2* as dialogue, interchanging and repeating them in any order.
3. Once you are confident, create an interaction of 6–8 lines that crescendo to a climax.
4. Repeat steps 1–3 with the lines for the head centre.
5. Repeat steps 1–3 with the lines for the will centre.

### Speech placement/iambic pentameter exploration 6—partner work with Shakespeare text

Using the above explorations to prepare, apply the work of the previous explorations to the following dialogues from Shakespeare.

### Heart centre

*Romeo and Juliet*, Act I, scene 5, rhyming iambic pentameter, based on sonnet form:

> *Romeo*: If I profane with my unworthiest hand
> This holy shrine, the gentle sin is this;
> My lips, two blushing pilgrims, ready stand
> To smooth that rough touch with a tender kiss.
> *Juliet*: Good pilgrim, you do wrong your hand too much
> Which mannerly devotion shows in this;
> For saints have hands that pilgrims hands do touch
> And palm to palm is holy palmer's kiss.
> *Romeo*: Have not saints lips and holy palmers too?
> *Juliet*: Ay, pilgrim, lips that they must use in prayer…

### Head centre

*The Taming of the Shrew*, Act 2, scene 1:

> *Petruchio*: Good morrow, Kate; for that's your name, I hear.
> *Kate*: Well have you heard, but something hard of hearing:
> They call me Katharine that do talk of me.
> *Petruchio*: You lie, in faith, for you are called plain Kate……
> Come, come, you wasp; I' faith you are too angry.
> *Kate*: If I be waspish, best beware my sting.
> *Petruchio*: My remedy is, then, to pluck it out.
> *Kate*: Aye! If the fool could find it where it lies.
> *Petruchio*: Who knows not where a wasp does wear his sting? In his tail.
> *Kate*: In his tongue.
> *Petruchio*: Whose tongue?

*Kate*: Yours, if you talk of tales; and so farewell!

*Petruchio*: What! with my tongue in your tail? Nay, come again

Good Kate, I am a gentleman.

*Kate*: That I'll try. (striking him)

*Petruchio*: I swear I'll cuff you if you strike again.

### Will centre

Channel the same Kate and Petruchio lines through your will centre.

## Advanced layering—transitions and combinations of centres and their placements

Now that we can integrate each speech placement with its centre, we are ready to explore transitioning more quickly as well as fusing different combinations of our three-fold functioning. On page 141 of *The Art of Speech*, the second stage of *by miner wafer* requires us to weave back and forth between the archetypal centres and their place-ments. The following Steiner text provides the opportunity to build on this. Lines 1–3 allow us first to ground each centre/placement in our instrument. Lines 4–6 invite us to move from one centre/placement to another in a single line and then attempt to inte-grate them. Line 7 invites us to integrate all three.

### Weaving and integration of speech placements and centres exploration 1—In the heart …

In my heart weaves warmth of feeling,

In my head light of thinking,

In my limbs strength of will.

Weaving of radiant light,

Strength of the weaving,

Light of the surging strength!

Behold the Human Being!

Rudolf Steiner

Always prepare full-bodily, only reducing your movement (10–1) when you are able to sustain your level 10 body of sensation.

1. Warm up with stages 1 and 2 of *by miner wafer*.

2. Apply the appropriate centre/placement to each line above:

   a. Our first version of 'weaving of radiant light' requires us to transform our instrument from heart/lips to head/teeth in the course of the single line.

b. Our second version requires us to integrate the two centres/placements so that we achieve warmth within the light and clarity within the warmth.

c. Likewise, the first version of 'strength of the weaving' requires us to transform our intrument from will/soft palate to heart/lips in the course of the single line. Our second version requires us to integrate the two centres/placements so that we achieve strength in the warmth and warmth within the strength.

d. Likewise the first version of 'light of the surging strength' requires us to transform our instrument from head/teeth to will/soft palate in the course of the single line. Our second version requires us to integrate the two centres/placements so that we achieve clarity within the strength and strength within the clarity.

e. In the final line we attempt to integrate all three: sustaining all three bodies of sensation simultaneously.

### *Weaving and integration of speech placements and centres exploration 2—partner work with Shakespeare text*

When you feel confident in layering the centres/speech placements, apply the above steps to our Shakespeare lines from *Speech placement/iambic pentameter exploration 6.*

1. For example, 'weaving of radiant light' prepares Romeo and Juliet to communicate warmth of love penetrated with clear thought and wit.

2. Likewise 'light of the surging strength' prepares Kate and Petruchio to communicate strength of will penetrated with clear thought and wit.

### *More examples of centre combinations*

These examples suggest other characters whose behaviour at times appears predominantly driven by two of the three soul functions. When you have warmed up with the appropriate steps from the previous *explorations*, explore different lines from their speeches with the following suggested combinations.

- Othello — predominantly will/feeling type.
- Iago — predominantly will/thinking type.
- Edmund in *King Lear* — predominantly will/thinking type.
- Lady Macbeth — with her intellect and will she has forged a suit of armour to protect a wounded, vulnerable heart. By the end of the play that armour has cracked open. Her heart is exposed and her thinking is in fragments.

Such images inspire us to layer centres/placement work with *imaginary centres* and an *imaginary body*. Pages 159–167 and 220–225 in *The Art of Acting* explore the distortion of the archetypal centres into their one-sided tendencies: how layering, for instance, an imaginary centre of a 'frozen brain' or 'eyes that slice like razor blades' with *stick*[*], allows us to create a character who is coldly rational and lacks warmth of heart; or how an imaginary heart-centre — a 'wet sponge', for example — layered with *veil*, suggests a sentimental character incapable of thinking clearly. However, such extreme examples demonstrate the need for a voice technique that allows us to express extremity of soul or character one-sidedness without the damage to our vocal instrument that excessive tension in the throat can cause when we instinctively distort our voice. We will see further on how Steiner's observations about *taste* provide a basis for extreme vocal tendencies.

The initiation journey undergone by many Shakespeare characters requires that they develop equal strength and harmony between the thinking, will and feeling functions of their soul. Portia, Rosalind, Cordelia, Imogen, Marina — all are heroines who passionately feel and yet display a clear intelligence coupled with an equally strong will. Edgar in *King Lear* and Malcolm in *Macbeth* both achieve such integration as they undergo the hero's journey. *Exploration 1* above is an excellent warm up to explore this aspect of such characters.

The flexibility to thoroughly transform our instrument as we combine or move between the archetypal centres/placements provides a firm foundation for creating all such characters who work towards their own development as human beings and function in their lives from such an integrated place: the Duke in *Measure for Measure*, Cerimon and Marina in *Pericles*, Paulina in *A Winter's Tale*, Prospero by the end of *The Tempest*, Cordelia in *King Lear*. When our imagination/breath/body/speech-instrument has been refined through working with the template Shakespeare offers us — and how the multiple dimensions of his characters are present in the words they speak — we are ready to apply our skills to a character like Gandalf, for example, in *Lord of the Rings*.

Benedictus and Maria from Steiner's mystery plays provide the opportunity to work with characters who have achieved the conscious integration of their thinking, will and feeling. Of course, when we work with a translation we are not supported by the integration of experience and words that English speakers find germane to Shakespeare's plays. Benedictus is a present-day initiate who speaks with deep love and compassion for the inner struggle of the pupil who has come to him for guidance. But his warmth of heart is penetrated with a clarity of thought that illuminates her turmoil, allowing her to understand the truth she has resisted in a way that frees her will to do what is required. Initially she is torn between conflicting emotions: her love for her friend and the inner voice that tells her it is time to separate and let Johannes find his way without her. Guided by Benedictus, layer by layer she exposes the illusions she had hidden from herself and which had driven her emotional dependency.

---

[*] See, *The Art of Acting*, Chapter 3.

Yet the clarity of thinking that enables Benedictus and Maria to make their way through the labyrinth until they reach the truth is only possible because each works within their inner world with the same will and focus that are needed in the outer world to build a bridge or tunnel through a mountain. Unless the characters achieve such intensity of inner work the scene contains nothing else that would engage us and sentences like those that follow, spoken by Maria, will sound like didactic platitudes:

> Normally human beings only find the strength
> to change what once united them
> by turning love into its opposite,
> tearing the loved one from their hearts in hatred.
> But I must abolish, by my own free will,
> the influence my soul
> has had upon my friend,
> while my love remains unchanged.

Or this reply of Benedictus:

> You'll find your way
> if you can recognise
> what you most valued in this love of yours.
> If you can understand what force
> is driving you unconsciously within your soul,
> you'll find the strength to do
> what duty asks of you.

Our challenge in these speeches is to bring such intensity of will into our thinking, such clarity of thought into our feeling, such warmth of heart into our will and thinking, that what appear as abstract concepts are transformed into living thoughts infused with feeling. Emotion need not be less dramatic or intense because it has been penetrated with the conscious work that is necessary to evolve beyond our instincts and our untransformed astrality.

### Weaving and integration of speech placements and centres exploration 3—Maria and Benedictus—individual and partner work

Building on the last explorations, apply the conscious layering of all three centres to the sentences above. A: Maria, B: Benedictus.

1.  Choose some tools for character development.* For example:
    a) Maria: conflicted *PGs*: 'I want to understand my motives' conflicted with, 'I want to conceal my motives from myself so I can continue to believe my love is pure', *qualities and sensations*: courageously, scared.
    b) Benedictus: *PG*: 'I want to help you reach the truth', *qualities and sensations*: compassionately, calmly, clear-sightedly.
3.  Layer your character preparation with *speech placement/centre exploration 2*. Apply the process to the sentences above.
4.  Make contact with your partner and engage each other in your inner journey through the words.
5.  Reflect back to your partner any moment you were not engaged, identify the cause and try again.
6.  Apply this process to the whole interaction: scene 2 of *The Soul's Probation*.

## Advanced work with the three styles and the centres

As explored in Chapter 6 of *The Art of Speech*, Steiner connects the vocal qualities arising from the speech placements with epic, lyric and dramatic styles. Working to consciously develop our capacity to channel will and thinking through our feeling; feeling and thinking through our will; and will and thinking through our feeling, has consequences far beyond command of the artistic styles. The process of crafting epic, lyric or dramatic texts enables us to work at a central challenge of our time. For now, it is enough to say that many human beings of the present struggle with the separation of their thinking, will and feeling, which in ancient times had functioned instinctively as one. Hamlet is the first great imagination in the English language, of the modern human being whose will is paralysed because his thoughts and feelings are conflicted. As our once integrated thinking, will and feeling continue to disintegrate, the agony of our condition will force us to raise them into consciousness so that we can learn to integrate them once again. This we can only do if our spirits become as active as those demonstrated by the characters of Benedictus and Maria. It is for this reason Steiner called our present time the age of the *consciousness* or *spiritual soul*. The mystery of the chicken and the egg appears again. For although working on the three styles requires capacities we have not or hardly yet developed, the work itself is what develops them. Our ability to integrate the speech placements with their related Chekhov *centres*, in the more complex ways developed in *speech placement/centre exploration 2*, makes it possible to approach the styles in a nuanced way.

---

* In Chapter 4 'Other states of being', we shall explore other tools for accessing such characters.

## *Lyric style*

Shelley's passionate 'Ode to the West Wind' demands the lyric style, yet we cannot fail to notice that the long and complex sentence structures that comprise each verse demonstrate how deeply he has penetrated his intensity of feeling with a clarity of thought only possible when we direct our will into our thinking. Nor can we do justice to the elemental power of the images without the full commitment of our will.

Our capacity to weave between and integrate these functions as we sense their changing combinations enables us to honour the thinking and the will dimensions of the poem and still maintain its lyrical integrity. We will use the fourth verse to explore these possibilities.

### *Style exploration 1—lyric*

This exploration involves sometimes engaging with a partner.

> If I were a dead leaf thou mightest bear;
> If I were a swift cloud to fly with thee;
> A wave to pant beneath thy power, and share
>
> The impulse of thy strength, only less free
> Than thou, O uncontrollable! If even
> I were as in my boyhood, and could be
>
> The comrade of thy wanderings over Heaven,
> As then, when to outstrip thy skiey speed
> Scarce seem'd a vision; I would ne'er have striven
>
> As thus with thee in prayer in my sore need.
> Oh, lift me as a wave, a leaf, a cloud!
> I fall upon the thorns of life! I bleed!
>
> A heavy weight of hours has chain'd and bow'd
> One too like thee: tameless, and swift, and proud.

1. Warm up your heart centre/speech placement.
2. Use Chekhov's *qualities of movement* to explore full-bodily the *will* component of the images.

3. Channel the will sensations through the will centre/placement into *noon air lark* etc. then into the word 'strength' in the line *strength of the weaving*.

4. Identify the central feelings and emotions: e.g. longing to be free, despair, exhilaration, anguish etc.

5. Use *qualities and sensations* to permeate your instrument with each in turn and find the vowel placement most aligned with each specific body of sensation.

6. Channel each emotion through your heart and lips placement into *by miner wafer/ by boom* etc.

7. Speak the whole verse channelling its feeling content through your heart centre/ lyric speech placement.

8. Condense all this sensation into 'of the weaving' in the line *strength of the weaving*.

9. Alternate full-bodily between your will and feeling centres/placements as you speak *strength of the weaving* until you feel both layers of sensation integrate and sense that you are channelling your will through your heart centre/lyric placement.

10. Now speak the whole verse while you move full-bodily so the will component in the images is channelled through your warmth of feeling and the consonants are no less active but sacrifice their elemental character to serve the vowel.

11. Find a partner and sit opposite each other. A, express each sentence in your own words. B, encourage A not to move on to the next until the thought is clear.

12. A, warm up your head centre/teeth placement *see fee shielding* etc and speak the whole verse again to B, communicating every thought with crystal clarity.

13. Channel this layer of sensation into speaking 'of radiant light'.

14. Alternate full-bodily between your warmth of feeling and clarity of thought as you speak *weaving of radiant light*, then integrate both qualities so that the incisiveness of *radiant light* is penetrated with the warmth of *weaving*.

15. Now speak the whole verse in this way, striving to channel clarity of thought through weaving warmth of heart.

16. Work through the whole verse again exploring full-bodily how to integrate the layers so that both the elemental will and clarity of thought and image are channelled through the warmth of feeling in your heart.

17. Repeat the process with each verse.

Of course, each lyric demands a different balance of our soul capacities. Some or parts of some may be more descriptive or contemplative, others more a simple pouring out of feeling. Some, like 'West Wind', demand activation of our will. But all require that we channel both our will and thinking functions through our heart and that our distinctive vocal qualities of strength and clarity be permeated by the warmth of feeling life embodied in the vowels.

## *Epic style*

Once again, the right balance in the integration of these elements depends on the specific text and must be arrived at through artistic intuition. This passage from Tennyson's 'Idylls of the King' that describes the final battle of the Round-Table knights is clearly in the epic style; objectively depicting the events. Yet the will activity that drives the images must be delineated by crystal clarity of thought and the sentence structures permeated with intense emotion: and all of these channelled through the storyteller's standpoint and intention in relating these events.

### *Style exploration 2—epic*

… and in the mist
Was many a noble deed, many a base,
And chance and craft and strength in single fights,
And ever and anon with host to host
Shocks, and the splintering spear, the hard mail hewn,
Shield-breakings, and the clash of brands, the crash
Of battleaxes on shattered helms, and shrieks
After the Christ, of those who falling down
Looked up for heaven, and only saw the mist;
And shouts of heathen and the traitor knights,
Oaths, insults, filth, and monstrous blasphemies,
Sweat, writhings, anguish, labouring of the lungs
In that close mist, and cryings for the light,
Moans of the dying, and voices of the dead.

1. Adapt the template from *style exploration 1*.
2. Use the Chekhov centres/Steiner speech placement tools to full-bodily explore and consolidate the thinking, will and feeling layers of the text.
3. Focus on channelling the images and thoughts through your will centre/placement, using *light of the surging strength* to prepare your instrument.
4. Focus on channelling the feeling content through your will centre/placement, using *strength of the weaving* to prepare your instrument.
5. Work through the whole text exploring how to integrate and balance the layers in such a way that the thoughts and feelings are channelled through the will in order to create the images.

In the lyric style the elemental nature of the consonants is absorbed into the vowels and serves their revelation of the inner life of soul. In the epic style, we reverse the process: the vowels are subsumed into the consonants' activity in order to objectively create the images. If we can achieve this, the listener is free to witness the events and feel their own experience freed from the storyteller's attitude. We could summarise the difference in this way: in the lyric style, image and thought dissolve in some degree into the feeling. In the epic style, feeling and thought condense into the image.

## *Dramatic style*

In contrast to the epic and the lyric styles, dramatic style demands the will and feeling functions of the character be channelled through the actor's thinking. At first glance this may seem counter-intuitive since we tend to think what makes something dramatic is intensity of action and emotion. Recall the emotional intensity of the murder or the sleepwalking scene in *Macbeth*. Or the final battle between the tyrant and Macduff. We are gripped by the drama's action and emotional intensity.

Yet Shakespeare does not simply want us to experience a powerful display of action or be moved by powerful emotions. He uses these to make us think about the mystery of life and destiny; how characters respond to the challenges that drag them down into the dark or awaken them to strive towards the good. He writes that we may grow in understanding of the human journey through what the characters experience. This we cannot do by simply feeling what they feel and watching what they do. We need to also understand the thought content of the words they speak: their words inform us of the sense they make of their experience by thinking.

In the monologue that follows Lady Macbeth invokes the powers of darkness. Sitting in the audience we need to sense her strength of will and feel her powerful emotions, yet unless that intensity and strength are channelled with precision through the words that are generated by her thinking, not only will the audience not understand what she is saying but they will not understand the play.

### *Style exploration 3—dramatic*

In dramatic style, action and emotion must be channelled through the thoughts. Consonant and vowel must be held in balance. The consonant must chisel and define the vowel, giving clarity to inner life. The vowel must hold its own, ensuring that the outer action is a vessel for the inner journey of the human being.

> *Lady Macbeth*: The raven himself is hoarse
> That croaks the fatal entrance of Duncan
> Under my battlements. Come, you spirits

That tend on mortal thoughts, unsex me here,

And fill me from the crown to the toe top-full

Of direst cruelty! make thick my blood;

Stop up the access and passage to remorse,

That no compunctious visitings of nature

Shake my fell purpose, nor keep peace between

The effect and it! Come to my woman's breasts,

And take my milk for gall, you murdering ministers,

Wherever in your sightless substances

You wait on nature's mischief! Come, thick night,

And pall thee in the dunnest smoke of hell,

That my keen knife see not the wound it makes,

Nor heaven peep through the blanket of the dark,

To cry 'Hold, hold!'

*Macbeth*, Act 1, scene 5

1. Adapt the template for *style exploration 1*.
2. Use the centre/placement tools to full-bodily explore and consolidate the thinking, will and feeling layers of the text.
3. Channel her will through the head centre/placement, using *light of the surging strength* to prepare your instrument.
4. Channel her emotions through the head centre/placement, using *weaving of radiant light* to prepare your instrument.
5. Work through the whole text exploring how to integrate and balance all the layers so that her emotions and her will are channelled through her thoughts and we do not only feel what she feels but understand her understanding of the situation.

## Speech placements and the sense of taste[2]

In Lecture 10 of the *Speech and Drama Course*, Steiner points to the potential of the taste sensations *bitter*, *sour* and *sweet* to awaken greater consciousness of the speech placements in our mouth. Since our taste buds are seated in the very part of our anatomy with which we speak, it is not surprising that the sense of taste directly influences vocal quality. Exploring *taste* provides an objective, technical foundation for expressing, without harm to our instrument, the extreme soul conditions that distort the voice. The following idioms bear witness to this layer of our psycho-physical experience; the instinctive connection between our *sense of taste* and broader moral and emotional experience:

> the experience left a bitter taste in my mouth
> he wept bitterly
> it was a bitter pill to swallow
> bitter wrangling
> bitter family feud
> a sweet person
> sweet face
> what a sweetheart!
> sweet dreams
> the sweet taste of success
> sour puss/sour grapes
> a love gone sour
> hope turned sour
> it soured the whole proceedings
> s/he's a bit of a sour apple
> don't look so sour
> good taste
> bad taste
> taste in clothes, in the arts etc.

These colloquial expressions suggest that sweet, sour and bitter exist within a broadly accepted spectrum of response despite the fact that constitutions differ and there are individuals who crave a bitter taste, or who exhilarate in sourness while others cannot tolerate a sweet sensation. To benefit artistically from exploring taste's potential, it's important to go beyond reactions of antipathy or sympathy. We must observe precisely how these tastes affect our mouths *and* our whole psycho-physical constitution, proving again the intimate connection of the soul with body, voice and speech.

Chekhov's full-bodied principle has taught us that when responsibility for tensions in the mouth and throat that generate our voice is carried equally by all parts of our instrument, we can express extreme sensations without the need to harm our throat. Then we do not merely press or *push these sensations into the voice* but our voice emerges from the same source that inspires the deeper intuitions of our characters or images: our fully penetrated body-of-sensation.

### Taste exploration 1

1. Each person set up their own 'taste station' around the outside of the space, leaving room to move within the centre of the space. Each 'station' should have samples of the following, which have been provided along with paper cups and plates and plastic spoons:
    - wormwood tea — bitter;
    - neat lemon juice and vinegar (separately) — sour;
    - honey and sugar (separately) — sweet;
    - water to neutralise the taste buds in between each tasting.
2. Explore each taste in turn (in any order), taking time to observe the sensations and instinctive sounds that arise.
    - What effect does each taste have on you?
    - In what part of your mouth is it most intense? How is this reflected in your voice?
    - How does it affect your body?
    - How does the sensation alter over time?
3. Record your observations, then expand your first reponses into full-bodied movement/gesture (level 10).
4. While you move release your voice instinctively. Then speak the word *sweet, sour* or *bitter* until it matches the exact sensation.
5. Explore which consonants and/or vowels align most closely with each taste sensation and most effectively express each taste.
6. When you have a full-bodied gesture that embodies each original sensation, including your response in mouth and voice, practise moving from one full-bodied taste sensation to the next. Once you can recreate the journey of sensation generated by each *actual* taste, *imagine* tasting it and still allowing it to permeate your instrument.

### Group or Partner work

7. Divide the group in half. Group A, demonstrate full-bodily and vocally your responses to the *bitter* taste. Group B, observe.
8. Swap.
9. Share your observations with each other.
10. Repeat step 7–9 with *sour* and then with *sweet*.

Compare your responses to the following:

### Sour

*My reaction is immediate, sucking me into a sudden sharp contraction. My body tenses, charged as though with an electric shock. Utterly awake at the clear edge of myself, my tongue asserts itself, defends its boundary, prevents my swallowing and being penetrated further. It is not altogether disagreeable, unpleasant, arousing rather — how shall I say? — a sharpening of consciousness, after the first diving-into-icy-water shock, an exhilarating clarity throughout my instrument.*

## Bitter

*It takes a moment longer for this taste to register, as though I need to process what I swallowed before identifying what I let inside me. By then, too late! Revolting! I have let it past my resistance and before I know it, no going back, it has lodged itself within my guts. Gag reflex kicking in, heaving from deep within to root of tongue to 'throw up', eject it, thrust it out. Resisting all attempts, insidiously seeping, already it has crept into my arteries and veins 'poisoning' my soul and body.*

## Sweet

*Sweetness softens me; I expand outside my skin, separate boundaries dissolve. Tasting at the front of, even tip of, tongue, awakens delicate sensations: first a fineness, then a 'not enough', a craving now, a wanting more and more. But then, too muchness turns against me; too much sweetness cloys.*

## Taste exploration 2

1. Warm up with your full-bodied *sweetness* gesture.
2. Sustaining the sensation improvise: *enter a garden, look around and pick a flower.* Express whatever sounds arise organically — exclamations, vowels, words or phrases.
3. Repeat with *sourness*.
4. Repeat with *bitterness*.

## Taste exploration 3

1. Still working full-bodily, pay attention to how each taste affects your mouth: tongue, teeth, palate, lips.
2. Explore which consonants and vowels and which of the three speech placements feel most aligned to each sensation in your mouth.
3. Create simple sequences of words composed of sounds that support your expression of each taste. Here are some suggestions:

Sour: sour steel … slits and slices

*The sharp sour sensation sucks my lips back to expose my teeth, hardening the surface and edges of my tongue, tensing them against my palate, reminding tensions in the mouth of the head centre/placement. Clarity distorted with a sour edge.*

Bitter: carve gruesome curses … ghastly cracks and hurts

*The sense of violation that invades each cell! Consciousness hardens at the root of the tongue pushing up against soft palate, arousing will to grasp it at its roots — this nausea of bitterness — and heave it from my guts!*

Sweet:  tongue tip

> delicately taste and tingle
> sweetly titillate and touch
> sweet morsel
> dissolving,
> drifting through me
> wanting more
> pouring more
> wanting more and more
> pouring more and more

*Consciousness expands from tip of tongue to lips: mouth remembering the placement, warmth of feeling streaming from my heart, expands beyond my lips to overflow my boundaries.*

4.  Integrate the exercises for the archetypal centres and their placements, *by miner wafer, see fee shielding, noon air lark* etc., with the corresponding exercises for each taste until the taste-sensations penetrate the full-bodied centre/placement work and vice versa.

## Taste exploration 4

1.  Recreate *taste exploration 2* and extend it to pluck petals from the flower.
2.  Use the speech exercises from *taste exploration 3* to prepare your placements and permeate the words *s/he loves me, s/he loves me not* with each sensation.
3.  Allow each taste to determine how your interaction with the flower ends.

## Taste exploration 5 — taste and character

Here are further opportunities to integrate your skills with centres, placements and their voice/speech qualities with tastes. Flashes of character may be invoked simply by the full-bodied preparation for each taste.[*] These can be strengthened by layering them with *centres* and other choices such as archetypes. For example: to create a simple sketch for Scrooge — old man and miser; and Tiny Tim — young boy and invalid.[†]

---

[*]  For a thorough exploration of character development, see *The Art of Acting*.
[†] See Chapter 6 for the exploration of the stages of life.

1.  With a partner, warm up taste sensations of *bitterness* and *sweet*.

2.  Apply them to the following exchange from Charles Dickens's *A Christmas Carol*, reversing roles when you have finished:

*Sweet*

> *Tiny Tim*: Merry Christmas, Mister Scrooge!

*Bitter*

> *Scrooge*: Bah! Humbug!

3.  Use this next example, to transition from saccharine sweetness into sour:

> *Lady Macbeth*: Look you like the innocent flower
> But be the serpent under 't.

Or express the bitterness in her reference to 'gall':

> Come to my woman's breasts
> And take my milk[3] for gall, you murdering ministers,
> Wherever in your sightless substances
> You wait on nature's mischief!

Once again, the taste sensations in themselves may well create a pathway into other aspects of the character that can then be translated into tools that can be layered with the taste.

4.  Look for other texts which indicate a taste sensation. For example, in the lyric style, Tennyson's lines from, 'The Lotos-Eaters':[*]

> There is sweet music here that softer falls
> Than petals from blown roses on the grass.

And this from Shakespeare's *The Merchant of Venice*, in the dramatic:

> *Lorenzo*: How sweet the moonlight sleeps upon this bank.
> Here will we sit and let the sound of music
> Creep in our ears.

Or Menenius' description of Coriolanus when he returns from his failed attempt to dissuade the exiled Roman from destroying Rome:

> The tartness of his face would sour grapes.

Or the fool from *King Lear* warning Lear not to trust Goneril:

> She will taste as like this as a crab does to a crab [*meaning the sour crab apple*].

---

* See, *The Art of Speech,* Chapter 6.

Macbeth's famous soliloquy invites us to experiment with bitterness:

> To-morrow, and to-morrow, and to-morrow,
> Creeps in this petty pace from day to day,
> To the last syllable of recorded time;
> And all our yesterdays have lighted fools
> The way to dusty death. Out, out, brief candle!
> Life's but a walking shadow, a poor player
> That struts and frets his hour upon the stage,
> And then is heard no more; it is a tale
> Told by an idiot, full of sound and fury,
> Signifying nothing.

As do Gloucester's lines from *King Lear*:

> As flies to wanton boys are we to the gods;
> They kill us for their sport.

### Taste exploration 6

When you are confident with layering and transitioning between the centres and their placements coloured with the tastes:

1. Layer* one taste sensation on another. For example, many of Cecily's and Gwendolyn's lines from Act 3 of Oscar Wilde's, *The Importance of Being Earnest* provide the opportunity to play with sour disguised as sweet or sweetness so exaggerated that it cloys. The girls have just discovered they are both engaged to Ernest. Although their relationship has soured, they behave 'sweetly' in the presence of the butler:

   *Gwendolyn*: Are there many interesting walks in the vicinity, Miss Cardew?
   *Cecily*: Oh! yes! A great many. From the top of one of the hills quite close one can see five counties.
   *Gwendolyn*: Five counties! I don't think I should like that; I hate crowds.
   *Cecily* (sweetly): I suppose that is why you live in town?

## Further areas of research

Having explored, through taste, some of the extremities connected with our threefold instrument and their contribution to developing a character, we identify some of the questions that still require further research in relation to the archetypal centres and their

---

* See, *The Art of Acting*, Chapter 2.

placements. We have discussed already Steiner's observation that the direct quality of speech required for dramatic style arises from the head centre/teeth placement.[*] Yet how might this relate to characters who function, either in their core or momentarily, in their will or feeling centre?

Perhaps we could regard the dramatic style of speech as the frame of a painting and the painting as the substance generated by the interaction of our characters. It is our task as artists to create integrity between our content and its frame. In this case, to achieve complexity and depth of character within the framework of direct dramatic interaction. No simple formula can possibly suffice; only patient work and willingness to wrestle with the ambiguities. Likewise we expand our ability to use the centres and their corresponding placements to achieve the epic and the lyric styles by integrating them with other layers of our work.

Mature artistry consists in weaving single skills to ever greater levels of complexity that continue to expand our field of research and practice. The following suggestions indicate some of the paths that open up when we combine the many basic skills available. Each is another step along the way to ground the inspirations granted us by talent in certainties we can depend upon. Clothed in these certainties we discover our artistic practice is not trapped in rigid forms but released into an infinitely rich and expanding web of intersecting pathways of experience.

### *Advanced layering exploration 1—epic style and the four qualities-of-movement*

I have created the following short passage to provide an opportunity to layer our will-centre/placement (which together form the basis in our instrument for epic style) with the four qualities-of-movement[†] and the elemental power of the consonants.[‡]

1. Warm up your will-centre with its speech placement exercises.
2. In turn, layer these full-bodily with moulding, floating, flying and radiating, and their corresponding speech exercises.
3. Apply the appropriate quality of movement/speech, layered with the will centre, to each passage in the text until you can tell the story in the epic style.
4. Then reduce the outer movement from level 10 to 1.

Once upon a time, in the depths of winter, everything grew so cold that even the mountains froze. The little birds in their nests could not move their wings to keep warm and the earth was in grave danger of dying.

---

A fiery spirit from the sun felt so sorry for the earth that he shot forth like a shining star, circled the snow peaks and iron crags and at last turned himself into a spear of flame that seared deep into the frozen heart of the earth itself.

At first it seemed that the fire had gone out. But then …

Slowly, slowly the ice began to melt. It melted and melted until all the rivers were flowing again and the great ocean itself could once more move in its tides with the moon.

And the little birds felt the warmth spread even into their wings. They fluffed their feathers and soared into the air and flew. The sky rang with their joyous cries and the souls of all creatures lifted up again into the light.

Dawn Langman

## Advanced layering exploration 2—lyric style and qualities-of-movement

The following lyric poem, found in one of Steiner's notebooks, provides an opportunity to channel floating and radiating with their related consonants through your heart-centre streaming through the lyric placement. [*]

> I would enkindle every human being
> with the spirit of the cosmos,
> that we might be as flames
> and unfold our being's essence as a flame.
>
> Others would take water from the cosmos,
> to quench that flame
> and make all being
> watery and dull within.
>
> O joy! to see the human flame
> burning brightly even when at rest.
> O bitterness, to see a human being
> become a thing
> bound
> when we would be free.

Judith Wright's poem, 'The Wattle Tree' provides an opportunity for layering all four elements and qualities of movement with the lyric style.

> The tree knows four truths—
> earth, water, air and the fire of the sun.
> The tree holds four truths in one.

---

[*] *The Art of Speech*, Chapter 6.

Root, limb and leaf unfold
out of the seed and these rejoice
till the tree dreams it has a voice
to join four truths in one great word of gold.

Oh that I knew that word!
I should cry loud, louder than any bird.
Oh let me live forever, I would cry.
For that word makes immortal what would wordless die;
and perfectly, and passionately,
welds love and time into the seed,
till tree renews itself and is forever tree—

Then upward from the earth
and from the water,
Then inward from the air
and the cascading light
poured gold, till the tree trembled with its flood.

Now from the world's four elements I make
my immortality; it shapes within the bud.
Yes, now I bud, and now at last I break
into the truth I had no voice to speak:
into a million images of the Sun, my God.[4]

## The Foundation Stone meditation

Developing the skills to consciously apply the speech placements with the archetypal centres in such complex ways and combinations transforms our instrument into an organ of perception that allows us to explore the macrocosmic mysteries at work in our microcosmic soul activities of thinking, will and feeling. In mighty pictures, the mantra known as *The Foundation Stone* invokes the supersensible realities at work within our everyday perception of ourselves as autonomous agents of our own emotions, thoughts and actions. Steiner's words evoke in us what we experience unconsciously in sleep or after death when, freed from our earthly bodies, we are released into the ocean of all-beingness. There we experience ourselves among exalted spirits whose own states of consciousness think and feel and will us into being; not, however, as obedient automatons but as creatures capable of being guided step by step towards maturity and spiritual autonomy.

There can be no profounder application of the integrated Chekhov psycho-physical technique with Steiner's speech formation. Our prepared body/soul/and speaking instrument becomes the organ through which we gain our first perceptions of the meditation's sacred content. The words articulate what normally remains unconscious. Our integrated methodology allows us to move beyond mere concepts that the intellect can grasp, enabling the psycho-spiritual substance of the mysteries to begin to penetrate our bodies and become direct experience.

What immediately strikes us when we meet the mantric words is that the speaker is not *a* human being in specific circumstances but *the* human being: our cosmic human archetype, the I AM Self. Therefore, the words provide us with our first opportunity (within the context of these books) to explore how our speech technique can differentiate between micro and macrocosmic levels of experience. Once again our instrument (body, soul and spirit) must evolve to finer levels of perception as we learn what is required for the divine creative powers of the Logos (our future Self) to speak through us.

Our challenge is to find the voice that sounds as from around us, speaking to us from the 'encircling round' and yet speaks *through* us. It is a voice that speaks both to and from our most intimate core of being, yet sounds with cosmic power (not to be confused with volume). In the face of such demands our commitment can only be to strive, knowing that we have a speech technique which has trained our instrument to channel consonants and vowels as bearers of the cosmic soul and spirit powers: that in *The Actor of the Future 2: Word Made Flesh* we came to know as the planetary beings and the starry beings of the zodiac.

In addition, we have Chekhov's psycho-physical technique to ground and support us as we expand our reach into their ever further spheres of consciousness. In *Word Made Flesh* we explored how eurythmy gestures for the planetary beings and the zodiac enable us to sense their objectives and activity. Now we can use them to further train our organ of perception, discerning how the faculties of thinking, will and feeling that are channelled through our threefold constitution are further gifts of the creator beings we invoke. In the Foundation Stone mantra we invoke them through the names of the Nine Hierarchies recognised in Christian esotericism.[*]

The meditation is structured in four parts.[5] Part one invites us to explore the words with full-bodied movement channelled through our *will-centre*, and the *epic* placement for our sounds.

---

[*] For a detailed exploration of the connection between the planetary beings, the spiritual hierarchies and the eurythmy gestures, see Chapter 5.

Human soul!
Thou livest in the limbs
Which bear thee through the world of space
Into the ocean being of the spirit.
Practice spirit recollection
In depths of soul,
Where in the wielding world creator life
Thine own I
Comes to being
Within the I of God
Then in the all world human being
Thou wilt truly *live*.

For the Father Spirit in the heights
Holds sway in depths of worlds,
Begetting life.
Spirits of Strength (Seraphim, Cherubim, Thrones)
Let there be sounded from the heights
What in the depths is echoed
Speaking:
*Ex deo nascimur.*
[From God humanity has being.]
The [elemental] spirits hear it
In East and West and North and South
May human beings hear it.

*Are you ready? Do you dare align the centre in your belly with the centre of the earth, risk being split asunder by the primal will? Moving full-bodily, rivers of life gush forth, sensations of the earth not yet as finished object but as molten still becoming swirling currents, continually coming into being. Sensations of some greater-than-your-conscious-self dynamic moving through your limbs — and can you really think you do this, any action by yourself? Sensations body forth, surging through muscle, sinew, just beneath the surface, just beyond the shore of your solidity, swimming in a universe of conscious action. Ride the current to its source in swirling galaxies beyond. Hold steady! Speak the words, refined in fire, cleansed of narrow selfhood, all desire. Channelled through the soft palate-portal leading to the mysteries of your digestion, transforming world-willed-into-being outside of you into world-willed-into-being within, will to act, create events — let the speaking grant you consciousness, steer you through sounding whirlpool words. In the beginning …*

*Figure 2 Starry beings of the zodiac (Seraphim and Cherubim) stream through the cosmic consonants*

*Figure 3 The planetary being Saturn (Thrones or Spirits of Will)*

Part two invites us to explore the words with full-bodied movement channelled through our *heart-centre*, and the *lyric* placement for our sounds.

Human soul!
Thou livest in the beat of heart and lung
Which bear thee through the rhythmic tides of time
Into the feeling of thine own soul being.
Practice spirit mindfulness
In balance of the soul,
Where the surging deeds
Of the world's becoming
Thine own I
Unite
With the I of the World.
Then midst the weaving of the human soul
Thou wilt truly *feel*.

For the Christ will in the encircling round
Holds sway in the rhythms of all worlds
Blessing the soul.
Spirits of Light (Kyriotetes, Dynamis, Exusiai)
Let there be fired from the east
What in the west is formed;
Speaking:
*In Christo morimur.*
[In Christ death becomes life.]
The [elemental] spirits hear it
In East and West and North and South:
May human beings hear it.

*Are you ready? Do you dare align your own heart to the world-heart-flaring-sun, risk losing consciousness? Moving full-bodily, rivers of love gush forth; and are your heart walls, valves, strong enough to hold the flood back, channel it through arteries, capillaries, at last deliver it to thirsty cells — this liquid sun, relentless tide of love, transcending sentiment that clings to forms unable to evolve? Sweep them away, burst the now-become-a-prison open, crack the obsolete! Ride the current to its starry source! Hold steady! Speak the words, refined in fire, cleansed of narrow selfhood, all desire. Warmed by lips let words caress but also steer you clearly through temptation's ecstasy to bless the world.*

*Figure 4 top left: Planetary being Jupiter (Spirits of Wisdom/Kyriotetes), centre right: Planetary being Mars (Spirits of Movement/Dynamis), bottom left: Planetary being Sun (Spirits of Form/Exusiai)*

Part three invites us to explore the words with full-bodied movement channelled through our *head-centre*, and the *dramatic* placement for our sounds.

Human soul!
Thou livest in the resting head
Which from the ground of the eternal
Opens to thee the thoughts of Worlds.
Practice spirit-vision
In quietness of soul
Where the eternal aims of Gods
World beings' light
On thine own I bestow
For thy free willing;
Then from the Human Spirit's ground
Thou wilt truly *think*.

For the Spirit's universal thoughts
Hold sway, in the beings of all worlds
Craving for light.
Spirits of Soul (Archai, Archangeloi, Angeloi)
Let this be prayed in the depths
And from the heights be answered;
Speaking:
*Per spiritum sanctum reviviscimus.*
[In the spirit's universal thoughts
The soul awakens.]
The [elemental] spirits hear it
In East and West and North and South:
May human beings hear it.

*And are you ready? Do you dare align your sometimes often furrowed brow — to the world-wide-cosmic web of consciousness. Moving full-bodily, rivers of light stream forth! And are your brain cells, synapses — precision-made to focus eyebeams, intersecting shafts of light projected from infinity, with pinpoint clarity — ready to ride the current to its source, receive that voltage from the universal mind? Hold steady! Speak the words refined in fire, cleansed of narrow selfhood, all desire. Their edges sharpened on hard palate's file, honed at the teeth, cut through all deception, mental laziness, boundaries that limit understanding, barriers to knowledge, expose expanding edges of the universe with crystal clarity and vast exhilarating joy.*

*Figure 5 top left: Planetary being Venus (Archai), centre right: Planetary being Mercury (Archangels), bottom left: Planetary being Moon (Angels)*

Part four is pure spirit lyric which invites us to weave, within that lyric form, between the three aspects of our being.

> At the turning point of time
> The spirit light of the world
> Entered the stream of earthly being.
> Darkness of night
> Light that gives warmth
> Had held its sway.
> Day-radiant light
> Poured into human souls;
> Light that gives warmth
> To simple shepherds' hearts,
> Light that enlightens
> The wise heads of kings.
>
> O Light Divine,
> O Sun of Christ,
> Warm Thou our hearts
> Enlighten Thou our heads
> That good may become
> What from our hearts we would found
> And from our heads direct
> With conscious will.

*From the primal will, the universal heart and mind, rivers of life and love and light release themselves into the world. And are you ready? Do you dare align yourself, risk annihilation of your closely clung-to separated self-identity? Hold steady! Speak the words refined in fire, cleansed of narrow selfhood, all desire! Let them bring you to the place where cosmic might and love and light contracted to a human span to show us how to weave between them as we make the journey home.*

Chapter 3

# Style and genre: tragedy, comedy, drama, clowning

## The origin of tragedy and comedy

Tragedy and comedy evolved as distinct dramatic forms in Athens in the fifth century BCE. Their separate streams flowed through the landscape of Western theatre for many centuries. Since the Renaissance the increased complexity of our evolving consciousness has caused the mingling of their waters. It could be argued, for example, that the first half of most of Shakespeare's final plays is tragedy. Yet they are known as comedies because the tragic elements are nearly all resolved in the second half. Closer to our own time, Anton Chekhov conceived his plays as comedies while Stanislavski regarded them as tragic, and Beckett called his *Waiting for Godot* a 'tragi-comedy'. Tracing these genres to their source will help us appreciate not only their significance within our human journey but also the suggestions made by Steiner and Chekhov for the differentiation of their speech and acting styles.

Theatre historians generally agree that the origin of tragic and comic forms in the drama of the Greeks lay in the choral odes or dithyrambs composed to celebrate the resurrection of the god Dionysus with the return of spring each year.[*] Once sung and danced by a chorus and its leader, outer evidence of how these hymns metamorphosed step by step into the dramatic art of an Aeschylus or Aristophanes is buried in antiquity. Nor is there material evidence that connects these early rites with the mysteries enacted in the temple drama of Eleusis, the occult centre to which the origin of drama has also been connected.[†]

Most scholars trace the derivation of the word *tragedy* from the Greek words *trágos* (male goat) and *ōidé* (song) meaning *goat song*, suggesting that perhaps a goat was offered as the prize to the composer of the winning chorus at the drama festival each year. Aristotle himself, on whose authority centuries of Western culture based its understanding of the way the drama functioned, analysed the best examples of its forms but offered no insight into what preceded them. There is so much we do not know that will probably never be verified by any outer evidence yet to be uncovered. Therefore I offer these imaginitive bridges to connect the fragments that survive. They

---

[*] *The Art of Acting*, pp. 268–279.
[†] *The Actor of the Future 1: Tongues of Flame.*

spring from a lifetime of investigation and immersion in the works whose genius preceded any rules extracted later by the analytic mind. Since the tragic paradigm has been explored already several times within these books,[*] in this present context I shall point to what I see as the central thread connecting the surviving fragments of our tragic theatre history, but give my main attention to the nature and development of comedy.

## Tragedy

Goat songs were sung by the followers of Dionysus in honour of his mysteries. They wore goatskins to represent the satyrs, the goat-like creatures that were the god's companions. Then came Thespis, the first recorded tragic actor who was presented with a goat for his winning performance of a tragedy. Future winners were also presented with a goat … why a goat? Scapegoat — the sacrificial animal, free of blemish, marked out to bear the sins of the community, its blood spilt on the altar, smoke from its burning flesh rising up as incense to the gods. These are some of the fragments of surviving ancient texts that theatre history has thrown into the mix when considering the origins of tragedy. Yet without external evidence to provide a context, they do not satisfy our need to understand how tragedy connects with them.

Present mainstream consciousness is largely disconnected from any sense that blood or flesh are more than complex chemical formations. From within its paradigm, we cannot imagine that the cosmos is a web of interweaving life and consciousness in which all the single threads of being sacrifice themselves that others might evolve. Our lack of gratitude for the beings which sustain and make our own existence possible, means we cannot understand the cultures who absolve their debts through gratitude and channel their participation in the Oneness-of-all-Life through sacred ritual. We dismiss ancient consciousness as superstitious and simply less intelligent than ours.

Throughout the ancient world, as direct perception of connectedness decreased, the ancient atavistic consciousness of oneness with all life and its recurring cycles of fertility through seasons, harvests, times of drought and plenty, faded. Rituals through which communities had once aligned their consciousness to the divine creative will, ceased to be understood and fell into decay.

---

*See pages 20-22 and Epilogue from *The Art of Acting,* and Chapter 1 of *The Actor of the Future 1:Tongues of Flame.*

Yet from this loss of primal consciousness embedded in blood sacrifice a new and precious sensibility emerged. Instead of the consecrated blood it recognised the consecrated *heart and mind* of one who underwent that sacrifice on everyone's behalf. An indication of this as it manifested in the Hebrew consciousness is found in Psalm 51 verse 17:

For the sacrifice of God is a broken heart and a contrite spirit.

This preparation in the Hebrew soul would metamorphose further into the Christian sacrament of bread and wine. In the Greek soul, this shift manifested in the metamorphosis of blood sacrifice into the artistic form of tragedy. In the new temple of the theatre, the sacrifice could be *imagined*. Through the protagonist, the representative of our humanity, the actor-priest, demonstrated how suffering shattered the 'average boundaries of the ego'.[6] Through what the *persona*, the illusory or separated self, experienced as 'death' was born the knowledge of the true immortal Self.[7]

Enacted by the priests in the temple drama at Eleusis, neophytes beheld in mythic form, how the human soul, Persephone, was carried down to Hades and the earth became a wasteland. Only when Demeter — her mother and the mother of all life — instructed Triptolemus, a mortal man, to descend into the depths and rescue her, could the earth recover. Thus initiating him into her mysteries, he returned Persephone to Paradise to be united with her bridegroom, the wholly immortal, resurrected god, Dionysus.[*]

Mists veil the transition from initiation knowledge, channelled only to deserving neophytes by priests within the hidden temple, to the first actors playing on the open stage before the whole community of Athens. But at some point Aeschylus, the father of Greek tragedy, dared to portray, in mythic form, Prometheus, sacrificed on our behalf and bound and tortured on the rocks of Caucasus, to demonstrate the crucifixion that the human spirit undergoes when, to win its freedom from the old unconscious union with the gods, it incarnates into a body and becomes enmeshed in matter. And yet despite his suffering, even as Zeus flings him to the farthest reach of Hades, Prometheus bears witness to his indestructable, immortal self, crying out, *He cannot kill me!* Some were fearful that in portraying through his trilogy the long plan of redemption for the human race, Aeschylus betrayed the mysteries: exposing to an uninitiated audience the occult truth — that human beings were destined to achieve divinity and become co-creators with the gods.

A generation later, coming closer now to earth, somewhere between myth and history, Sophocles portrayed the destiny of Oedipus: the king who killed his father and married

---

* See also *The Actor of the Future 1: Tongues of Flame*, Chapter 1, and the DVD series 'A Dramatic Journey through the Evolution of Human Consciousness', disc 1.

his own mother, not knowing what he did. His unacknowledged sin spread pestilence throughout the land he ruled, destroying many of his people; yet at last accepting his responsibility, he purified his soul of hubris and after years of penance died a *wondrous death* that blessed the community who sheltered him. All tragedy thus far portrayed the pain of separation from the gods that was the necessary price to bring our human consciousness to birth, and suggested that the suffering itself contained the seed of our journey back to Oneness.

In the third generation, Euripides, less trusting of divine compassion, wrenched himself from faith in outworn gods who disdain our pleas for mercy, and was flung back on himself, discovering the infinite compassion of the human heart for earthly suffering.

Four centuries further on, Seneca, schooled in Stoic discipline, reworked all the Greeks with Roman fortitude and portrayed the emergence of divinity within the conscience of the moral human being: human virtue on its own in the battle with depravity and vice. Initially the tutor to his future emperor, Nero subsequently sentenced him to death and ordered Seneca to commit suicide; a sacrificial victim on the altar of his life. But his tragedies became the model for Renaissance tragedy and its perpetuating, bloody cycles of revenge.

To shatter that paradigm, as he knew he must, Shakespeare needed first to utterly immerse himself in it. This he did in *Titus Andronicus*. Having thus explored a world devoid of mercy, he earns the right to lead us step by step through all the early plays, weaving in and out of comedies and dramas that while they make us face in some degree the darker aspects of our nature, yet also offer some escape into a happy ending; some temporary consolation. Until in *As You Like It* we cannot avoid the fact of evil any longer. There he makes us teeter on the edge of the abyss where we can go no further without the willingness to plumb its depths. And so, on our behalf, Jaques leaves the play — refusing to attend another doomed-to-failure wedding, refusing to pretend it's all okay and collude with the illusion there can ever be a truly happy ending if we bypass the necessity not just of confronting evil but of penetrating and transforming it. And so Shakespeare plunges with us into the abyss — yet one more brother-killing-brother-Hamlet-hell. Yet even in the deepest pit he does not abandon us and the stars of his resurrection language beckon, pointing beyond a static theology of good and evil to a new theology of transformation.

Thus he does not allow us to emerge from tragedy — *Macbeth, Othello, Lear* — to enjoy another happy ending till he can show us, step by step, through *Cymbeline, A Winter's Tale, Pericles* and finally *The Tempest*, how to make that transformation real that will deliver us from Hell.

And ever since, somewhere between the promise of the happy ending and the loss of hope, the path of tragedy continues to unfold, predicated as it is on our experience that suffering feels real to the separated self and that until we understand the parables appearance teaches us, we must experience its pain. [*]

# Comedy

Perhaps we are puzzled that comic plots and characters should be as rooted in the sacred Mysteries as their tragic counterparts. According to the myth of Eleusis, the goddess Demeter was inconsolable at the loss of her daughter, Persephone. Being Earth Mother, her tragedy becomes the earth's when drought and famine take hold everywhere. After searching far and wide, she arrives in Eleusis disguised as an old woman and is engaged by the royal household as a nurse. An old servant, Baubo, tries to lift her spirits by telling her obscene jokes and stories. Finally in desperation, Baubo lifts her skirt, which provokes a smile in the great mother.

What Baubo showed varies in different versions of the story. As with all myths, each account reflects how a different aspect or degree of consciousness expresses its grasp of the realities embodied in its images. And so, what was revealed when Baubo lifted up her skirt is sometimes portrayed as her genitalia and sometimes as the child Iacchus, the baby Dionysus, who leapt into the Earth Mother's arms and gave her hope that her daughter would be rescued. Whether we understand the former image simply as a source of coarse amusement or as a reminder to the goddess that her mysteries are celebrations of fertility and therefore of life's triumph over death, Baubo causes Demeter to smile. With renewed hope, there at Eleusis, she institutes her mysteries and provides initiation for the neophytes who come to try and find a way to deal with tragedy. The mystery of Baubo's gesture is perhaps connected with that surrounding the Sheela na gigs; those ancient carvings from the Celtic Mysteries of ancient Ireland. Perhaps also, we can wonder at their resemblance to images of the vocal chords when they are open or closed and vibrating as we speak. As discussed in Chapter 5 of *The Art of Speech* Steiner's research has connected the evolution of the larynx of the future to the transformation of our sexuality.

The jests of Baubo, the goddess of humour, their connection to fertility, the triumph of the life-force over death and tragedy, are the seeds of the comedic stream in Western culture. Our puzzlement that opportunities for laughing at obscenities were included in the sacred rites most honoured in the ancient world indicates how two millennia of repressive Christianity make it difficult to understand a culture where sexuality was not

---

[*] See *The Actor of the Future 1: Tongues of Flame.*

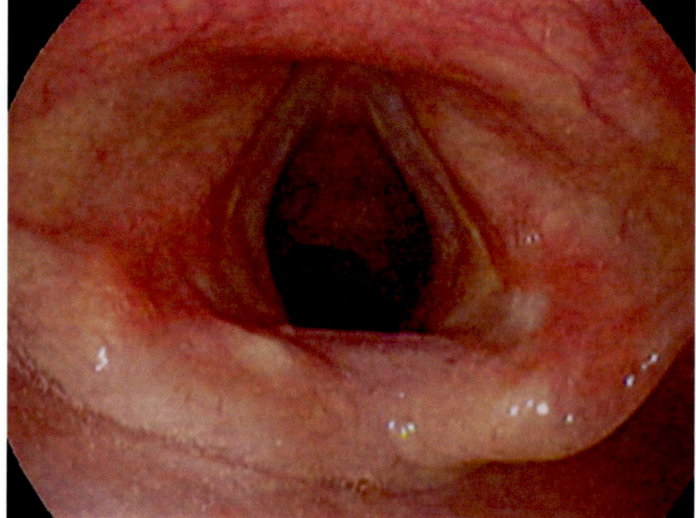

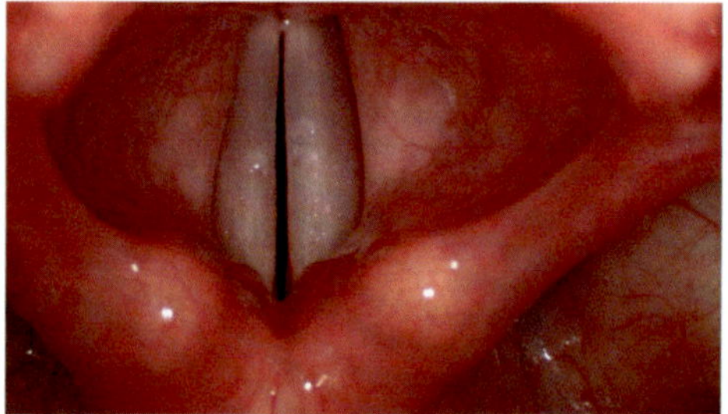

*Figure 6 Images of the Sheela na gig showing their relation to the vocal chords*

regarded as a sin but an expression of the One Life's divine renewal of creative force: no less sacred and demanding of inclusion than any other. Yet at the same time, nor was it any less susceptible to the abuse that springs from excess or depravity than any other aspect of creation when stripped of sacredness by a consciousness incapable of apprehending it. The exaggerated phalluses worn by comic actors were the male counterpart of Baubo's gesture and expressed the joyous celebration of fertility: life's eternal triumph over death. Thus the comedic pathway to the healing of the human tragedy provokes the audience to laugh no less at the absurdities resulting from distortions of our sexuality than any of our other foolishness. In *Lysistrata*, Aristophanes invokes the goddess Baubo, showing the power that women could exert to end the absurdity of war if they withold their sexual favours and refuse to lift their skirts until the men of their community are willing to make love instead of war.

*Figure 7 Vase with scene from Aristophanes', Birds*

## *Aristotle's lost commentary on comedy*

Aristotle's observations about tragedy, passed on through centuries of Western culture, influenced the evolution of the tragic genre. Although his better-known *Poetics I* makes reference to comedy, his analysis is sparse and, until recently, left scholars able only to infer from other works what his more extensive exploration might reveal. Since then however, fragments of *Poetics II* that have been found and pieced together confirm that Aristotle had as high regard for laughter's power to educate the soul as he had for the terror and compassion kindled by the tragic muse.[8]

Half a century before these fragments were identified, Steiner intuited what would later be confirmed as Aristotle's central insight: comedy leads the audience through a complicated plot arising from absurd extremes of character and situation that are guided by some sure, miraculous hand to a resolution of what had seemed could never be resolved.[9] A 'sure, miraculous hand' suggests a Being, not an abstraction. Perhaps the comic genius who untangles even the most tangled threads of destiny and finds a way to weave them to a satisfying resolution is a Someone we can get to know.

Certainly the great comic texts hint at a wise and loving cosmos that, while exposing with unflinching honesty the follies and mistakes we make along our path towards maturity, beholds us also with affection and a gentle eye. As witnesses, hurled back and forth by our laughter at the absurd complications in which their foolishness has landed them, we are curious to find a way out for the characters we cannot help but wish a happy ending. For in spite of, or just possibly because of their stupidity or foolishness, we love them and see them not as sinners to be punished but as children who must learn from their mistakes. Further intuiting the content of *Poetics II*, Steiner tells us that it was the goal of comedy to expand our apprehension of life and broaden our humanity.

Such a content was also intuited by Umberto Eco, the Italian novelist and scholar. In the mediaeval murder mystery, *The Name of the Rose*, Eco explored what the consequences might have been if the content of this controversial document, *Poetics II*, had been revealed in the repressive culture of the mediaeval Catholic church. Let us imagine, he posits, that Aristotle's treatise, written by the greatest mind yet known, had survived but, for reasons justified to Church authorities, its whereabouts had been concealed. A series of murders is required to keep that whereabouts and even the knowledge of the manuscript's existence, hidden. What could such a treatise possibly contain that the Church could perceive it as a threat? The novel contains several conversations between William, the liberal Franciscan monk sent to the abbey to investigate the deaths, and the ancient cleric, Jorge, who is subsequently proved to be the murderer. Here, for example, Jorge defends the suppression of all laughter.

> Laughter, for a few moments, distracts the villein[10] from fear. But law is imposed by fear, whose true name is fear of God. This book could strike the Luciferine spark that would set a fire to the whole world, and laughter would be defined as the new art, unknown even to Prometheus, for cancelling fear. To the villein who laughs, at that moment, dying does not matter: but then, when the license is past, the liturgy again imposes on him, according to the divine plan, the fear of death. And from this book there could be born the new destructive aim to destroy death through redemption from fear. And what would we be, we sinful creatures, without fear, perhaps the most foresighted, the most loving of the divine gifts?

We remember that one of the goals of initiation at Eleusis, out of which the annual theatre festival evolved, was to bring about assurance of eternal life and thus relieve the neophytes of fear of death.* Comedy played no less an important role in the festival than tragedy. We remember also that the purpose of the festivals was to honour Dionysus, the god who embodied the ecstatic energy the Greeks found as necessary to their lives as order and restraint.† After all, what is chaotic, unpredictable, wild, untamed and dangerous is also the creative energy existing in the universe, one form of which is sexuality.

What must we do with such a power? In *The Bacchae*, Euripides had shown the tragic consequence of refusing to accept its contribution to the universe. The Greeks knew it made no sense to control it by suppression. And so, through comedy, everything obscene was held up to the light, nothing pushed into unconscious realms, there to become an 'unthing'[11] unacknowledged, seething in the dark, waiting for its moment to arouse and wreak revenge. Rather let humour, in its wisdom, claim and celebrate the role of the obscene within the whole; for how useful is a view of life excluding half of our experience?

## *Aristophanes'* The Frogs

The comic genius of Aristophanes administered this healing medicine in Athens in the fifth century BCE. There was no absurdity or foolishness he was not prepared to examine and expose; no belief about the gods or human beings, human institutions and authority was exempt from the probing scalpel of his wit. *The Frogs* portrays Dionysus, the patron god of theatre, as so desperate for art of higher quality and so depressed by the mediocrity of what is presently on offer that in order to hear some decent poetry, he braves the terrors in the Kingdom of the Shades to find the good poets who have long since died! This is the comic conceit within which Aristophanes exposes aesthetic snobbery and some of the contradictions and absurdities inherent in popular religious teaching and belief.

The comic vision of the god Dionysus, who disguises his effeminate nature by dressing as the hero Hercules in order to discourage trouble on his journey to the underworld, might well have been considered blasphemous by some. Not to mention the fiasco at the entrance to the underworld where he constantly exchanges garments with his slave, each time hoping either to avoid being punished by the Shades who harbour grudges toward Hercules or to receive the gifts of those who owe the hero favours. Flung

---

* *The Actor of the Future 1: Tongues of Flame*, Chapter 1.

† See Chapter 7 for a detailed exploration of these two extremes.

back and forth between his master's contradictory commands, at one moment having to pretend he is the great hero Hercules and in the next reverting to the humble slave, Xanthus finally refuses to comply again or to relinquish his identity as Hercules and suggests that the gatekeeper whip his 'servant' for his lies. Hoping to avoid the whipping, Dionysus reveals his true identity. [12]

> I'm warning everyone not to torture me. I'm a god. If you touch me you'll have yourselves
> to blame.

Trying to maintain his power, Xanthus, claims that he (the slave) is the god and Dionysus (the god), his mortal slave. To back his claim he suggests the keeper whip them both. It will be absolutely clear, he claims, which one is the god because:

> ... if he's really a god he won't feel anything.

Therefore if either winces or reacts, even in the tiniest degree, it will expose his mortality. In what must rank with the greatest comic scenes, Dionysus and Xanthus submit to being whipped, each attempting to out-do the other in suppressing any sign of pain. But through the audience's laughter, the mystery of what it means to be a human being is explored — and what it means to be divine. Is it possible a god can suffer?

For centuries, Christian theology, and what have been regarded as its heresies, have endlessly revolved around the questions: was the son of man divine or was the son of God 'merely' human? For if he were divine, why did he allow himself to suffer rather than exert his power to destroy his enemies? How can we believe someone is a god who suffered torture on the cross and died? And yet unless he had experienced the same suffering and death as other human beings, how could he understand our pain or be with us when we die? Aristophanes does not attempt to give us answers but, with amused and kindly eye, unravels us through laughter, causing us to teeter on the edge of the same existential ambiguity that Hamlet will tragically internalise on our behalf two thousand years later: *What should such fellows as I do, crawling between earth and heaven?*

But, quite apart from content, the comedic *style* itself reveals an occult truth. In contrast to the fear and hatred of creation that Jorge elevates to a theology — one that excuses murder to defend itself — through laughter we learn we are forgiveable. Of course we must weep at the tragedy of what we lose when we defy and then forget the gods. But we must also laugh as the gods do, at how loveable we are in the foolish ways we try to cope when we forget.

And we *can* laugh because comedy reminds us that at the Last Judgement there is no pain, no cruelty, no punishment. We can laugh no matter what *appears* to happen, who *appears* to suffer or to die, or drown in the tempest because we know that in the end, as Prospero assures Miranda, *there's no harm done*. There will be a happy ending, not dependent on any of the norms for virtue or success or happiness determined by society. Indeed, comedy lets us view our greatest follies and mistakes, the illusions we have about ourselves and our reality, from the same perspective of forgiveness that enlightened gods must do. Such a way of seeing would be dangerous indeed to a Church whose authority depended on the fear of punishment for sin.

## *The Second Shepherds' Play*

In a Christian context, the ultimate relationship of comedy to this enlightened understanding of redemption is explored in the well-known *Second Shepherds' Play* of the *Wakefield Cycle*. Like all such plays in the mediaeval cycles,[13] it depicts the angels' announcement to the shepherds of the birth of Jesus and their visit to the holy child.[*]

Into this archetype the Wakefield version weaves the story of a sheep stealer, Mak, who tricks the shepherds into trusting him to guard their flock while they are sleeping. He steals a sheep and takes it home. He and his wife, Gill, wrap it in swaddling and hide it in the cradle. They plan that if the shepherds come to search their house, Gill will pretend she is in labour. Of course, the shepherds do arrive and when they hear the agonising shrieks and groans that issue from the cottage, are initially convinced by Mak explaining that his wife is giving birth. As they depart however, overcome with tenderness for the new babe within and shame that they suspected Mak to be the thief, they return to give a gift to the child. Mak and Gill are unmasked when the shepherds find their missing sheep is in the cradle. To punish Mak, they toss him in a blanket. Could there be a more potent image in which to embody the comic paradigm, that regardless of our human constructs of punishment and sin 'underneath are the everlasting arms'[14] that, despite all appearances, will ultimately never fail to catch us in their safety net of love? At any rate, exhausted from this effort the shepherds fall asleep and at this point the angel visits them, announcing Jesus' birth in Bethlehem.

In this story, many threads of consciousness create a tapestry that glows with loving kindness. As Jorge recognised, we cannot tremble with the fear of punishment for sin when the consequences of our actions are hilarious, the hope for all benign; the hearts of hardworking, decent human beings, so able to be touched with tenderness and generosity. And any in the audience who think they can pronounce on what is good or evil are confounded, when the one inhabiting the cradle (whose horns, long snout and cloven hooves belong traditionally to the devil) at the same time is the lamb, who takes away all sin and judgement from the world. Who can say who suffers more, the punisher who

---

[*] See Chapter 6.

must inflict chastisement or the punished — Mak who must be hurled by the shepherds between earth and heaven on his journey to become a human being, or the shepherds who toss him in the blanket and must endure their aching muscles afterwards? Yet it is their honest human hearts, still able to be stirred by the mystery of birth, that hear the angel and are not ashamed to bring their mundane gifts to offer to the child in Bethlehem: a ball, a bob of cherries and a bird. These are the 'simple shepherds' hearts' whose warmth alone can melt the winter of the earth.[*]

The play depicts the parallel realities of earth and heaven. There are two dwellings. One is the earthly home of Mak and Gill where we act out the illusion of our deprivation, and disguise and hide what we have stolen out of fear. The other is the shelter where the holy child is born. Such parallel realities would not be seen again for many centuries, until the comic masterpieces, the films, *The Great Dictator* and *The Life of Brian*, were shown around the world. In the first, Charlie Chaplin inhabits both the character and world of the little Jewish barber caught up in the horrors of the Nazi persecution of the Jews, and the parallel reality in which the megolomaniac dictator, Adenoid Hynkel, lives out his fantasy.

## The Life of Brian

Judged as profane by those, like Jorge, who fear to laugh at the patent contradictions and absurdities confronting us in so much of the Christian church's history, tradition and beliefs, Monty Python's *The Life of Brian*, like the *Second Shepherds' Play*, also moves between two levels of reality. Brian is an ordinary mortal man who keeps turning up at the wrong place or time (crossing paths with the parallel reality which his divine counterpart inhabits) and is mistaken by the crowds for the Messiah.

One of the great comedic moments explores the mystery of resurrection. Brian, once again mistaken for the saviour, is crucified along with many others, one of whom, on the cross next to Brian, cannot restrain his toe-tapping impulse. Gently he begins to whistle, then to sing, 'Always look on the bright side of life'. Increasing numbers of the crucified join in until Brian is unable to resist. Admonished by his friend with, 'Come on, Brian, cheer up,' he adds his jaunty song and whistle to the last triumphant chorus, in the face of which the agents of evil and authority are powerless. We can only feel compassion for the soldiers and officials who, utterly bewildered, try without success to gain control over the divine comedy in which they find themselves.

The revelation that suffering and death are illusions that can be transcended threatens all establishments that depend on fear for their authority. This is the

---

[*] From the fourth verse of Steiner's *Foundation Stone Meditation* quoted in Chapter 2.

subversive power that comedy, whose roots are in the mysteries, has always wielded and which the Jorges of the world, who stand to lose their power, persecute and struggle to suppress.

## A Midsummer Night's Dream

Shakespeare's genius veiled this inclusive vision in layer upon layer of disguise so that his subversiveness, even if suspected, remained elusive and defied detection. Surely gales of laughter at the foolishness, the sheer absurdity of Bottom's portrayal of the tragic death of Pyramus would have shaken the foundations of the Globe. These must have been confusing to the spies and authorities and perhaps even drawn from them, if not a laugh, at least a smile. Awake to any hint of deviant theology, how could they have missed the blatant heresy of Bottom's words (unless perhaps helpless with laughter of their own) who as he stabs himself, collapses in the mock throes of death and extracts the last drop of melodrama, speaking even after he is dead?

Now I am dead. Now I am fled. My soul is in the sky.

Indeed, his very corpse rose up and would have danced had not *cool reason*, in the voice of Theseus, proclaimed an end to the entertainment (that those less rational would never want to end) of the ignorant mechanicals.

By exposing moral defects and absurd behaviours as ultimately harmless foolishness, the genius of comedy enables us to laugh at what the conditioned mind condemns as evil. Our laughter bubbles up from an alternative theology whose source is all-embracing love. It massages the narrow cells constructed by the fearful mind until they are soft enough to relinquish their dogmatic edge and admit the revolutionary paradigm. This love distinguishes what I regard as golden comedy, whose roots are in the mysteries, from comedy whose savage wit and satire cruelly attacks its enemy and has its roots in hatred.

## In practice

In Chapter 9 of *To the Actor*, Michael Chekhov has suggested how to differentiate the styles of *tragedy*, *clowning*, *comedy* and *drama*. In Lecture 16 of *Speech and Drama*, Steiner offers *tragic* and *comic meditations* as a way to differentiate the moods and speaking styles for tragedy and comedy. He sensed how each distinctive mood can be accessed and channelled through specific sequences of vowels. I think it fair to suggest that Steiner was concerned to broadly differentiate the two contrasting moods. It was not his aim, as Chekhov's was, to further differentiate these categories or place them in relation to the style that Chekhov called *dramatic*.

If we explore both frameworks, we discover they enrich each other; what Chekhov differentiates as *comedy*, *high comedy*, *farce*, *vaudeville* and *circus* or *clowning* are differing degrees of tendencies within the spectrum Steiner names as *comic*. Chekhov also pointed to a difference between *heroic tragedy* and *tragedy* that moves towards *dramatic*. He made it clear that these nuances exist within a broader spectrum that encompasses the two fundamental styles, and within which even more degrees might be identified.[15] This shows that Chekhov viewed the range of styles as a continuum that we can learn to move within, and not as inflexible divisions to be dogmatically applied.

My own experience has not included opportunities for vaudeville or circus and I have minimal experience of clowning.[16] Therefore, I shall share my work with Chekhov's broader indications, showing how the processes that he devised provide the foundation that allows us to appreciate and fully implement the Steiner meditations and adapt them to the more specific styles within each genre. To plough the field and prepare it for these seeds, let us first explore the instinctive responses that prompt us to designate experience as *tragedy* or *comedy*.

## Tragic/comic style exploration 1

1. For a month or two, immerse yourself in observations of your life and events around you and watch films and plays and news reports through the lens of each perspective. Identify the elements that make you label someone as a *clown*, *comedian* or *tragedy* or *drama queen* or an event as a *farce* or *drama*, *comedy* or *tragedy*.
2. When you have identified these aspects of your own experience, ask others how they understand these terms.
3. Share your observations and conclusions with a partner and your group.

## Tragic/comic style exploration 2—partner work

On the basis of your observations, improvise the following scenario in any order that you choose: as a drama, comedy and tragedy.

1. A and B, set out on the same path from opposite directions. Finally you come face to face where the path is only wide enough for one of you to pass. What happens next?
2. Share your observations as actor and as audience. Consider the following questions and ideas as you discuss what about a situation or experience or your response makes you designate it as comic, tragic or dramatic.

You have probably recognised that this scenario belongs to the backstory of the tragedy of Oedipus. Unaware the stranger was his father, he killed the man who blocked his way on the narrow path at the Crossing of Three Ways. Does the fact that the same situation can be played in different ways demonstrate that what makes it tragic, comic or dramatic is not the situation but our view of it? Are these genres the result of our attempt to express these different views of our experience? Do the following thoughts relate to your experience?

We call a situation *tragic* when it causes more pain than our ordinary consciousness can grasp. We feel overwhelmed by a degree of suffering that appears disproportionate or undeserved, as though delivered by some power in the universe in comparison to which we feel that we are powerless. The Ancient Greeks still experienced it was the gods who ruled their destiny. Even as late as the Renaissance many felt it was the power of the stars. From a materialistic perspective, we view it as something like the 'weight of circumstance', absurdity or chance. But however changing consciousness conceives it, we sense that something greater than ourselves controls our lives.

In his *Poetics*, Aristotle wrote that the purpose of the art of tragedy was to purify our soul (our emotional or astral body) through *catharsis*. This was accomplished when the suffering, caused by the moral defects of the tragic hero, aroused *terror* and *compassion* in the audience who witnessed it.

Terror was a stern reminder of the guardians whose greater will upheld the moral fabric of the universe whose violation does not come without a cost. It served to shrink the arrogance or *hubris* that tempts the ego to exert its will in opposition to

*Figure 8 Greek tragic mask*

the gods. The contraction of the soul through terror would then be balanced by *compassion* that expands our hearts with fellow feeling for the suffering protagonist.

In our times, when freedom is viewed increasingly as a right that should extend to everyone, it is difficult to understand that this expression of humanity's evolving ego, was still quite new in the fifth century BCE.* We know the ego is a two-edged sword that wreaks havoc in its egotistical expression even as it grants us selfhood. For the Greek psyche, this complex nature of the ego was embodied in the myths relating to the god Dionysus. Those who were still inspired by temple wisdom to leadership of their communities knew that it was vitally important to create a culture that would educate the primitive expression of the ego until the I AM or Higher Self could descend into

---

* See *The Actor of the Future 4: One More Time* for a more detailed exploration of the evolution of consciousness through the different culture epochs.

the human being to begin the transformation from within. Thus the art of tragedy was introduced; through terror and compassion it ministered the antidote to the destructive aspects of the ego in the human beings of that time. And of the animals important to that culture was there any that more clearly showed the gesture of the ego than the single goat, separating from the herd to scale the highest peaks; any other creature whose dismemberment as sacrificial victim could more aptly represent the sacrifice of the god Dionysus whose own dismemberment was the sacrifice the One Self had to make along the path to freedom? Consider this passage from Euripides' *The Bacchae*:

> Oh what delight is in the mountains!/ There the celebrant, wrapped in his sacred fawnskin,/
> Flings himself on the ground surrendered,/ While the swift-footed company streams on./
> There he hunts for blood, and rapturously/Eats the raw flesh of the slaughtered goat.[17]

Goat song … *tragos* … *oide* … tragedy.

*Figure 9 Greek comic mask*

On the other hand, that we can laugh at the same follies and stupidities which, seen through a different lens, result in tragedy, ultimately stems from the largely unconscious existential trust that somewhere on another level we are safe. Shakespeare reminds us that, in some way, no matter how intense the tempest raging in our souls and the extremes to which it drives us, 'there's no harm done'. No one is *really* going to die and even if, in the worst scenario they do, the corpse of Pyramus sits up, reminding us that death is not the end: 'Now I am dead. Now I am fled. My soul is in the sky'.

This implicit sense of ultimate security allows us to endure the excruciating consequences of our foibles and peculiarities. We can laugh at how ridiculous we are, knowing, with some instinctive sense, that we are not condemned to death for our failings. On the contrary, 'every tear shall be wiped away'[18] as after all the centuries of separation, the human family will come together for the marriage at the end of time.[19] Such is the occult wisdom that inspires the weddings (often more than one) with which so many comedies conclude.

Within that part of the continuum concerned with the serious reality and inescapability of suffering and death, Michael Chekhov places *tragedy* as the form that has its source in a world conception that includes supersensible realities. *Drama* on the other hand, deals with that same serious reality and inescapability of suffering but stripped of any other-wordly context. If we stay in that same part of the continuum (that recognises only the physical dimension of reality) but are able to detach from pain through laughter, we come to the form identified by Chekhov as *comedy*. Exaggeration of the comic tendency results in *farce*. Finally we come full circle to the boundary where other-worldly beings once again participate in our reality — *clowning*. There the clowns' absurdities are so extreme it is as though they are possessed by other creatures. So relentlessly tormented are they by their crazy circumstances that we cannot help suspecting there are Puck-like beings, who delight in working mischief and witnessing 'what fools these mortals be', as they frantically career from one bewildering perception to another trying to make sense of a world that seems on purpose to oppose and even mock their most heroic efforts. Bravely they smash themselves against the walls of their material perceptions to find themselves spent at last and powerless, yet against all odds, still alive to tell the tale and share with their audience the intimate confessions of their dark side or their helplessness. Oblivious to what works within them or behind the scenes, clowns are no more able to resist these powers or overcome their obstacles than their tragic counterparts can successfully resist those gods or powers that control their destinies.

Within this framework we can now appreciate the tools that Chekhov has provided to differentiate these styles.

## Dramatic style

Dramatic style allows us to portray actions that are serious, performed by characters who experience that what they do or what is done to them proceeds entirely from the world of their material perceptions and the emotions that arise accordingly. Everything is human-sized and, according to the naturalistic paradigm, there is no sense of any non-material dimension of reality. Chekhov suggested this style is best achieved by truthful portrayal of sincere emotion. *Qualities and sensations* is the perfect tool for this. Feel free to choose your own but here are some suggestions with which to explore the Oedipus scenario (described in *style exploration 2*) in dramatic style.

### *Dramatic Style exploration 1—partner work*

1. A and B, both prepare the qualities *impatiently* and *arrogantly*.* When you can confidently alternate between them, layer them together.

2. When you are ready to sustain this complex layering, improvise the Oedipus scenario again. A and B approach each other on the narrow path. The tension builds as neither gives way to the other. Finally A forces B off the path, causing his death, and continues on his way.

# Tragic style

To achieve the *tragic* style we imbue our actions with the weight and foreboding we associate with tragedy. Confirming some of Steiner's indications in the *Speech and Drama* course, Chekhov suggests this can be achieved if we work with a predominantly slower *tempo*† occasionally punctuated with fast or staccato moments. While doing this, we must sense a presence that observes our lives and actions with the power to influence our destiny. Here is a way to cultivate that sense.

### *Tragic style exploration 1*

1. Devise a set of simple actions; for example, enter the space, turn and look around, take some steps, then sit, continuing to look around, stand and back away, then exit.

2. Perform your sequence with a partner watching you. You (A) are aware that every detail of your action is observed. There should be no direct interaction. B, strive for objective interest, not coloured with an attitude.

3. Reverse roles.

4. Share your experience. How does being watched affect your actions? Does it make a difference if you are watched from the side, behind or above? If there is more than one observer, how are you affected?

5. Respond to a presence or to presences who are not just objectively observing you but willing you to act in a specific way. Chekhov quotes the following examples: the witches in *Macbeth*, the furies in the *Oresteia* and the ghost in *Hamlet*.

6. Without the physical presence of your partner or the group observing you, recreate the sense of being watched or influenced and sustain it while repeating your action sequence from step 1.

7. Try your action sequence several times, alternating *with* and *without* the sense of that presence watching you. Show your partner or the group and share your observations.

---

* *The Art of Acting*, pp. 176–178.
† *The Art of Acting*, pp. 104–115.

### Tragic style exploration 2—partner work

1. Warm up with the qualities prepared before: *impatiently, arrogantly*.
2. Warm up slow tempo punctuated with fast or staccato movements.
3. Layer steps 1 and 2 together.
4. Layer steps 1 and 2 with the sensation of being watched.
5. Sustaining these integrated layers, play the Oedipus scenario again — first just with each other, then for an audience.
6. Share your experience. How does it relate to Chekhov's observation that our sense of being in the presence of a power greater than ourselves creates the atmosphere of tragedy?

## Comic style

Comic characters are mostly not aware that they are funny, nor are they attempting to be funny. On the contrary, the circumstances can be painful, even excruciating. Yet comic actors make us laugh. Chekhov's observations help us analyse how they elicit this response. First, he observed, they *exaggerate* behaviour that is absolutely truthful and sincere, allowing us to see how ridiculous we are when we behave that way. This task of comedy to mirror the ridiculous was observed by Aristotle in *Poetics 1*.

### Comic style exploration 1

Exaggerate the quality of *arrogantly* or *impatiently*, till it becomes ridiculous. Be careful that you don't confuse exaggerating with being insincere. Although extreme, the quality must always be emotionally truthful.

*Chekhov's tools to achieve the comic style*

Chekhov suggested that if we radiate in the six directions at once within an atmosphere of joyous expectation such as a child might feel while waiting for a party or a festival, in addition punctuating a predominantly faster tempo with slower or more legato moments, and all the time maintain a sense of ease, we will achieve the comic style.[20]

Reading the instructions for the task we feel the impossibility of doing it. If we attempt it anyway, we discover that not only does it generate the high octane energy the comic style requires but it lifts the actor into the very situation in which comic characters so often find themselves: overwhelmed by the impossible demands of life even as they strive heroically against all odds. Chekhov's tools for comic style place the actor in the archetypal comic situation. Most of these tools can be regarded as familiar friends we can apply already. Therefore we will explore the new suggestions first. We will use the well-known game 'wink-murder' to prepare our body of sensation for the comic consciousness.

### Comic style exploration 2

1. Play several rounds.[21]
2. Become aware that you are playing a scenario that would be terrifying were it 'real' yet the knowledge that it is a game generates a mood within which you feel safe to experience emotions like anxiety and fear, urgency, suspicion, terror and suspense, maliciously intending to do harm, pretence of innocence, and even an agonising death. Knowing that no harm can come to you, you can allow yourself to take them to extremes (as you try to avoid and identify the murderer before becoming the next victim yourself).
3. Play another round and become aware of the sensations that compose that mood.
4. Detach yourself from the content of the game and sustain those sensations while you move around the space.
5. Step out of them and move around. Step back into them again. Do this several times.
6. Describe them to a partner or the group. Do you experience a sense of lightness, of being lifted outside of your body, a sense of detachment from the situation while at the same time being totally awake to it?
7. Compare these sensations with those generated in the tragic and dramatic and *style explorations* that preceded these comic ones.

### Comic style exploration 3—atmosphere

1. Warm up with wink-murder.
2. Follow the steps described on pages 179–184 of *The Art of Acting* to create and then respond to an atmosphere of ease and joyous expectation, such as a child feels waiting for a festival.
3. Compare the sensations generated in step 1 with those generated in step 2.

Can you observe also how the sense of being lifted slightly outside of your body is what grants the detachment that you (*the actor*) need from the excruciating circumstances and absurd behaviour with which the *character* is totally identified?

Here is a way to begin exploring how to radiate the above sensations in the six directions all at once.

### Comic Style exploration 4—radiating in 6 directions

1. Warm up *radiating* and *staccato*.
2. Radiate full-bodily, first left, then right, then left and right together.
3. First radiate above, and then below, then above and below together, then left and right, above, below together.

4. First radiate in front and then behind, then behind and front together, then in six directions all at once.

5. Layer these sensations with those aroused in comic explorations 2 and 3 — radiating them in six directions all at once.[22]

You will probably observe it is impossible to do this perfectly! This does not mean we should not try. It is just such heroic struggles with life's impossible demands that constitutes the stuff of comedy.

## Comic style exploration 5—layering

1. Radiate in six directions in your real or imaginary wings.

2. When you are warmed up, sustain full-bodied movement level 10, enter and cross your real or imaginary stage. Exit and release.

3. In the wings, radiate in six directions, layer this with the *atmosphere* of joyous expectation — *what will happen next?*

4. Sustaining both, enter and cross your real or imaginary stage. Exit and release.

5. Observe each other and share your observations.

6. Repeat steps 1–3 reducing your movement from level 10–1. As you do so, explore how the level of movement relates to the level of exaggeration that in turn determines the range of style within the genre: the spectrum between naturalistic comedy and farce.

## Comic style exploration 6—Oedipus

1. Warm up and layer all the basic tools:
   a) Create the *atmosphere**of joyful expectation.
   b) Warm up the qualities *impatiently* and *arrogantly*.
   c) Exaggerate them not forgetting to sustain a sense of *ease*† and *lightness*.
   d) *Radiate*‡ all this in six directions.

2. Improvise the Oedipus scenario again sustaining all the layers of sensation and letting them determine the events. Remember to enjoy the hopelessness of your attempt and not let this diminish your endeavours.

You may come to the conclusion that you cannot do it! It's impossible to radiate in six directions all at once, let alone to layer this with goodness knows how many other tools and situations! Our wondrous discovery, however, is that although we are doomed to fail,

---

* *The Art of Acting*, pp. 179–184.
† *The Art of Acting*, page 118 and 234.
‡ *The Art of Acting*, pp. 64–66.

it is precisely our heroic and unshakeable resolve, our earnest striving in the face of overwhelming hindrances and everything!!! — to *radiate* an *atmosphere of joyous expectation* in *six directions* as we cross the space, all the while remembering to move *arrogantly and impatiently* in a *predominantly faster tempo*, punctuated with *a few slower and legato moments*, and don't forget the *sense of ease*!!! — that is the very thing that makes us laugh and somehow generates our love for the human beings confronted with such impossible demands.

We can explore the more exaggerated styles of farce and slapstick if we apply our inadequate attempts at all of the above (but nevertheless with movement level 10 commitment) to such classic formulae as 'slip on a banana skin' or being chased by an angry bee or lion, then chasing and confronting it.

## Comic style exploration 7—slapstick

1. Repeat steps 1–3 of *comic style exploration 5*, but as you cross the stage, slip on a banana skin, recover, exit, then release.
2. Warm up the qualities *courageously* and *anxiously*. Exaggerate their tendencies to level 10.
3. Sustaining level 10, repeat step 1, first in one quality and then the other.
4. Repeat the preparation for step 1 but now apply the tools as you chase or are chased by an angry bee. Rimsky-Korsakov's *Flight of the Bumble Bee* will inspire the tempo needed.
5. Repeat step 4 but this time layered with the alternating qualities *courageously* and *anxiously*.

## Comic style exploration 8—fight, flight and freeze
### Individual

1. Inspired by *Flight of the Bumble Bee*, run across the space heroically sustaining as many of the tools as you are able to at movement level 10.
2. Stop the music suddenly and *freeze* while sustaining the sensations of movement level 10.
3. When the music starts again, move again at level 10 sustaining all the comic tools that you are able to!!! but this time you are running from the bee: *flight* mode.
4. Stop the music suddenly, *freeze* again, sustaining the sensations of movement level 10.
5. When the music starts again, move again at level 10 sustaining all the comic tools that you are able to!!! but this time turn heroically and face your enemy: *fight* mode.

### Partner work

Once you are confident with steps 1–5, play with a partner.
6. Approach from opposite directions and explore how freeze, fly or fight, can alternate.

## *Comic style exploration 9—speaking*

Your goal is a precisely integrated speech and movement comic monologue in which each gesture supports the crafting of each syllable with clear intention.

### *Individual*

1. Warm up* your speech instrument with:

> towhit twinkle twas
>
> twice twigged tweaker
>
> to twenty twangy twirlings
>
> the zinnia crisper
>
> zither zooming shambles
>
> this smartened smacking smuggler
>
> sneezing snoring snatching.

2. Work through each choice of freeze, flight and fight, finding precise full-bodied gestures to accompany each line and syllable until you have three full-bodied monologues with which to practise speaking in the comic style.

### *Partner work*

3. Once you have achieved this, explore all the possibilities of interaction arising from the interplay of freeze, flight or fight, exchanging single lines or sections with a partner to create a full-bodied comic dialogue in which each word or syllable affects your partner with the same precision of intention you achieved alone.

## *Comic style exploration 10—text application*

1. Adapt this process to explore these lines, from Act 3, scene 4 of *Twelfth Night*. Practise each phrase and sentence until you integrate your full-bodied gestures with the language according to the following suggestions.
2. Experiment with all three roles, rotating them in groups of three so everyone attempts them all.

> *Sir Toby*: [fight] (*to Sir Andrew*) Why man he's a very devil, I have not seen such a virago. I had a pass with him, rapier, scabbard and all and he gives me the stuck-in with such a mortal motion that it is inevitable; and on the answer he pays you as surely as your feet hit the ground. They say he has been fencer to the Sophy.
>
> *Sir Andrew*: [freeze/flight] Pox on it! I'll not meddle with him…

---

* *The Art of Speech*, page 124.

*Sir Toby*: [fight] Aye but he will not now be pacified.

*Sir Andrew*: [freeze/flight] Plague on it, and I thought he had been valiant and so cunning in fence, I'd have seen him damned e're I'ld have challenged him. Let him let the matter slip, and I'll give him my horse, grey Capilet.

*Sir Toby*: [fight] (*to Viola*) There's no remedy Sir. He will fight with you for his oath's sake.

*Viola*: [freeze/flight] Pray God defend me: a little thing would make me tell them how much I lack of a man.

*Sir Toby*: [fight] (*to Sir Andrew*) Come Sir Andrew, there's no remedy; the gentleman for his honour's sake will have one bout with you…Come on, to it.

*Sir Andrew*: [freeze/flight] Pray God he keep his oath. (*draws*)

*Sir Toby*: [fight] (*to Viola*) There's no remedy Sir.

*Viola*: [freeze/flight] I do assure you, 'tis against my will……Pray sir, put your sword up if you please.

*Sir Andrew*: [freeze/flight] Marry, will I sir, and for that I promised you, I'll be as good as my word. He will bear you easily and reins well.

# *Clowning*

The clown reminds us that our personalities are not our own to the degree *cool reason* would have us think. Chekhov reminds us that behind our belief that we are rational creatures in control of our destinies, a whole other world is at work. In contrast to the numinous tragic presence, a sub-world plays with us: laughing at our ignorance of its existence, at our presumption of our own importance, and that we take ourselves so seriously. *Lord, what fools these mortals be!*[23]

By inviting the audience to share their confidence, clowns make it bearable for us to recognise what goes on behind our carefully constructed, civilised personas. If we were clairvoyant we would see the forms our untransformed astrality assumes, hovering in the lower astral world. But, until we are, the clown reveals to us the sometimes grotesque and pathetic beings inhabiting our auras and possessing us: drawing our attention to what we might not wish to acknowledge is a part of us.

In demonstrating how to play with these beings rather than condemn and punish them, clowns broaden our understanding of the forces that inhabit our subconscious life and thus begin the transformation of what would, unacknowledged, continue to wreak havoc.

This is especially important in the case of the darker clowns, who are possessed for example by the archetype of 'rage', 'vindictiveness' or 'ruthlessness'. To embody such an archetype successfully, a clown must investigate its qualities with ruthless honesty, a scrutiny no less devoted to the truth, than that of scientists in a laboratory. The clown is the part of us able to observe that aspect of the human soul clearly and without fear or favour, but not identify with it. Instead the clown stands beside it, observing its own behaviour and takes the audience into its confidence to share that observation. *Look! See what I am doing, how badly I behave, how blatantly and unapologetically I expose this aspect of my soul. Now however shocked you may appear to be, do you recognise this in yourself?* It is the self, conscious of itself and demonstrating it is conscious of itself. Whether it be the whole body costume, the exaggerated face or the micro costume of a nose, like the motley of former times, it grants permission to the clown to expose the truth without the fear of punishment. In his portrayal of Adenoid Hynkel, for example, in the film *The Great Dictator* (available on Youtube), Charlie Chaplin has explored the archetype that repeatedly possessed the soul of Hitler.

In the case of the positive archetypes, Patch Adams stated unreservedly that clowning is the trick that allows him to get close enough to pour Love into the wounded souls whose pain might make them normally resist it.

As mentioned earlier, my experience of clowning has been minimal and I direct the reader to Chekhov's wonderful analysis on pages 142–143 of *To the Actor*. However, here are some explorations I have based on Chekhov's thoughts about possession by sub-human beings.

### *Clowning style exploration 1*

1. Warm up and sustain full-bodily the qualities *anxiously, impatiently, arrogantly* etc.
2. Magnify their tendencies (even to beyond level 10!!!) until you have become that quality, consist of nothing but that quality and your instrument has taken on the

actual form of arrogance, impatience or anxiety; as though the being of arrogance, impatience or anxiety has totally possessed you.

3. Using the same process, experiment with the seven deadly sins in Marlowe's *Dr Faustus* (Act 2, scene 3).

4. Improvise the pranks Puck plays on hapless creatures as described by the fairy and himself;[24] identify some qualities, prepare them as in steps 1 and 2, reverse roles back and forth. Alternate the prankster with the victim until the physical reversals transform into dynamics that are played out in the victim's body/soul who has to struggle with the sub-human beings who possess them.

Observation of ourselves and others reveals that when we invoke the comic spirit, whether in life or art, it grants us the capacity in the present and in retrospect — even as we find our foolishness exposed — to step outside ourselves, observe ourselves and demonstrate in some degree from subtle to extreme, that we are conscious of our own absurdity.[25]

## Steiner's meditations for tragic and comic styles

Through the preceding explorations we achieve the full-bodied psycho-physical awareness that allows us to explore and appreciate the genius of Steiner's tragic/comic meditations. Named in this way, he clearly intended them as mantras that, spoken and embodied, have the power to invoke the tragic or the comic muse. In this way they perform the function of all meditation — to be a portal through which the meditant connects the earthly here and now with the cosmic levels of experience. In doing so, the actor is a priest who mediates the mysteries through the sacraments of tragedy or comedy.

These mantras are born out of Steiner's insight that the spectrum of the vowels based on their placements in the mouth from back to front, connects to the spectrum of sensation that our souls interpret as the comic or the tragic mood. Before we explore their power to evoke these moods it might be helpful to survey the chart that shows each vowel sequence and its place within the total spectrum.

*Outer circle—anticlockwise direction—phonetic symbols, followed by an English example of the vowel, indicate the placements of the vowels from the back of the mouth, through the boundary of the teeth in the middle, to the furthest forward placement on the lips.*

*Inner cirlce—indicates movement back and forth within the sequence of vowel placements from which arise the tragic and comic moods—with examples from Steiner's meditations.*

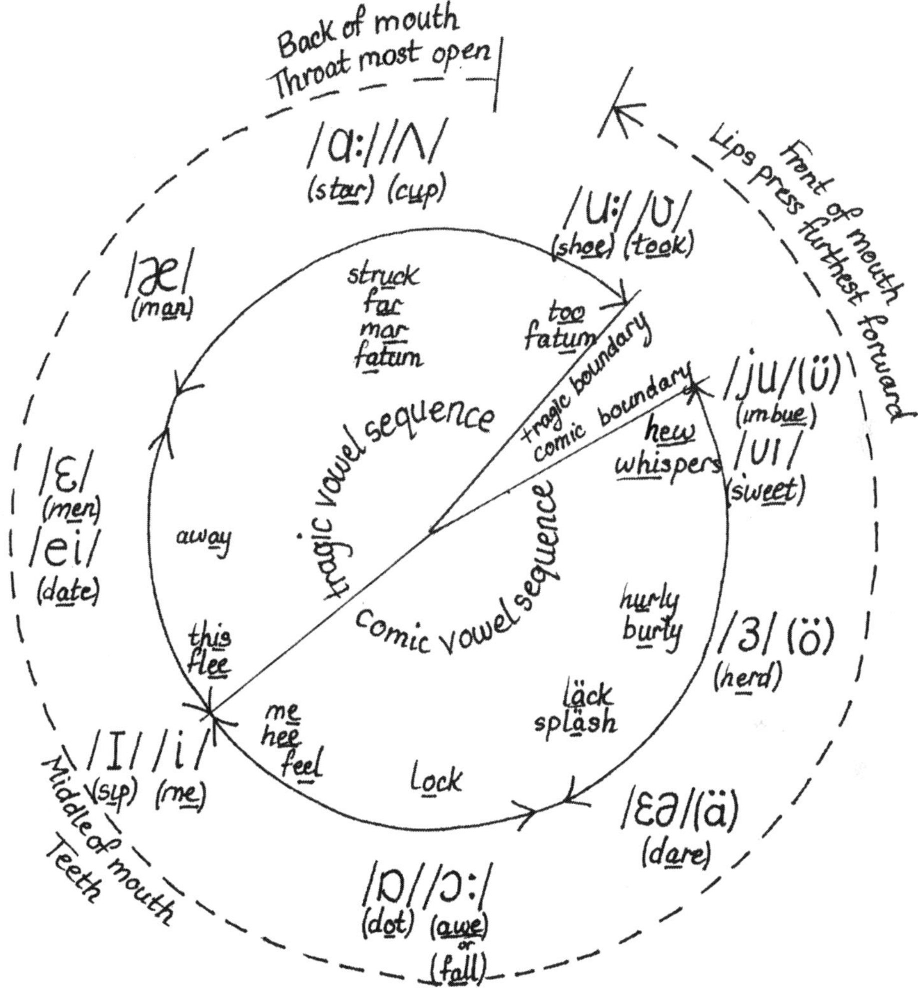


NB: Umlauts over the English 'läck' and 'spläsh' indicate that the short English 'a' can be spoken with the spaciousness of 'ä'.

NB: Phonetic symbols next to umlauted vowels indicate the nearest English equivalent to those vowels.

*Figure 10 Circle of Vowels*

## *The Tragic style*

To appreciate the wisdom guiding Steiner's choice of vowels that prepare our souls to mediate the tragic mood, it will be helpful to recall the following:

- Tragedy was born out of the *Mysteries* [*] to demonstrate the human being's journey to self-knowledge.
- The representative of the community, the tragic hero or protagonist, acts out of overweening pride (hubris) that causes the ego to believe that it has god-like power and authority but is not morally accountable. This finds expression in the gesture of the vowel /i:/ (m<u>e</u>).
- The consequence of hubris is the 'catastrophe' that demolishes the character's constructed self. Mystery language described this as the death of the persona on which the second birth depended: the birth of the immortal self or spirit. In *Oedipus Tyrannus*, Sophocles makes this clear in the words Tiresias speaks to Oedipus:

  This day brings you your birth and death.

- Greek consciousness conceived the catastrophe as punishment by the gods for daring to compete with them. The initial resistance of the ego to being shattered by the blows of fate finds expression in the vowel /ɛ/ (m<u>e</u>n) and the English diphthong /eɪ/ (f<u>a</u>te).
- The surrender to the presence of a power greater than the ego's hubris finds expression in the vowel /ɑ:/ (m<u>ar</u>) while the terror that the ego feels at its impending doom finds expression in the vowel /u:/ (t<u>oo</u>). Steiner has used the Latin word '*fatum*' which means 'destiny' or 'fate' because it contains both vowels. Together they provide the opportunity to tinge the /ɑ:/ with /u:/. This combination is repeated several times within the verse and achieves the vocal colouring appropriate to tragedy: fear-tinged awe or awe-tinged fear.

Holding the above in our consciousness while we sustain Chekhov's tools for tragic style in our body of sensation, we approach the mantra.

## *Tragic meditation—style exploration 1*

> <u>Ah</u> F<u>atu</u>m!
>
> Y<u>ou</u> have struck me t<u>oo</u> f<u>ar</u>!
>
> Th<u>is</u> wa<u>y</u> f<u>a</u>tes m<u>ar</u>!
>
> Fl<u>ee</u> awa<u>y</u>!
>
> F<u>ar</u> t<u>oo</u>!

The sequence of vowels[†] in this mantric verse reveals the tragic hero's archetypal journey, allowing Chekhov's tools for tragic style to manifest in speech. The text moves back and forth between the vowels /ɑ:/ and /u:/ intersected by /i:/ and /eɪ/.

---

[*]  *The Art of Acting*, pp. 20–22.
[†]  See Appendix B for the table of phonetic symbols referring to the vowels indicated here.

## Ah Fatum!

*Figure 11*

*You have struck me too far*

*Figure 12*

Figure 13

# Flee away

Figure 14

*Far too*

Figure 15

# *Far too*

Figure 16

/ɑ:/ (<u>A</u>h F<u>a</u>tum!)

Beginning with /ɑ:/

*I, the protagonist, feel my boundaries dissolve as I approach the threshold where I sense a greater presence looking on, to whose all-seeing gaze I must surrender.*

*Figure 17 Vowel mood /ɑ:/*

Moving now towards /u:/ (Fat<u>u</u>m! Y<u>ou</u> )

*I feel myself contract — a tinge of fear pulls me back into myself as I recognise that I approach the threshold.*

*Figure 18 Vowel mood /u:/*

Moving back again to /ɑ:/ then /u:/ then /ɑ:/ again.

Ah Fat<u>u</u>m!

Y<u>ou</u> have str<u>u</u>ck me t<u>oo</u> f<u>ar</u>.

*Awe alternating now with terror, stirs. My actions have not gone, are not undetected. I begin to sense the power of something that will change my world forever. Events are no longer under my control.*

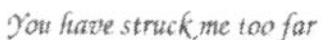

/i:/ (m_e th_is, fl_ee) and /eɪ/ (w_ay, f_ates, aw_ay)

*Assert myself* /i:/

*Dare to resist, to strike back at the gods* /eɪ/

*even as my boundaries dissolve again in /ɑː/*

*Assert myself again, /iː/*

*hit out defiantly, resist my fate, escape! /eɪ/:*

*Moving back again to /a:/: (f<u>ar</u>)*

*If I fly to the ends of the earth I cannot escape. I finally surrender to their presence and accept my destiny.*

*And once again to /uː/ (t<u>oo</u>)*

*Awe and fear at what the gods accomplish.*
This was Oedipus, greatest of men. Behold what a great tide of misfortune has swept over him![26]

We can sense in the image on the left, the /ɑː/ (f<u>ar</u>) gesture tinged with /uː/ (t<u>oo</u>) while on the right the /uː/ is tinged with /ɑː/. Through practising this mantra our body of sensation transforms into a vessel for the tragic muse to fill.[27]

### *Tragic meditation — style exploration 2*

1. Create a full-bodied vowel sequence based on /i:/ and /eɪ/ which expresses the assertion of the ego in the world in expanding alternation. This vowel prologue prepares you for the first line of the text with its sense of foreboding.
2. Working full-bodily, you sense a presence overshadow you — /ɑ:/ and /u:/. Alternate the vowels until you can colour /a:/ with /u:/ to generate that ominous sense that tragedy is imminent.
3. Now assert yourself with a full-bodied gesture of defiance — /i:/, /eɪ/ — only to surrender once again in fear-tinged awe, in awful fear — /ɑ: /, /u:/.
4. Recreate this journey but now insert the mantric words, permeated with this archetypal sequence of the tragic vowels.
5. Explore the mantra as a monologue and address it to the gods. Does sustaining the full-bodied gestures at level 10 give a sense of the classical Greek style?
6. As you reduce the gestures (10–1) explore how the acting style becomes more naturalistic.
7. Once you have mastered the archetypal journey embedded in the text, layer it with appropriate *qualities and sensations, objectives* etc.
8. Work with a partner and explore the text as a dialogue between two human characters or between a human being and a god.

## Comic style

To appreciate the wisdom underlying Steiner's choice of vowels relating to the comic style it will be helpful to remember how the I heroically asserts itself against all odds /i:/ (m<u>e</u>) until the levels of uncertainty /ɜ/ (h<u>ur</u>ly b<u>ur</u>ly) alternating with excruciating agony /ju/ (h<u>ew</u>) and /uɪ/ (<u>whi</u>sp<u>er</u>s) … interspersed with more heroic efforts to survive /i:/ (m<u>e</u>) build to a monumental climax of disaster only to reveal that after all 'there's no harm done' /ɛə/ (spl<u>a</u>sh).*

### *Comic meditation — style exploration 1*

<u>I</u>nside m<u>e</u>

I c<u>a</u>n f<u>ee</u>l

How l<u>i</u>nk lock h<u>ew</u>

And lock lack h<u>ee</u>

H<u>ur</u>ly b<u>ur</u>ly m<u>erely</u>

<u>Whi</u>sp<u>er</u>s

Spl<u>a</u>sh!

---

* Here I have used the English diphthongs to replace the umlauted vowels on which Steiner based the German text. The connection between the German vowels and their equivalents in English has been explored in Chapter 1 of *The Art of Speech* and will be explored again in Chapter 8.

*Figure 19*

*Figure 20*

*Figure 21*

*Figure 22*

*Figure 23*

*Figure 24*

*Figure 25*

*Figure 26*

*Figure 27*

*Figure 28*

Figure 29

Figure 30

*Figure 31*

Here I have presented alternative ways to approach the climax at the end. If the stage represented by Figure 30 is treated as the climax then the release that follows it, represented by Figure 31, can be treated as a sort of anticlimax. On the other hand it is possible to also approach the release itself as the climax: an endless falling into blissful oblivion after all the tension.

## Comic meditation—style exploration 2

Inside me
I can feel
How link lock hew
And lock lack hee
Hurly burly merely
Whispers
Splash!

1. It will help to appreciate the progression of vowels [/ɪ/ (<u>i</u>nside) /i:/ (m<u>e</u>, f<u>ee</u>l, h<u>ee</u>) /ɜ/ (h<u>ur</u>ly b<u>ur</u>ly) /ju/ (h<u>ew</u>) /uɪ/ (<u>wh</u>ispers)] out of which the verse has been constructed if we remember the archetypal journey of the comic character. Perhaps we are anxious, angry, arrogant, shy or greedy. If we exaggerate the outer expressions of these qualities, radiating them full-bodily in six directions [all the while slightly excarnated in an atmosphere of joyous expectation and, in addition (just in case you forgot!) in a faster tempo with a sense of ease!!!!!] we can demonstrate just how absurd it is to be so greedy, anxious, arrogant, shy or angry etc. because — no matter how extreme or disproportionate within the scale of reality perceived by the dispassionate observer, no matter how confused we are or how much chaos we create, how ongoing or extreme the list of crises, how close to catastrophic doom — *there's no harm done.* We can never really harm another nor be harmed by them. Everything will turn out alright in the end. This is the safety net (the blanket in which Mak was tossed) that grants us courage to invoke the comic muse and hurl ourselves into the abyss of craziness.

2. Working full-bodily, express the stages of this journey in the vowels that follow.

*Whatever it is, whoever I am, however arrogant, or absurd etc., radiate its quality (in six directions) out into the space — /ɪ/ (<u>i</u>nside) /i:/ (m<u>e</u>, f<u>ee</u>l, h<u>ee</u>).*

*Now the consequences — foreseen of course by everyone except myself — appear; con-fusion multiplies, doubt, uncertainty, absurdities spiral out of my control; what will happen now? Lips contorting as they twist back and forth between —* /ɜ/ *(h*u*rly b*u*rly)*[28] /uɪ/ /ə/ *(wh*i*sp*er*s) and* /ju/ *(h*ew*)* /uɪ/ *(*wh*i*sp*ers).*

*Try harder to control it; more* /ɪ/ *and* /i:/ *(wh*i*spers, m*e*rely)*

*Even w<u>o</u>rse than I imagined /ɜ/ and /ə/, /uɪ/ (<u>whisp<u>e</u>rs</u>)*

*Hesitation alternating with unbearable, excruciating, escalating tension; (<u>whisp<u>e</u>rs</u>) twisting, contorting, squeezing me between /uɪ/ and /ɜ/and /ə/.*

*Alternating faster, intensify the repetitions: (whisp<u>e</u>rs): confusion /ɜ/and /ə/, (h<u>ew</u>): excruciating agony /ju/, <u>whi</u>: /uɪ/, desperate attempts to put things right, assert myself again /i:/, more confused than ever /ɜ/ and /ə/, more excruciating agony /ju/, /uɪ/, until — just when I think it couldn't possibly get any w<u>o</u>rse — surely the tension must have reached its climax /ɜ/ — finally it b<u>u</u>rsts /ɜ/!!!!!*

*Blessed release, relief spreads over everything: diphthong/æ/ expands the surface area of /æ/ (spl<u>a</u>sh).* There's no harm done!*

3.  After playing with the vowels, single words and syllables we are ready to speak the mantra and invoke the comic muse.

Inside me
I can feel
How link lock hew
And lock lack hee
Hurly burly merely
Whispers
Splash!

## Comic meditation—style exploration 3

1.  Recreate the full-bodied archetypal journey as described in step 2 of *comic meditation style exploration 2.*
2.  Integrate it with the comic mantra. Play with the lines, flexibly repeating them in any order as often as you like until the escalating tension of the unresolved complexity builds to its climax at the end.
3.  Treat the text as a comic monologue.
4.  Use the mantra to invoke the comic muse before you plunge into the chasing/being chased by bee scenario accompanied by *Flight of the Bumble Bee.*
5.  Treat the mantra as a dialogue. A is the tormentor, B the tormented. Play with repetition, alternation, single lines, sections and whole text.

---

* The English rendering *splash* needs to be spoken with the sensation of the diphthong /eə/(d<u>are</u>) in order to convey release.

6. The final climax could occur on *whispers* or on *splash*. Play with both. *Splash* as the final climax or as the release of tension that follows the final climax which occurs on *whispers*.

7. Layer the text with *qualities and sensations*, e.g. *threateningly, pompously* etc.

8. To expand your expressive range explore what happens when you layer the text with *moulding, floating, flying* and *radiating; expanding/contracting* and *staccato/legato* and the *seven archetypal gestures* that embody the revelations of speech, as explored in volume 2.

9. Having used the mantra to invoke the Comic Muse,[29] explore how it prepares you to attempt the following speeches. They need not be gender specific. The first is Helena's from *A Midsummer Night's Dream*. Exploit her use of /ɪ/, /iː/, /ə/and /ɜ/ and /ʊɪ/ — /ju/ — /uɪ/ to extract the comic possibilities.

> … Dem<u>e</u>treus,
> The more <u>you</u> b<u>ea</u>t m<u>e</u> I <u>wi</u>ll fawn on <u>you</u>.
> <u>U</u>se m<u>e</u> but as your spaniel; sp<u>ur</u>n m<u>e</u>, strike m<u>e</u>,
> Neglect m<u>e</u>, lose m<u>e</u>; onl<u>y</u> <u>g</u>ive m<u>e</u> l<u>ea</u>ve,
> Unw<u>or</u>thy as I am, to follow <u>you</u>.
> What w<u>or</u>se a place can I beg <u>i</u>n your love,
> And yet a place of high respect w<u>i</u>th m<u>e</u>,
> Than to b<u>e</u> <u>u</u>sed as <u>you</u> <u>u</u>se your dog?*

The second is from the Prologue to Shaw's, *Androcles and the Lion*. Androcles, who has become a Christian, is fleeing Rome with his wife in order to escape persecution. They come upon a lion in the forest.

*Androcles: (quaking, but keeping between the lion and Megaera)* Don't you come near my wife, do you hear? *(The lion groans. Androcles can hardly stand for trembling.)* Meggy: run. Run for your life. If I take my eye off him, it's all up. *(The lion holds up his wounded paw and flaps it piteously before Androcles.)* Oh, he's lame, poor old chap! He's got a thorn in his paw. A frightfully big thorn. *(Full of sympathy.)* Oh, poor old man! Did um get an awful thorn into um's tootsums wootsums? Has it made um too sick to eat a nice little Christian man for um's breakfast? Oh, a nice little Christian man will get um's thorn out for um; and then um shall eat the nice Christian man and the nice Christian man's nice big tender wifey pifey. *(The lion responds by moans of self-pity.)* Yes, yes, yes, yes, yes. Now, now *(taking the paw in his hand)* um is not to bite and not to scratch, not even if it hurts a very, very little. Now make velvet paws. That's right. *(He pulls gingerly at the thorn. The lion, with an angry yell of pain, jerks back his paw so abruptly*

---

* I have not underlined all the unstressed syllables which add to the build-up of stress through their tendency to turn into the neutral vowel /ə/ when spoken, e.g.: 'and' 'the' 'as' 'a' 'of'.

*that Androcles is thrown on his back.*) Steadeee! Oh, did the nasty cruel little Christian man hurt the sore paw? (*The lion moans assentingly but apologetically.*) Well, one more little pull and it will be all over. Just one little, little, leetle pull; and then um will live happily ever after. (*He gives the thorn another pull. The lion roars and snaps his jaws with a terrifying clash.*) Oh, mustn't frighten um's good kind doctor, um's affectionate nursey. That didn't hurt at all: not a bit. Just one more. Just to show how the brave big lion can bear pain, not like the little crybaby Christian man. Oopsh! (*The thorn comes out. The lion yells with pain, and shakes his paw wildly.*) That's it! (*Holding up the thorn.*) Now it's out. Now lick um's paw to take away the nasty inflammation. See? (*He licks his own hand. The lion nods intelligently and licks his paw industriously.*) Clever little liony-piony! Understands um's dear old friend Andy Wandy. (*The lion licks his face.*) Yes, kissums Andy Wandy. (*The lion, wagging his tail violently, rises on his hind legs and embraces Androcles, who makes a wry face and cries.*) Velvet paws! Velvet paws! (*The lion draws in his claws.*) That's right. (*He embraces the lion, who finally takes the end of his tail in one paw, places that tight around Androcles' waist, resting it on his hip. Androcles takes the other paw in his hand, stretches out his arm, and the two waltz rapturously round and round and finally away through the jungle.*)


## *Advanced layering and style*


*Advanced style exploration 1—vocal tempo and dynamic in the comic style*
In *comic style exploration 9*, we discovered how easily this exercise for vocal flexibility can be adapted to the comic style.[*]

    To whit twinkle 'twas
    Twice twigged tweaker
    To twenty twangy twirlings
    The zinnia crisper
    Zither zooming shambles
    This smartened smacking smuggler
    Sneezing snoring snatching.


1.  Warm up *tempo* and *dynamic*.
2.  Focus on a sequence of action fast/staccato punctuated by slower moments/legato.
3.  Warm up *radiating* an atmosphere of *joyous expectancy* in 6 directions.

---

[*] *The Art of Speech*, page 124.

4. Warm up *to whit twinkle 'twas* etc., as described on page 124 of *The Art of Speech*.

5. Integrate these layers.

6. The first three lines suggest radiating in all six directions with a faster tempo and staccato moments. Layer into these lines such qualities as *mischievously* or *teasingly*.

7. In the lines 'the zinnia crisper, zither zooming shambles' the voiced /z/ enables us to build the comic tension by digging deeper into density and confidently carve our way through all resistence. Play with layering these lines with qualities like *threatening* or *relentlessly pursuing*.

8. The /s/ and /m/ combination in 'this smartened smacking smuggler' makes us tread carefully, the sole of each foot sensing deeply with each step, trying not to make a sound as we would if we suspect that our presence is or might be sensed. Play with layering this line with qualities like, *carefully*, *warily* and *surreptitiously*.

9. The /sn/ combination in the final line 'sneezing snoring snatching' inspires us to leap out of hiding and pounce on our assailant with each /sn/ at the same time using it to spring away, well clear of any danger or reprisal. Layer the last line with qualities like *scarily*, *courageously* and alternating these with *warily*.

10. Experiment with changing tempo and dynamic in each line.

11. Apply the text to the chasing/being chased by a bee scenario alternating between qualities *heroically* and *nervously*.

12. Play with a partner, exchange lines and sections to create a dialogue and improvise with all the possibilities above.

## Advanced style exploration 2—expanding and contracting*

### Tragic style

This next exercise applies *expanding* and *contracting* to condense the archetypal journey of the tragic hero, an Oedipus or Lear, for example, into a text based on the complementary qualites of p and b.[†]

    Power proudly (x 3 — expanding in 3 stages)
    Being broken (x 3 — contracting in 3 stages)
    Prayer penetrating (x 3 — expanding in 3 stages)

---

* The following exercise is based on the expansion and contraction exercises described in *The Art of Acting*, pp. 98–100.

[†] *The Art of Acting*, pp. 97–100, *The Art of Speech*, pp. 41,78.

1. Warm up *expanding* and *contracting*.
2. Warm up the tools for tragic style; *sense of superhuman presence, slower tempo, tragic meditation* etc.
3. Warm up the quality-and-sensation of *arrogantly* and layer it with *expanding* in three successive stages; at each stage speaking:

   Power Proudly

4. Warm up quality-and-sensation *brokenly* and layer it with contracting in three successive stages until the ego is reduced to nothing; at each stage speaking:

   Being Broken

5. Warm up quality-and-sensation *humbly* and layer it with expanding again in three successive stages, at first tentatively and then with a strength born of humility; at each stage speaking:

   Prayer Penetrating

6. Explore how Steiner's tragic meditation and this exercise enrich each other.

## Advanced style exploration 3—Comic style

The following idioms demonstrate how instinctively we use the same expanding and contracting qualities of /p/ and /b/ to express our sense of the ridiculous:

Piddling pimple!
Piffling piffle!
Pompous pedant!/Pompous prick!
Preposterous! How perfectly preposterous!
Poppycock!/pure poppycock!/'he is the very pineapple of perfection'.[30]
Blimey!/bother!/blooming bother!/botheration!/blooming bungle!/bumbling around/bumbling idiot/bit of a bumbler/bit of a bummer!/bunbury.[31]

1. Warm up the comic tools and layer them with *expanding* and *contracting*.
2. Layer these with now familiar qualities like *arrogantly, shyly, anxiously, aggressively, ashamedly* and any others that appeal. Have fun with all their different combinations.
3. Insert the above words or phrases using /p/ as you expand full-bodily, to support your voice to radiate into the space without pushing from your throat.
4. Use /b/ as you contract full-bodily in order to support your voice so it doesn't disappear inside your instrument.
5. Play with a partner in all the combinations of expanding and contracting layered with the other tools.
6. Exchange the words and phrases as a dialogue.

## *Advanced style exploration 4—revelations of speech in tragic style— individual & partner*

1.  Warm up the full-bodied archetypal speech gestures.*
2.  Warm up the tools for tragic style including the tragic meditation.
3.  Explore all the gestures in the tragic style.
4.  Use the seven gestures in tragic style to explore your interaction with a partner.

## *Advanced style exploration 5—revelations of speech in comic style— individual and partner*

1.  Warm up the full-bodied archetypal speech gestures.
2.  Warm up the tools for comic style including the comic meditation.
3.  Explore all the gestures in the comic style.
4.  Use the seven gestures in comic style to explore your interaction with a partner.

---

* *The Actor of the Future 2: Word Made Flesh*, Chapter 1.

### *Advanced Style exploration 6—exercising all the styles*

*Dramatic style*

1.  Warm up a series of qualities and sensations, for example, *fearfully, courageously, sadly, shyly, hopefully.*
2.  When each one is prepared, enter your performing space and cross it in that quality.
3.  Exit and release.

*Tragic style*

4.  Layer your quality with the tools for tragic style.
5.  Enter and cross the space.
6.  Exit and release.
7.  Sustaining your quality in *tragic* style, enter the space and perform your *Ah fatum!* monologue.
8.  Exit and release.

*Comic style*

9.  Now layer your quality with the tools for comic style.
10. Enter and cross the space.
11. Exit and release.
12. Sustaining your quality in *comic* style, enter the space and perform your *Inside me…* monologue.
13. Exit and release.
14. Layer your quality with the tools for *clowning* style (you are possessed with the being of courage, greed etc.) and cross the space.
15. Exit and release.
16. Sustaining your state of possession, enter the space and perform your *Inside me…* monologue.
17. Exit and release.
18. Introduce a simple action as you cross the space, eg: stopping and turning, sitting or kneeling, finding a letter and repeat steps 1–8.

## Combinations

19. Repeat steps 1–9. Add to your sequence of actions and layer it with one change of quality, then two etc. (e.g. *fearfully* to *hopefully to sadly* etc.).

## *Advanced style exploration 7—further application of the styles*

We will now apply our tools to three small interactions that provide the opportunity to differentiate between the styles of drama, tragedy and comedy. By allowing each interaction to unfold from the gestures of *giving and receiving* layered with the same *qualities and sensations* it will be very clear how the tools for style transform the other factors. Working full-bodily:

1. Warm up *giving and receiving.*[*]
2. Warm up the qualities of *tentatively* and *courageously.*
3. When you can alternate between them and also layer them together, layer *giving and receiving* with these qualities.

*Dramatic style — partner work*

Apply these layers of sensation to this excerpt from the end of Ibsen's *A Doll's House.* Nora prepares herself for the most courageous deed of her life: to leave her husband. As a step in her journey of emancipation she *gives* back her wedding ring to her husband. Torvald, still in a state of shock, *receives* it from her. Then he *gives* his back to her and she *receives* it.

> *Nora*: Look here's your ring back. Give me mine.
> *Torvald*: That too?
> *Nora*: That too.
> *Torvald*: There it is.

## Tragic style—partner work

1. Warm up the tools for tragic style.
2. Layer them with steps 1–3 above.
3. Apply these layers of sensation to the moment from *The Trojan Women* by Euripides when the Greek ambassador Talthybius approaches Hector's widow, Andromache. He *gives* and she *receives* the news that her son, the child Astyanax, has been sentenced by the Greeks to be hurled from the citadel of Troy.

> *Talthybius*: Your son must die.
> *Andromache*: Oh!

## Comic style—partner work

1. Warm up the tools for comic style.
2. Layer them with steps 1–3 above.

---

[*] *The Art of Acting,* pp. 137–138.

3. Apply these layers of sensation to the following excerpt from Anton Chekhov's one act comedy *The Bear*. The widow Popova is determined to challenge Smirnov to a duel. Because she has never held a gun and does not know what to do with it, she *gives* it to Smirnov and asks him to show her how to use it. He *receives* it from her realising he has fallen hopelessly in love with her feisty spirit. He *gives* her the information she requires to use it which she (also realising she is in love) in turn *receives*.

*Popova*: (*she enters carrying the pistols*). Here they are, the pistols… But before we begin, be good enough to show me how to fire. I've never had a pistol in my hands before…

*Smirnov*: (*examining the pistols*). You see, there are several sorts of pistols … There are special duelling pistols, that's the Mortimer make with capsules. But these pistols of yours are Smith-Wessons, triple action with extractor… Beautiful pistols! They're worth at least ninety roubles the brace… You must hold the revolver like this…

## *Advanced style exploration 8—clowning—partner work*

*A Midsummer Night's Dream* provides the opportunity to explore transitions between comic style and clowning. We can do this if we make the choice that when Bottom (comic style) is 'translated' by the ass's head Puck places on him (Act 3.2) he is possessed by the spirit of the ass (clowning) (Acts 3.1, and 4.2) and when Puck removes it and Bottom is restored to himself (final speech of Act 4.1) he shifts back again into the comic style. Here are some suggestions.

1. Warm up with the comic meditation and return to it throughout the following process whenever you feel the need to reconnect.
2. Study the qualities of an ass, incorporating them full-bodily.[*]
3. One of Bottom's fundamental gestures is to *give* to and receive the world in a *bull-dozing* ('bully bottom') kind of way. Therefore warm up *giving* and *receiving* and the *bulldozing quality*, then layer them.
4. When he first *receives* the ass's head (although unknowingly) he *gives* his next lines with typical *ebullience, enthusiasm* and *dominating confidence*.
5. Deserted by his friends, he is increasingly *possessed* by the spirit of the ass (begin transition into clowning). Initially confused, he alternates between *giving* (singing *confidently* to allay his fear) and *receiving tentatively* as he allows the strange sensations to possess him, alternating comic style and clowning until the spirit of the ass has totally possessed him.
6. During his encounter with Titania and the fairies he *receives completely* the spirit of the ass (clowning); his assinine behaviour is woven through with *humble deference, respect and gratitude* for the nature beings and everything they *give* to him.

---

[*] *The Art of Acting*, pp. 168–174.

7. When he finally wakes up and the ass's head has been removed he returns to his customary self (comic style) and alternates beween *confidently giving* as he forms his plan of action and *receiving tentatively* as he recalls the dream that altered his reality forever.

## Advanced style exploration 9—playing death

*Comic style*
*A Midsummer Night's Dream* also provides the opportunity to die in comic style.
1. Warm up the *Three sisters* with its speech exercise 'what use wail and weep' etc.[*]
2. Warm up the comic tools and meditation.
3. Warm up qualities like *grief-stricken* and *heroically.*
4. Layer steps 1 and 3 with the comic tools and meditation.
5. Apply all these layers of sensation to the deaths and final speeches of Pyramus and Thisbe in Act 5.

*Tragic and Dramatic Style*
*Romeo and Juliet* provides the opportunity to die in tragic or dramatic styles.
1. Repeat steps 1 and 3 above replacing step 2 with the tools for tragic style.
2. Apply these layers of sensation to explore the deaths of Romeo and Juliet in Act 5.
3. Remove the layer of the tragic style and play their deaths in the *dramatic* style.

## Advanced style exploration 10—the Ubus and Macbeths

Alfred Jarry based the characters of Pa and Ma Ubu from his *Ubu Plays* on Macbeth and his wife. These two sets of characters allow us to explore the same dynamics of behaviour in comic, tragic and dramatic styles with the opportunity to explore as well the comic/clowning interface.
1. Contrast the wife's taunting of her husband in Act 1, scene 7 or Act 2, scene 2 of *Macbeth* with the opening scene of *Ubu Roi*.[†]
2. Identify such qualities for the wife as *mocking, manipulating, ambitious,* with an objective/PG such as *I want to dominate.*
3. And for the husband: *ambitious, conscience ridden* with conflicted objectives/PGs such as *I want to be king. I want to be a loyal subject, good person* etc.
4. Play the Macbeth scene in dramatic style by expressing emotions and objectives honestly and naturalistically
5. Play the Macbeth scene in the tragic style by layering the same with the tragic tools: tempo, sense of being watched etc.

---

[*] *The Art of Acting,* pp. 122–123.
[†] See pp. 25–26 of *The Actor of the Future 1: Tongues of Flame.*

6. Play the Ubu scene in the comic style by layering the gestures and qualities with the comic tools (tempo, exaggerating all the qualities and gestures etc.).
7. Play the Ubu scene in the clowning style by letting the characters be possessed by the grotesque astral forms of ambition, greed, mockery, doubt etc.

Finally, based on Steiner's suggestions for the vowels that help prepare us for the comic mood, the following lines invite us to explore the comic possibilities in /i:/ (m<u>e</u>) and /uɪ/ (s<u>wee</u>t) and /ju/ (imb<u>ue</u> or f<u>ew</u>) and /ɜ/ (h<u>ear</u>d), and will perhaps inspire you to create your own.

### Advanced style exploration 11—more speech exercises for vowels of the comic sequence.

1. Warm up with Chekhov's tools for comic style (see chart that follows).
2. Based on /i:/ and /uɪ/:

Tweedledum and Tweedledee's
Relationship was somewhat twee.
Unless one had the wit to see,
The only way to prove
Which one was which between them
Was if one was whiskered, one was smooth.

3. Based on /ju/ and to be spoken with a Scottish accent:

While their humour can be crude,
And sometimes even somewhat lewd,
A Scot is really quite a prude
Because their accent's never rude.

4. Based on /ɜ/:

Things once bad, when turned to verse
Can only go from bad to worse
Even causing lips to purse
Making our expressions terse
And our conclusions more perverse.

5.  Based on English diphthong /ɛə/ : nearest to ä:

> When life's more than I can bear,
> Causing me to tear my hair,
> Because it simply isn't fair,
> Then I like to sit and stare:
> All day long without a care,
> Gazing into empty air.

If we return to the circle of vowels we can see how, for both the tragic and the comic vowel sequences, /i:/ (m<u>e</u>) marks a boundary. We know that just as we achieve a sense of self through /i:/ we equally can say that the sense of self achieves expression in the /i:/. With this in mind we can sense how the tragic vowel sequence encompasses a journey that reaches from the paradisal past /ɑ:/ (f<u>a</u>r) through separation /eɪ/ (f<u>a</u>te) and the primitive experience of ego /i:/ that results in suffering and pain in order to prepare the way for death and the resurrection of the higher I. This suffering and pain is the karmic burden that we carry from our past that must be acknowledged and for which our I AM must take responsibility. Our soul senses this in the dark, foreboding mood of /u:/ (t<u>oo</u>).

Having achieved the boundary of /i:/, the vowel placements of the comic sequence play predominantly at and forward of the teeth, straining back and forth between each other and the /i:/ but never finally achieving the completion of the circle in the /u:/. It is as though in order to sustain the detachment demanded by the comic style, the moment we would venture near /u:/'s serious foreboding mood we are bounced away from it again so we can always stay in comedy's transcendent realm.

In the final chapters we will further penetrate the relationships between the vowels and planetary beings and recognise how even the tragic and the comic moods that the soul experiences on the ego's journey to maturity are not any less the gift of macrocosmic powers than any other aspect of the soul's experience.[*]

---

[*]  In this chapter I have not addressed the form referred to as Comedy of Manners. I have chosen to explore this in the context of human cultural evolution that is the focus of volume 4.

# Summary of styles and tools

| Style | Qualities | Most helpful tools |
| --- | --- | --- |
| Dramatic style | Honest emotions true to the character and given circumstances. | 1. Chekhov's tools for building character.<br>2. Qualities and sensations. |
| Tragic style | Honest emotions true to the character and given circumstances, but sensing that a greater presence observes you and participates. | 1. Tools for building character.<br>2. Qualities and sensations.<br>3. A sense of the greater presence.<br>4. Predominantly slower tempo and dynamic punctuated by faster moments.<br>5. Steiner's vowel moods and the tragic meditation.<br>6. Speech style supported by expanding and contracting in relation to b/p polarity. |
| Comic style | Character manifests one predominating psychological feature. | 1. Tools for building character.<br>2. Qualities and sensations. Exaggerated tendencies.<br>3. An atmosphere of joyous expectation.<br>4. Radiate that atmosphere in six directions with a sense of ease and lightness.<br>5. Predominantly faster tempo and dynamic, punctuated by slower moments.<br>6. Steiner's vowel moods and the comic meditation.<br>7. Speech style supported by expanding and contracting in relation to b/p polarity. |
| Clowning | Possession by non malevolent and humorous sub-human beings. | 1. Transitions from one state of emotion to another don't need to be justified.<br>2. But must be sincere and truthful nonetheless. The clown must utterly believe in them. |

## Steiner's Being of World Humour

*Figure 32*

In the top left corner of Steiner's wooden sculpture, the *Representative of Humanity*, a figure witnesses the cosmic drama being played out in the human soul, observing the I AM striving to maintain the balance between Lucifer who tempts it to disdain the earth and Ahriman who tempts it to believe that matter is the sole reality.

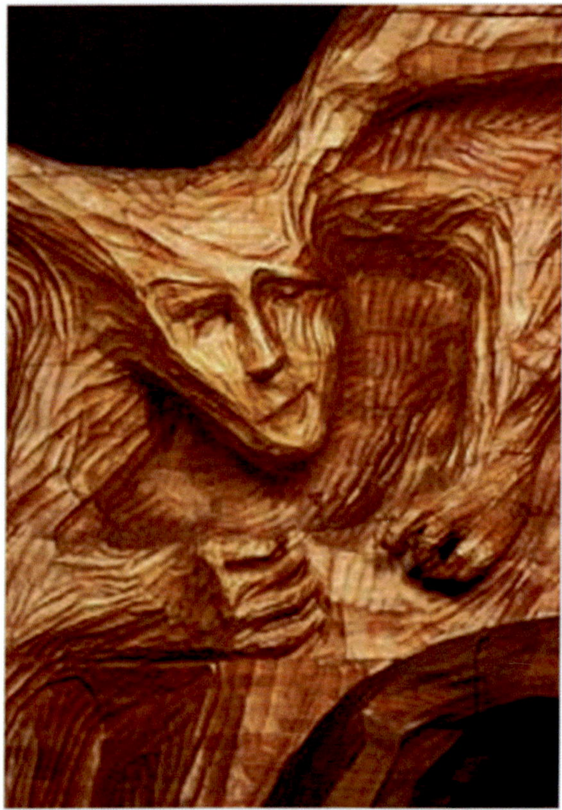

*Figure 33* Being of World Humour

Steiner calls this the Being of World or Cosmic Humour. By including it in such a work, he suggests that its perspective on this battle for the human soul cannot be excluded from the universe.

A close examination shows that the two halves of the figure and the figure's face are very different. In fact we could say that the two halves embody a conflicted soul in which two opposing states struggle to exist together. Recognising this will lead us to a deeper understanding of the wisdom in Steiner's choice of vowels that most articulate the soul's experience of comedy. In Chapter 8, I explore in detail these three umlauted vowels (which do not appear in their pure form in the English language) each of which, as we shall see, results from the fusion of two entirely separate placements in the mouth.*

---

* See pp. 53–57 of *The Art of Speech* for a preliminary exploration of these vowels.

If we isolate the right side (from the viewer's perspective) of the figure, reverse it and create an image consisting of the two right halves, then we look into a face suffused gently from within by warmth of heart, detatched benignly from what the right side beholds but nonetheless, as arms and hands suggest, accepting and embracing it.

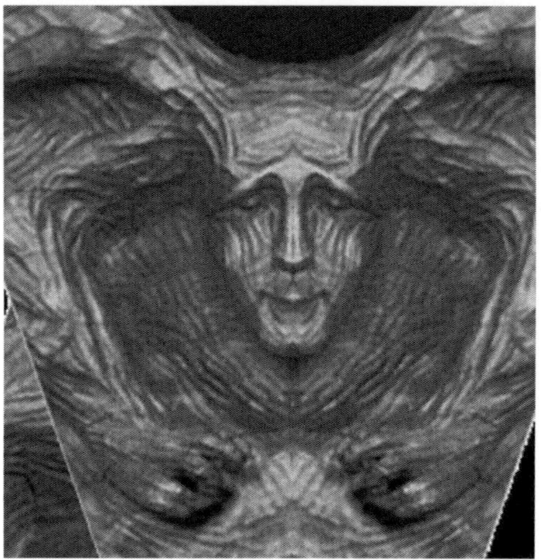

*Figure 34* Being of World Humour, *two right halves and two left halves*

If we isolate the left side (from the viewer's perspective), reverse it and create an image of the two left halves, we look into a face, the focus of whose eyes reveals an unrelenting, stern and utterly awake intelligence ready to fix with eagle-like perception on any detail of the confrontation taking place beneath, and as the contracted tensions in the arms and hands suggest, only too ready to react.

*Figure 35 Artist's impression of the above (whole figure)*

*Figure 36 Artist's impression of the above (face only)*

The two contrasting halves together demonstrate what constitutes the genius of great comedians. Inspired by the spirit of world humour, they possess both clear perception of the follies and delusions that result from our entanglement with matter, and the love that, from its higher standpoint, embraces and forgives us all.

I apply my comic tools, use the meditation to invoke the muse, inspire my full-bodied exploration of each face, and enlist my illustrator's help. Here are her mad attempts to capture my insane endeavours to embody my discoveries.

### Being of world humour exploration 1—it's as bad as you feared and even worse!

Exploring this side of the face reveals how the soul, convinced it's entanglement in matter must be real, catastrophises its perceptions.

1. Incorporate figure 37, exaggerate its tendencies.
2. Radiate the tendencies in six directions all at once. The quality might perhaps be something like *fiercely awake* with an objective like *I want to expose/do battle with/engage with hypocrisy and self delusion/the 'slings and arrows of outrageous fortune'*. And while you're at it, don't forget the predominantly faster tempo, AND a sense of ease!
3. Twist the lens still further, using the mantra to invoke the comic muse... *inside me I can feel* etc... your body of sensation tells you you have now become the hapless victim of the world's determination to defeat you: *Disaster! Catastrophe! And just as I was thinking things couldn't possibly get any worse*!

Sustain your body of sensation and improvise losing a key or sock, escalating through a scale of qualities: from annoyed, to worried, frantic, through to desperation.

*Figure 37 'It's as bad as you feared and even worse'.*

*Figure 38 'Everything's fine! I'll just pretend this is not happening'.*

### Being of world humour exploration 2—Everything's fine! I'll just pretend this is not happening.

1. Incorporate figure 38, *exaggerate* its tendencies.
2. *Radiate* the tendencies in *six directions* all at once. The *quality* might perhaps be something like *dreamy, drifting dreamily above concerns of earth, blissfully removed.* And while you're at it don't forget the *predominantly faster tempo, atmosphere of joyous expectation* and a *sense of ease*!
3. Then twist the lens still further with the comic mantra … *inside me I can feel* etc. … Exploring this side of the face sense your soul dissolve in *sweetness/bliss*, deny 'reality'. *Floating* and *expanding* ever further from the earth, your body-of-sensation tells you: *I'm powerless to change the situation so I'll close my eyes and just pretend it isn't happening. If I ignore it it will go away and everything will be just fine! It's not the end of the world after all!*

*Partner work*

4. Once you're confident with integrating and sustaining as many of the layers as you can, A, work with one gesture, B, with the other. Engage each other and explore the interaction that results.
5. Reverse roles.
6. Work alone again. Alternate the roles, internalising both and find a single gesture that embodies each.
7. Increase the alternating tempo until the two bodies of sensation merge, resulting in the simultaneous experience of both perspectives.
8. Find a movement/gesture sequence that embodies all the possibilities: sometimes one predominates, sometimes the other, sometimes they wrestle equally within your soul.
9. Use this sequence to warm up to the lost key/sock scenario again.
10. Now perhaps you can sympathise with Beethoven and appreciate his Rondo titled *Rage over a Lost Penny*. Use the music to accompany your key or sock scenario, adapt it to a penny if you wish, or perhaps to the ongoing challenge that kinks in the garden hose present to your attempts at watering .

### Being of World Humour exploration 3—The Spirit of Love

When we incorporate both aspects of the image in this way and layer them together, we can also have a sense that the one aspect is not so much avoiding the reality 'down here' but gathering its separate parts into the higher harmony in which it dwells. I am reminded of the words from the Old Testament: 'underneath are the everlasting arms',[32] and Charlie Chaplin's portrayal of Adenoid Hynkel (Hitler) that enables us to view such a figure with compassion.

*Figure 39 'Everything's fine! There's no harm done.'*

### The Spirit of Mockery

However when we see the two contradictory perspectives jammed together as in figure 40, we recognise the spirit of mockery. It is a tragic figure that embodies the dark clowns we fear. Those who were close to the actor Heath Ledger after his brilliant portrayal of the Joker in the 2008 film *The Dark Knight* describe how his inability to free himself from the archetype with which he had identified himself, was one of the factors that led to his tragic death. Such events remind us that actors need to find objective tools that allow them to approach such characters with empathy and yet remain observers of the figures they create.

*Figure 40 Spirit of Mockery*

### *Being of World Humour exploration 4—spirit of mockery*
Adapt the *Being of World Humour explorations 1* and *2* to explore the character embodied in this figure.

If the two conflicted halves collide and jam together squeezing out the heart so it cannot penetrate them with its warmth and mediate between them, then the demon of mockery and ridicule … *nudge, nudge, wink, wink* … possesses us. Its brand of humour cannot heal because it feeds on the hatred and despair arising from our sense that we are powerless and, as a consequence, intends to hurt.

*Figure 41 Spirit of the 'Earth Brain' face only*

For each perspective is susceptible to the very powers whose battle for the human soul
it witnesses. Honest recognition and truthful exposure of our foolishness can be twisted
by Ahriman into the mocking humour that attacks with cruelty and icy hate. Lucifer can
tempt us to turn a blind eye to our faults, distorting loving kindness into the belief that
we can irresponsibly discount our frailties without the need for moral reckoning. When
these tendencies collude in us, we can blissfully delude ourselves that we are better than
we are but have the right to expose the foolishness of others from the moral high ground
we assume is ours. In these distortions of the two sides of the comic face the lower form
of comedy is born, whose archetype appears as the *Spirit of the Earth Brain* in *The Portal
of Initiation*.[33] This scene provides the opportunity to use the *Being of World Humour
explorations* as a basis for this character.

*Figure 42*

## *Further reflections*

While exploring the *World Humour* figure, each face stirred in me a memory of something I could not identify at first. Then, in the stern gaze of the left-side face, I recognised eyes that had haunted me since I first saw a photograph of Samuel Beckett's face: he whose destiny it was to stare remorselessly into the abyss of emptiness our present age demands we face, and penetrate it consciously in order to articulate its terrors.[34]

*Figure 43 left: two left halves face, right: Samuel Beckett stares into the abyss.*

Yet, other images of Beckett's face reveal another side of him. In his eyes we can also recognise the warm gaze of the right-side face. We see the love and infinite compassion with which this great artist beholds the comic dimensions of the human tragedy, exploring the burlesque comedy routines employed by Vladimir and Estragon in their clownlike, desperate attempts to dodge those terrors, making it impossible not to love his foolish characters as he does.

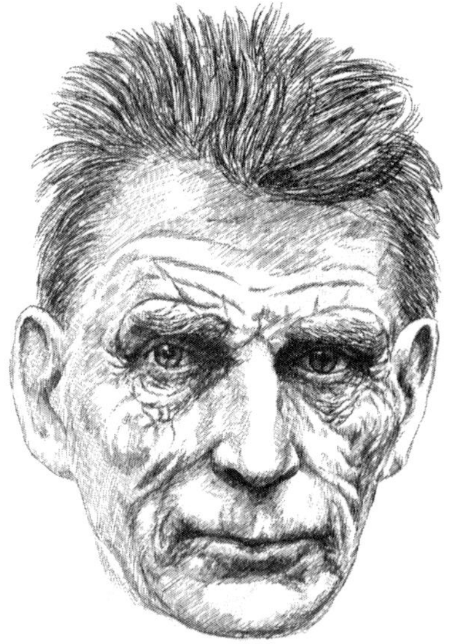

*Figure 44 Samuel Beckett's compassion*

Beckett designated *Waiting for Godot* as a tragi-comedy. The two sides of experience that Ancient Greeks expressed discretely in the comic and the tragic masks now appear together in one face, embodying the complex nature of reality with which our consciousness has had to deal increasingly since Shakespeare's time. This complexity, which no longer neatly fits into the ancient categories, is nowhere more comically expressed than by Polonius in Act 2, scene 2 of *Hamlet*, when he struggles to announce the genre of the players' work:

> The best actors in the world, either for tragedy, comedy, history, pastoral, pastoral-comical, historical-pastoral, tragical-historical, tragical-comical-historical-pastoral, scene individable, or poem unlimited. Seneca cannot be too heavy, nor Plautus too light.

Finally, these intimations led me to identify the countenance that had been haunting me behind the right-side face. In the eyelids folding gently round what they behold, embracing it with tender warmth, compassion and the Love that goes beyond appearances, I recognised Leonardo's portrait of the Christ. *There's no harm done.*

*Figure 45 left: Leonardo da Vinci,* Portrait of Christ, *right: two right halves*

### *Being of World Humour exploration 5—monologue of the comic muse*

1. When you have warmed up your instrument with the tools for comic style, consciously connect with your *heart centre*, penetrating all the other layers with warmth of heart.
2. Use the comic meditation to invoke the muse, explore the different facets of her being and express them in your own divine comedic monologue.

Here is my attempt:

*Oh no! No no! Not again! I don't believe it! What am I to do with you my darlings? I hunch my wincing shoulders, hold this little O, this planet in my helpless-to-do-anything-but-let-you-slip-through-my-fingers grasp.*[35] *I'm afraid my left eye's ruthless honesty just won't let me not see what you've gone and done again, relentlessly holds self-deception up to ridicule, pierces far into the cosmic distances of stern necessity … I know it has to be this way until you learn. All the same my right eye just can't bear to look — can't bear to feel how you must feel if you could only see yourself — discreetly pulls the curtained eyelid down, respects your privacy, your right to carry on like this, display your foolishness in front of everyone, continue to disgrace yourself in — does it really have to be this too excruciating way? Conflicted micro-gesture muscles in my face twist and grimace. I wince for you my darling little manikins and ladykins! Love you to bits but what am I to do as I watch you sliding down the slippery slope of maya yet again … to be honest I can't really call it sliding … have to say it … call it what it is … silly! … there I've said it now … You really are a silly billy! … and in the face of all advice as well to go … to leap and even hurl yourself like that, completely reckless off the very edge! But what can I do, Beloved, except to pierce the veil of your illusions with my left eye's infinitely penetrating gaze, embrace you with my right eye's infinitely loving all shall be well, forgiving half-smile face?*

So Lear's fool held up the mirror to his master:

Thou'ldst make a good fool nuncle. All thy other titles thou hast given away. That one thou wast born with…If thou wert my fool nuncle, I'd have thee whipped for being old before thy time…Thou should'st not have been old until thou had'st been wise…

### *Being of World Humour exploration 6—Launcelot Gobbo*

In this spirit we can play with Launcelot Gobbo, Shylock's servant in Shakespeare's *The Merchant of Venice*. In his speech that follows we recognise the archetypal drama from the sculpture played out in the psyche of our comic anti-hero as the two opposing powers wrestle in his soul.

*Launcelot Gobbo*: Certainly my conscience will serve me to run from this Jew my master. The fiend is at my elbow, and tempts me, saying to me, 'Gobbo, Launcelot Gobbo, good Launcelot,' or 'good Gobbo', or 'good Launcelot Gobbo, use your legs, take the start, run away'. My conscience says, 'No; take heed, honest Launcelot; take heed, honest Gobbo'; or, as aforesaid, 'honest Launcelot Gobbo; do not run; scorn running with thy heels.' Well, the most courageous fiend bids me pack; 'Via!' says the fiend; 'away!' says the fiend, 'for the heavens rouse up a brave mind,' says the fiend, 'and run.' Well, my conscience, hanging about the neck of my heart, says very wisely to me, 'My honest friend Launcelot, being an honest man's son,' — or rather an honest woman's son; — for, indeed, my father did something smack, something grow to, he had a kind of taste; — well, my conscience says, 'Launcelot, budge not.' 'Budge,' says the fiend. 'Budge not,' says my conscience. 'Conscience,' say I, 'you counsel well'; 'Fiend,' say I, 'you counsel well': to be ruled by my conscience, I should stay with the Jew my master, who, God bless the mark! is a kind of devil; and, to run away from the Jew, I should be ruled by the fiend, who, saving your reverence, is the devil himself. Certainly, the Jew is the very devil incarnal; and, in my conscience, my conscience is but a kind of hard conscience, to offer to counsel me to stay with the Jew. The fiend gives the more friendly counsel; I will run, fiend; my heels are at your commandment; I will run.

## Concluding thoughts

We all know people who see life through the comic lens and others who incline more naturally to focus on the tragedy. In life as well as art we may tend more in one direction than the other. Cultivating both sets of skills expands our stylistic capabilities beyond our natural disposition, developing a range of sensibilities that allow us to flexibly respond to the complex web of tragic/comic nuances of which our life is woven, which many of the greatest scripts demand and which, like the work of *Hamlet's* players, cannot be confined to one dogmatic category. For as Michael Chekhov wrote in *To the Actor*:

> For as soon as you develop them [the styles] within you, they themselves will find expression through the labyrinthian corridors of your creative spirit.

It is well known that Anton Chekhov viewed his plays as comedies while Stanislavski found them tragic. Perhaps they were both right. Each of Chekhov's plays is filled with moments we can view through either lens: the excruciating interaction, for example, in Act 4 of *The Cherry Orchard*, when Lopakhin is left alone with Varya in order to propose to her. At the last moment just before they both depart forever into distant lives and places, she is sent into his presence on the understanding he intends, at last, to marry her. When their conversation never gets beyond discussion of the weather and their work arrangements, each attempts to flee the terrifying gulf that opens up between them by engaging in a frantic search for something — perhaps the galoshes Trofimov had lost or perhaps it is a nothing she invents to rescue both of them from their excruciating agony. The scene is full of tragic and comedic possibilities.

### *Comic, tragic, dramatic style exploration 1—partner work*
Use Chekhov's tools to build some layers of your character: *centres, qualities and sensations, PGs and objectives, atmosphere* etc.
1.  Learn your line:

> *Lopakhin*: It's cold outside. Three degrees of frost.
> *Varya*: I hadn't noticed. Besides our thermometer's broken.

2.  Warm up your character.
3.  Warm up with the tools for dramatic style.
4.  Approach each other in dramatic style and explore your interaction through this lens.
5.  Warm up with the tools for tragic style.
6.  Approach each other in the style of tragedy and explore your interaction through this lens.
7.  Warm up with the tools for comic style.
8.  Approach each other in the style of comedy and explore your interaction through this lens.
9.  Share your observations.
10. Explore the scene again investigating how the tragic and the comic elements might interweave.
11. Expand the interaction to include everything that takes place from Lopakhin's entrance to his exit.
12. Identify other opportunities in Chekhov's plays to explore this tragic/comic interplay of life's complexities.
13. Identify such opportunities in other plays. For example in *Waiting for Godot*, Vladimir and Estragon engage in comedy routines to escape the tragic emptiness of waiting ... *Nothing to be done* ... In *King Lear*, the fool administers the tragic truth to Lear through the healing medicine of humour: *Thou'st make a good fool nuncle. All thy other titles thou hast given away. That one thou wast born with.*


As the 'creative spirit' in the Michael Chekhov quote expands beyond the bounded-in-a-nutshell consciousness of Kali Yuga, mastering the tragic genre will school our sensibilities to recognise the signals the tragic muse provides to enable us to find our bearings in the pain we suffer as we make our way towards our true humanity. It will teach us not to cringe, like Beckett's Vladimir, from the terror that tells us we approach the sacred threshold, but to understand what it presages. In the new temple of the world, the illusory persona of the earthbound ego trembles as it senses the Presence of its greater counterpart, the I AM Self, draws near. It can choose to surrender to the little death or else resist and thus, in time, attract the escalating catastrophic blows that shatter it.

Understanding the archetype of tragedy as embodied in its ancient form enables us to recognise its metamorphosed elements as they appear to present consciousness, and to weave their threads within the complex tapestry of our contemporary art and daily life. To surrender, with infinite compassion, to the pedagogy of the Higher Self; to engage in the 'mental fight' to know ourselves and *why we are here and why we suffer*, is the pathway of the tragic hero/heroine. Then, like Oedipus, who demonstrated how to transform tragedy into a blessing for the earth, actors of the future will pour blessing through their art.

The ancient form of comedy also continues to dissolve and metamorphose. By mastering its genre we school our sensibilities to recognise its radiant glimmers wherever they appear, even in the deepest pit of Hell. And actors of the future will bear witness to the unconquerable spirit's urge to *always look on the bright side of life*.

A clear example of this complex tragic/comic tapestry is Terence McNally's play, *A Perfect Ganesh*. Two middle-aged women from America travel to India hoping for enlightenment. There they confront their conditioning and the unhealed wounds that imprison them in painful patterns and unresolved relationships. The elephant-headed god Ganesh from the Hindu pantheon feels the suffering of human beings caught in the world of maya and when the pain becomes unbearable, takes on human form in order to be helpful. The troubled characters remain, however, unaware that they are interacting with a god. In between his helpful interventions, we see Ganesh on stage, with divine compassion empathising with the pain of human beings trapped in their material perception. Head buried in his hands, closing his eyes in order not to see their suffering, he intones, over and again: *Oh no! Oh no! Oh no, no no!*

Theatre came into the world to bear witness to the complex mysteries of human selfhood: the death and dismemberment of Dionysus enacted through the tragedies and his resurrection in the comedies. These dual tasks are re-enacted yet again in Shakespeare's final play, *The Tempest*. Prospero's untransformed hatred and instinct for revenge calls forth a tempest that appears to wreck the ship that carries all his enemies. As the ship goes down, all the parts of the dismembered Self cry out, *We split! We split!* ... and a myriad of splintered egos, all battling for survival in the

Figure 46 'Everything's fine! There's no harm done.'

maya of this world, appear to drown. So convincing is their anguish to Miranda who, like Ganesh, so *suffers with those that [she] saw suffer*, that she cries out to her father to allay the storm and end their pain. Prospero, shaken by the depth of her compassion, tries to reassure her that *there's no harm done*. To make this true, he must reconcile the untransformed dynamics in his soul he had projected onto those around him. Only when he finally embraces Caliban, that 'thing of darkness', is the purpose of the comedy fulfilled and the audience allowed, with Gonzalo, to 'rejoice beyond a common joy'. Thus it was that in the Egyptian temple dramas, Isis gathered the dismembered pieces of Osiris and with her healing rituals restored him to new life, ensuring in Greece too, an epoch later, that a new incarnation of the god, the twice slain and twice reborn Dionysus, stepped forth as the bridegroom of Persephone, the soul. *

These myths touch upon the cyclic nature of our evolution which over and again requires that we pass through death to birth, through dark to light, through tragedy to comedy. Perhaps these mysteries provide another clue to the ancient link between the goat (*tragos*) and tragedy.

## The goat

Let us think not only of the earthly animal but of the cosmic being whose archetype it bears. This archetype was perceived by the old clairvoyant consciousness as the activity of macrocosmic beings whose body was condensed into the constellation Capricorn and whose will to serve our human evolution is embodied in the consonantal power of /l/. Through the gesture of this consonant my body of sensation quickens, resonating with its cyclic mystery, again and again descending into darkness and raising it again into the light until at last 'All shall be well'.[36]

---

* For a detailed exploration and connection of the ancient imaginations central to the drama's birth, refer to the Epilogue in *The Art of Acting*.

*Figure 47 Eurythmy gesture consonant /l/*

Inhabiting the gesture of the macrocosmic being Capricorn, I sense its objective for the earth and the divine necessity of separation. I feel from its lofty height, how consciousness detaches from itself in order to behold itself from outside in the other. I sense as well the long will that holds us through the cycles we perceive as death and tragedy until we ourselves attain that lofty view: the divina commedia. *

---

* See *The Actor of the Future*, 4 for an exploration of the culture epochs and their connection to the constellations.

*Figure 48 Starry being Capricorn*

Perhaps St John's vision of the wedding feast at the end of time 'when every tear shall be wiped away' was prophetic of the seventh cultural epoch that will evolve under the guidance of the macrocosmic being Capricorn, just as our present fifth epoch is evolving under Pisces and the coming sixth cultural epoch will evolve under the guidance of the macrosomic being Aquarius.* Perhaps we can imagine that the journey to the goal of comedy in that far future epoch, began with the long climb up the mountain in the Age of Aries when our perception of tragedy began. Perhaps St John's imagination of the wedding feast was the cosmic archetype inspiring Chekhov to suggest the comic atmosphere of joyous expectation such as a child experiences waiting for a festival.[37] At any rate, Chekhov's inspiration for this tool springs from the very origins of comedy and is intrinsically connected with the word itself, emerging as its does from the Greek words *kômos* and *ōidé* meaning a song of revelling and celebration.

If we return to the circle of the vowels we are confronted with the gap between the boundaries of /ɑ:/ and /u:/ which in the original approach to style remains unbridgeable. However, in the tragic half we feel /u:/ as the Saturnine resistance stemming from the burden of our past that we must carry with us until it is transformed. In the comic half we feel /u:/ as a future we strain towards but are not yet able to attain.[38]

Perhaps this mystery points us to the two levels of comedy we saw reflected in the right-side face and figure. On the one hand we achieve the comic style by lifting out of or detaching from the pain. On the other hand, as Shakespeare's final plays suggest, healing and serenity are finally achieved only when the pain and conflict of the tragedy have been embraced. In these plays forgiveness is the quantum leap that alone can cross that gap to join the two halves of the circle and bring the movement from tragedy to comedy into a continuum. There the past that has been healed becomes the future that will in turn become a new past for a further cycle of becoming. Of course, Shakespeare has mastered all the levels of comedic style. For example in *The Tempest* he moves from the clowning farce of Caliban and Stefano and Trinculo to the delicate humour of first love in the Ferdinand/ Miranda scenes, to the divina commedia of Prospero's forgiveness which releases everyone. And in *The Winter's Tale,* he moves from the kindly humour of the shepherds, earthy and utterly devoid of malice, through the cynical and mocking humour of Autolycus, to the divine comedic humour: the forgiveness ritual with which Paulina restores Leontes to Hermione and orchestrates a second wedding feast.

The divine compassion that empathises with the tragedy of human pain is embodied in the figure of Ganesh, from Indian mythology. Stories of Krishna, on the other hand, reveal the other face of Love. Instructing his disciples in the true nature of reality,

---

* The connection of these larger cycles to the constellations of the zodiac will be explored in depth in *The Actor of the Future 4: One More Time.*

Krishna reveals that all appearances are manifestations of Himself. Asked if there would ever be an end to the deception, he simply laughed.

In his comic masterpiece *The Magic Flute*, Mozart explores this mystery. To the dualistic consciousness the plot can seem confusing, exploring as it does the complex interwoven nature of reality where good and evil, suffering and joy, are revealed as aspects of each other. Yet even while the abstract intellect struggles to make sense of these confusing elements, the music sweeps our souls beyond confusion to the realm where Krishna's laughter bubbles irrepressibly.

In *The Lady's Not for Burning* (1948), Christopher Fry explores the absurd comic/tragic ambiguity of our existence. Thomas is a disillusioned soldier hoping to end his life by convincing the community that he is guilty of a criminal offence that warrants hanging. Jennet is a great-hearted whacky lady condemned to be burned as a witch for her unconventional behaviour and because her father was an alchemist. When both prove unsuccessful at convincing their gaolers to change their minds, and at making any sense of their dilemma, Thomas suggests:

*Thomas*: For God's sake, shall we laugh?

*Jennet*: For what reason?

*Thomas*: For the reason of laughter, since laughter is surely

The surest touch of genius in creation..

Would *you* ever have thought of it, I ask you,

If you had been making man, stuffing him full

Of such hopping greeds and passions that he has

To blow himself to pieces as often as he

Conveniently can manage it—would it also

Have occurred to you to make him burst himself

With such a phenomenon as cachinnation?

That same laughter, madam, is an irrelevancy

Which almost amounts to revelation.


At first sight it seems that Dante was no humorist. His *Divina Commedia* appears to offer little opportunity for the laughter we commonly associate with comedy. To the comic mind, however, the commitment to the endless cycles of behaviour with which the damned maintain the lifestyle choices to which they have become accustomed and which constitute their stay in Hell, certainly appears absurd and even farcical. Indeed the poet hints on more than one occasion that since the harrowing of Hell, the gates are open and there is no outer reason why anyone who chooses could not leave.[39] The comic genius immediately senses, in the horrifying torments of the damned, material that lends itself to exploration not only in the genre of 'black comedy' but in the whole range of comic styles.

*Figure 49 Michelino,* The Comedy Illuminating Florence

In its name and structure no other single work has conveyed so potently that only after the descent to Hell and journey through the fires of purgatorio are we able to ascend at last to the bliss of final union. Once again we cannot help but recognise that comedy and tragedy cannot exist without each other.

Joy and woe are woven fine,
A clothing for the soul divine;
Under every grief and pine
Runs a joy with silken twine.
It is right it should be so;

Man was made for joy and woe;

And when this we rightly know,

Safely through the world we go…

from 'Auguries of Innocence' (1805) by William Blake.

For as Steppenwolf discovered in Hermann Hesse's novel of that name:

For the first time I understood … the laughter of the immortals. It was a laughter without an object. It was simply light and lucidity. It was that which is left over when a true man has passed through all the sufferings, vices and mistakes, passions and misunderstandings and got through to eternity and the world of space … And above [this music of Mozart and Bach] there quivered a never-ending and superhuman serenity, an eternal divine laughter … And suddenly I heard this fathomless laughter around me. I heard the immortals laughing …

# Chapter 4

# Other states of being

The canon of Western drama is full of human characters whose consciousness no longer inhabits a material body, and non-human unembodied characters whose consciousness differs from our own. Greek drama demanded actors play divinities, semi-divine beings, mythological creatures and elemental beings; mediaeval drama the parts of God, archangels, angels, devils, souls in Hell or Heaven. Shakespeare's plays: *A Midsummer Night's Dream*, *Hamlet*, *Macbeth*, *Pericles*, *Cymbeline* and *Richard III* to name but a few, require a range of characters not human or physically embodied: ghosts, divinities (Jupiter in *Cymbeline*, Artemis in *Pericles*, Juno, Ceres and Iris in *The Tempest*), elemental beings/ fairies. Goethe's *Faust*: God, Mephistophiles, elemental spirits, mythological beings, archangels, human souls in Paradise. Shelley's *Prometheus Unbound*: divinities, elemental spirits, spirits of time, earth and moon. Thornton Wilder's *Our Town*: human beings after death, *Skin of our Teeth* and *Pullman Car Hiawatha*: archangels, spirits of time and planets. Steiner's *Mystery Dramas*: Lucifer and Ahriman, other beings not in physical embodiment. *Angels in America*: an angel, continental spirits, souls of discarnate human beings.

The inspirations of our greatest dramatists and poets have always provided us with clues that lead to a truthful penetration of the subconscious depths within the souls of the human characters we play. Mainstream psychology confirms the complex dynamics that weave within the psyche and determine so much of our behaviour. However, the suggestion that these dynamics might be influenced by beings invisible to earthly senses, such as those portrayed in mediaeval images of souls tormented and led astray by devils, or visited by angels, is dismissed as superstition. Representing such non-human beings, or non-incarnated human beings, or the forces working in our souls as *beings* at all, is tolerated so long as these can be explained as products of artistic fantasy or symbolic figures in which, throughout the ages, the human soul has traditionally clothed its understanding of non-material reality.

Such figures have always been agreeably portrayed using the conventions and devices with which theatre has persuaded us to 'willingly suspend our disbelief'.[40] Thus we are engaged by the make-believe of theatre: actors with distorted voices, wearing masks, dressed in strange but all too earthly garments, the *deus ex machina* of the Greeks, gods on stilts in Brecht's *Good Woman of Setzuan*, fireworks at the mediaeval mouth of Hell, Shakespeare's choruses or Thornton Wilder's stage manager inviting us to use imagination, explaining the theatrical conventions to their audience, the modern technology of stage and film; all serve to stimulate imagination, reminding us *there are more things in heaven and earth … than are dreamt of in* [our present day] *philosophy*.[41] The world would be a poorer place without Starveling's glorious and hopelessly inadequate portrayal of the moon.[42]

For art to leave us free, it must respect our right to choose what we experience. Therefore it must never blur the boundary between what life can thrust upon us unprepared and the experience agreed to when we choose to cross that theshold, as audience or actor, in order to enter the artist's imaginative realm. Such theatrical conventions as described above, mediate between the artist's fantasies or direct experience of super-sensible realities and their audience, some of whom at least must be invited by delight or wonder, willingly to entertain such possibilities which thrust upon them uninvited, might prematurely threaten or violate their boundaries.[43]

Alongside these conventions, however, on the path towards the theatre of the future, as human faculties for supersensible experience continue to expand, increasing numbers of us will demand theatrical techniques based on an objective source of knowledge of the supersensible realities. As our integrated Chekhov/Creative Speech and eurythmy methodologies allow us to investigate them with artistic truthfulness, we will learn to trust the insights arising out of Steiner's research into beings other than those imagined by the separated ego-constructs of the self.[44] As human consciousness continues to expand in our post-Kali Yuga Age, actors will need to expand beyond the excavation of the intricate psychology of human souls that they normally investigate. We will need processes and powers that hone our body-of-sensation into an organ of perception for the consciousness of beings that may be more or less evolved than us, or vastly different from ourselves. Audiences of the future will find actors unconvincing who are only able to project their everyday personas onto other orders of creation.

Steiner's spiritual-scientific research provides us with methods by which we may explore, discern and communicate more consciously the insights of our greatest dramatists and poets.* His observations that the orders of divine creative beings (referred to in Christian esotericism as the Spiritual Hierarchies) correspond to the planetary beings of our solar system and the starry beings of the zodiac, allow us to identify such lofty beings who are often loosely lumped together and generically referred to as angels, archangels and the like, with more precision. Our methodology stirs sensations of dynamics and energies behind the world of physical phenomena, awakening the level of spiritual cognition Steiner called Imagination. Beyond this, it grants us

---

* We laid the basis for this work in *The Actor of the Future 1: Tongues of Flame* and will continue to develop it in Chapter 6.

intimations of the consciousness of beings who express themselves through these dynamics, thus awakening the level of spiritual cognition called by Steiner, Inspiration. Then, as our methodology transforms our instrument still further our will becomes available to channel theirs, awakening the level of spiritual cognition called by Steiner, Intuition. This unfolding path of conciousness reminds us yet again of the privilege our actor's art bestows on us.

On page 96 of Lecture 4 of the *Speech and Drama* course, Steiner suggests:

> … in a dialogue with spirits, the being of the spirit, which can only be there at all in the degree to which the human being is able to focus a right conception of it must still be more powerfully present to that human being than would be necessary if [s/]he were having a dialogue with another human being.

Therefore he recommends that working on a dialogue with spirits can prepare the actor for scenes of human interaction. At first glance we might wonder what would make this necessary. Surely an interaction with another human being is self-evident? Yet how often are we conscious that the other that I meet in life or in a script is not the body-bound identity perceived by earthly senses but a spiritual being? In our everyday encounters, the physical presence of the other in the space can delude us into thinking we perceive their beingness when in fact we only recognise their shell. Their body does the work for us, so to speak, deludes us into thinking that we meet the other being and relieves us of the need to exercise our consciousness in order to achieve and sustain that 'right conception' of them.

Exploring Hamlet's meeting with his father's ghost on the battlements at Elsinore, I discovered that in order to maintain my perception of that disembodied presence I needed to listen to the speeches of the ghost with a level of attention that I only exercise in life in my most evolved encounters. Such a quality of listening and being present and responsive to another is the primary requirement for actors who must be tuned in to what their fellow actors are creating — so *believing* its reality that an audience believes it *through* them.

Steiner's research and our methodology will help us focus our attention on that 'right conception' of the spirits we portray or with whom we interact, whether they be human or beings of another kind. This is a level of encounter that the actor must achieve regardless of the character's capacity for that degree of consciousness. Behind all everyday appearances weave the supersensible realities of those (ourselves included) who are invisible to ordinary sense perception. Through our practice the actor of the future is invited to develop organs of perception that allow us to to intuit these dimensions (even when there seem to be no clues provided) whether in the dramas of our daily lives or those performed on stage and film.

These are faculties that can discern levels of reality beyond the forms in which material perception clothes them. They will allow us to create on stage not fantasy but the substance of supersensible reality. Thus the drama of the future will evolve into its next cycle of development.

Until then, the evolution of this work requires collaboration between actors and eurythmists as we experiment with integrating drama and eurythmy to portray the supersensible events and beings at work within our human dramas. So where can we begin? For English speakers, the genius of Shakespeare provides intimations of the deeper wisdom that could guide our explorations. Clues to supersensible dimensions are threads of gold that weave throughout the tapestry of Shakespeare's language but without a methodology that makes them gleam, cannot illuminate the text.

The following examples from his plays invite us to explore a range of different spirits and how to use our methodology to form that 'right conception' of them.

### Nature spirits exploration 1—Shakespeare's fairies

### Peaseblossom, Moth, Cobweb and Mustardseed

These are Shakespeare's names for the fairies who wait on Bottom in Titania's fairy kingdom in *A Midsummer Night's Dream*. He has chosen four of the humblest, seemingly least significant phenomena of nature; things that *cool reason*, capable only of assessing outer form, would dismiss (if it would notice them at all) as not warranting our serious attention. Shakespeare invites us to look again, listen to their voices, learn their names and address them, as Bottom does, with the respect that should be due to any conscious being: *good mistress, good monsieur*.

1. Find, observe and draw a moth, a cobweb, peaseblossom and mustardseed.
2. Write down your observations in the third-person, then exchange the third-person pronouns (s/he/it — him, her, it) with the first-person (I/me etc) and craft what you have written as a monologue.
3. Focus on Moth. *Incorporate* your observations* and explore your first-person monologue full-bodily.
4. Use your body of sensations to identify the psycho-physical tools (gravity/levity, qualities-of-movement, tempo/dynamic, centres, expansion/contraction, PG and objective, consonants and vowels etc.) that will release the processes that have condensed into and been embodied by your moth.
5. Explore each process thoroughly and move between them until you sense the psycho-physical being of a moth.
6. Consolidate this in a full-bodied movement sequence, level 10.

---

* *The Art of Acting*, pp. 184–189 and 227–230.

7. Condense the full-bodied journey from level 10–1, as close to the perceived body of a moth as your human intrument is able to achieve.

8. Release the full-bodied level 10 activities again, from which the perceived body had condensed.

9. Move back and forth between the perceived body of the moth and the released supersensible activity. Speak your name, your monologue and experiment with any of Titania's commands to wait on Bottom that are appropriate. Sing to him, lay him down to sleep, *hop in his walks, gambol in his eyes*, feed him fruit and berries, steal the honey bags from bees *and light them at the fiery glow-worm's eyes*, attend him on rising, *pluck wings from painted butterflies and fan the moonbeams from his sleeping eyes*.[45]

10. Sustaining your body of sensation, cast the spell that Titania orders you to place around the sleeping Bottom, keeping him from harm:

> You spotted snakes with double tongue,
> Thorny hedgehogs, be not seen;
> Newts and blind-worms, do no wrong,
> Come not near our fairy queen.
> Philomel, with melody
> Sing in our sweet lullaby;
> Lulla, lulla, lullaby, lulla, lulla, lullaby:
> Never harm,
> Nor spell nor charm,
> Come our lovely lady nigh;
> So, good night, with lullaby.
> Weaving spiders, come not here;
> Hence, you long-legg'd spinners, hence!
> Beetles black, approach not near;
> Worm nor snail, do no offence.
> Philomel, with melody, & c.

11. Repeat steps 2–10 with a peaseblossom, mustardseed and cobweb.

12. Play with other lines from these scenes.

### *Nature spirits exploration 2—four elements/qualities of movement*

Lectures 1 and 2 of Steiner's *Spiritual Beings in the Heavenly Bodies and in the Kingdoms of Nature* are packed with descriptions that our *sensitive membrane* will not be able to resist translating, with the help of Chekhov's tools, into full-bodied processes. These provide us with the means not only to explore the content of the lectures but to create such characters as:

- beings of earth, water, air and fire;
- beings who bring about alternations of the seasons/changes in the weather.

1. Start by closely observing and describing an event in nature. For example: describe precisely in third-person your sense impressions of a storm, an eclipse, a sunrise, a shower of rain, a drought, a springtime flowering.
2. Refine your description and replace your third-person pronouns with the first-person (I, me etc.). Now your description is transformed into a monologue that shifts your consciousness towards the realm of being. Explore your monologue full-bodily, using qualities-of-movement, expansion and contraction, tempo and dynamic, consonants and vowels. As you get to know this being perhaps it will reveal its objective/s to you through your body of sensation, allowing you to give expression to it in a PG (psychological gesture).
3. Polish your integrated speech and movement monologue.

On this basis explore these characters and texts:
- Ariel from *The Tempest.*
- Puck and the first fairy from Act 2, scene 1 of *A Midsummer Night's Dream.*
- Oberon and Titania from Act 2, scene 1 in *A Midsummer Night's Dream.*
- Gnomes and Sylphs from scene 2 of Steiner's fourth *Mystery Drama.*
- Ariel and the chorus of nature spirits from Act 1.
- Nymphs and Peneus from the scene on the Lower Peneus in Act 2 of Goethe's *Faust Part 2.*
- Earth and various nature spirits from Shelley's *Prometheus Unbound.*

Figure 50 *The Representative of Humanity*

# Lucifer, Ahriman and the I AM

Steiner's research allowed him to perceive that an essential aspect of our human evolution comes about only through the intervention of two macrocosmic beings whose opposing tendencies require us to balance their activity within our souls. Making use of names assigned in ancient cultures that also recognised their roles, he called them Lucifer and Ahriman. Without their challenge we could not achieve the freedom and maturity of spirit that are the goal of human evolution. He embodied the archetype of this dynamic in his wooden sculpture, the *Representative of Humanity*. In the centre is the I AM who balances and regulates their influence.

Ahriman's objective could be stated thus: *I want to draw human beings so deeply into matter that they believe that it alone is real and spirit does not exist.* Lucifer's objective could be stated thus: *I want to draw human beings away from earth, free of all concern with matter, which is only an illusion, maya.* This latter tendency tempts us to pluck the fruits of our existence prematurely because we feel we need not engage with the resistance that the earth confronts us with and learn what our entanglement in matter has to teach. The objective of the human archetype, the I AM, could be stated thus: *I want to experience myself by learning how to work with the gift that each one offers and how to balance their potentials, neither rejecting nor being overwhelmed by either one.*

The force of gravity draws us down towards the weight and density of earthly matter and provides stability. Levity draws us upward and allows us to expand beyond our earthly limitations. In the *Art of Acting*, we explored the activity required to balance these two poles of our experience.[*] Out of this *imaginative* level of our exploration stir the first intimations of the level of cognition Steiner designates as *inspiration;* subtle sensations inform us, if we give them our attention, that gravity and levity, and our ability to balance them, are not mere abstract forces but activities and states of consciousness of macrocosmic beings whose will it is to draw us down, to lift us up or find the balance in between.

We are ready to investigate these intimations further.

## *Gravity and levity exploration 1*

1. Re-explore the gravity/levity explorations in *The Art of Acting*.
2. When the sensation of being dragged down by gravity is at its most intense, imagine that force is exerted by 'someone' whose objective is to drag you down.
3. Full-bodily reverse roles with that imaginary 'someone' and embody their dynamic.

---

[*] *The Art of Acting*, pp. 118–122.

4. Express in your own words the objective it arouses in you and search for a PG that embodies it.

5. When the sensation of being drawn upwards by the light is at its most intense, imagine that force is exerted by 'someone' whose objective is to draw you up away from earth.

6. Reverse roles and, as above, express their dynamic, identify the objective it arouses and search for a PG that embodies it.

### Gravity and levity exploration 2—partner work

1. A, stand neutral and available, B, lie on the floor and drag A down to earth. A must be defeated but provide enough resistance so that B must work to win.

2. After doing this with full-bodied physical engagement, recreate full-bodily the energies and gestures of the interaction but without making contact physically.

3. Reverse roles.

4. A, lie on the floor where B defeated you. If possible, B, stand on a higher level and, without touching A, but exerting all your will, draw A upwards from the earth. A must provide enough resistance so that B must work to win.

5. After doing this with full-bodied physical engagement, recreate full-bodily the energies and gestures of the interaction but without making contact physically.

6. Reverse roles.

### Gravity and levity exploration 3—partner work—transition into speaking

1. Recreate *gravity and levity explorations 1 and 2*.

2. Experiment with words and phrases, vocal qualities, consonants and vowels that most clearly align with your body of sensation that expresses your objective to draw your partner up or drag your partner down.

### Gravity and levity exploration 4—in groups of three

1. A, stand between B and C, neutral and available.

2. B, try to drag A down, C, to draw A up.

3. B and C continue to compete for A who must find the strength to stay upright and balance them. After doing this with full-bodied physical engagement, recreate the dynamics of the interaction full-bodily but without making contact physically.

4. Rotate the roles until each person has experienced each one.

5. Continue to explore in your own words the subtext that arises from your interacting bodies of sensation.

*Figure 51 Images of Lucifer*

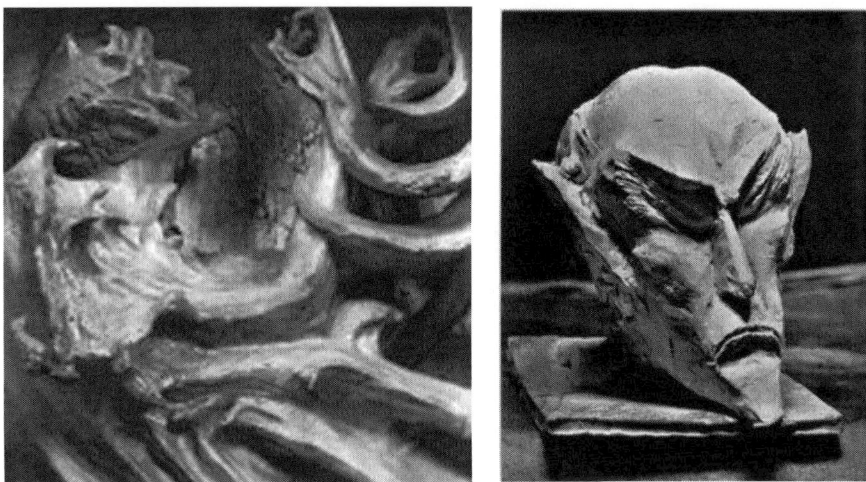

*Figure 52 Images of Ahriman*

## Gravity and levity exploration 5—in groups of three

1. Study the sculpture and incorporate it, taking turns to play each role.
2. Allow the full-bodied work of *gravity and levity explorations 1–4* to flow into your sculpture, bringing it to life.
3. Explore what other tools are drawn into the field that is generated by the body of sensation of each being: expanding/contracting, qualities-of-movement etc.
4. Examine the details of the faces. Treat their expressions as level 1 microgestures that can be expanded into full-bodied gestures level 10. Integrate your gestures with those embodied in the sculpture.
5. Move between the levels 10–1.
6. Integrate what you discover with steps 1–3. What objectives are revealed?
7. Condense all your work into a PG for each being. Continue to explore your own words for the subtext that arises.

### *Gravity and levity exploration 6—apply to text*

1. Use these as the basis for exploring the characters of Lucifer and Ahriman in Steiner's *Mystery Plays*.

2. Expand your understanding of these beings by reading other works of Steiner,[46] and explore how to integrate this with your psycho-physical preparation.

3. Experiment with your knowledge of the consonants and vowels to find voices that express these two extremes. Lucifer's voice seduces us with warmth and bliss by dissolving the consonants into vowel substance. Ahriman's voice obliterates all inwardness, hardening the vowels into consonants.

4. Use your PGs from *gravity and levity exploration 5* to explore the following texts from Scene 4 of *The Portal of Initiation:*

*Lucifer*: O human being, know yourself.

O human being, experience me.

You've wrenched yourself away

from spirit guidance,

and you have fled

into free earthly realms.

You've sought your own true being

in earth's confusion;

to find yourself

proved your reward

and proved your fate.

Me you have found.

Spirits desired

to cast a veil before the senses;

I tore the veil apart.

Spirits desired

to follow only their own will in you:

I gave you your own will.

O human being, know yourself.

O human being, experience me.


*Ahriman*: O human being, know me.

O human being, experience yourself.

You have escaped

from spirit darkness,

and you have found

the light of earth.
So suck the power of truth
from my solidity.
I harden stable ground.
Spirits desired
to rob you of the senses' beauty.
I activate this beauty
in solid light.
I lead you onward
into essential truth.
O human being, know me.
O human being, experience yourself.

### *Gravity and levity exploration 7—tendencies in human characters*

1. Identify in texts human characters who seem influenced by either Lucifer or Ahriman, and any who strive for or achieve a balance.

2. Integrate what you have learned from *gravity/levity explorations 1–6* with the other layers of your character creation. Explore how your full-bodied work affects these other layers. For example:

   - *Lucifer*
     Gayev in *The Cherry Orchard.*
     Timon in the first half of *Timon of Athens.*
     Romeo in the balcony scene from *Romeo and Juliet.*
     Helena and Johannes in Steiner's *Portal of Initiation.*

   - *Ahriman*
     Lopakhin in *The Cherry Orchard.*
     Iago in *Othello.*
     Shylock, *Merchant of Venice.*
     Demogorgon in *Prometheus Unbound.*
     Timon in the second half of *Timon of Athens.*
     Strader in *The Soul's Awakening.*[47]

   - *I AM*
     Benedictus and Maria in Steiner's *Mystery Dramas.*
     Sir Thomas More in *A Man for all Seasons.*
     Cordelia in *King Lear.*
     Cerimon in *Pericles.*

### *Gravity/levity exploration 8—Benedictus and Maria*

1. Revisit *weaving and integration of speech placements and centres exploration 3 — Maria and Benedictus — individual and partner work*, in Chapter 2.
2. Take the gesture of the central figure in the sculpture as a PG for Benedictus and Maria.
3. Layer the body of sensation that arises from it with the work arising from step 1.
4. Explore their dialogue.

*Figure 53 The I AM*

# Imagining theatre in the future—working on a scene from Shakespeare's *Cymbeline*

Shakespeare's *Cymbeline* traverses many levels of reality. In the final act the central protagonist, Posthumus Leonatus, is tormented with remorse and grief that his command to have his wife killed in revenge for her perceived unfaithfulness has (so he thinks) been carried out. He tries to end his life by exposing himself repeatedly to the possibility of death in battle in the Roman army's war against the Celts in Britain. At last, imprisoned and exhausted with despair, he falls asleep. There in the realm that lies beyond our world of everyday perception he encounters the souls of his parents and his brothers, the deceased family of the Leonati. Because they remain imprisoned in their own unprocessed suffering and the love that keeps them bound in anguish to the one who still remains on earth, they are not free to make their further journey through the spheres. It is a karmic community woven inextricably together from the ties of blood and the pain resulting from untimely death through grief, or childbirth or battle. It has left them uncomprehending of their lives that were unconsummated. Now, like iron filings attracted to a magnet, their souls are brought together through the pain of Posthumus who, through his own unprocessed agony would seek to prematurely end his life. They plead on his behalf with Jupiter, chief of the Roman gods, to pity their beloved child and brother who had to grow up as an orphan, before he was adopted by Cymbeline, the British king and brought up as his son. We learn that Posthumus received his name because, while still a baby in his mother's womb, his father, on whose person and descendants the king had bestowed the title Leonati in recognition of his loyalty and courage as a warrior, had died of grief on learning that his two older sons were killed in battle. And then, in giving birth to Posthumus, his mother also died of grief.

In answer to their pleas Jupiter, mounted on an eagle, descends from Olympus and reprimands them for their lack of trust in the highest source of love that determines our experience on earth in order that we grow in wisdom and maturity. He foretells that all will turn out well and ascends to Olympus on his eagle, leaving them a tablet which he commands they give to Posthumus. On it is inscribed the prophecy that Posthumus will be again united with the one he loves and that many ancient feuds and unresolved relationships in Rome and Britain will finally be healed through Posthumus' ordeal. Through this assurance the souls of his family are liberated and able to move on. Posthumus awakens from his dream and finds the tablet, but unable to interpret it, can make no sense of his experience.

I have seen two live professional performances where the scene we are considering, Act 5, scene 4, was performed with brilliant ensemble choreography, sincerely and without technological enhancement. Yet although I was moved by the sincerity with which the emotions of the gods and discarnate human beings were portrayed, they did not awaken in my consciousness any intimations that the beings at work beyond our everyday perception had reality beyond their value as symbolic or allegorical devices.

Digital technology, developed since, would no doubt turn this scene into a stunning spectacle. Yet we must ask whether such effects awaken genuine perception of the spirit or merely trap us in material appearances, keeping us addicted to the need for ever more intense sensation?

It would be our goal, that through this methodology:

- we could one day represent not just symbolic figures but create the very substance of supersensible experience, of the mystery dimensions that glimmer through the clues that Shakespeare's words provide; [*]
- we could evolve our capacities to discern and communicate the more than mortal forms and thoughts and feelings and emotions of those discarnate souls whose karma is woven inextricably with Posthumus;
- we could reveal something of the wisdom hidden in the names of Jupiter and eagle, the mysteries at work within the name of Posthumus, that clearly speaks of one who undergoes initiation through the mystic death in order to experience the second birth and who is born under the influence of the Lion constellation: Leo (Leonatus).

For surely we cannot think that the genius of Shakespeare, as he draws near the consummation of his vision in his final plays, would choose such images or language arbitrarily. No less arbitrary would have been his choice to base the story of the play in historical events that took place in Britain when Caesar Augustus was Emperor of Rome. To an audience, only recently exposed to the Bible in their native tongue, the name of Caesar Augustus that appeared in Shakespeare's text must have resonated in their minds with the opening words of the newly authorised translation of St Luke's Christmas story which would in time become a most beloved and familiar text:

> And it came to pass in those days, that there went out a decree from Caesar Augustus, that all the world should be taxed.

For an English audience such resonance would have placed this drama, connected so intimately with their own identity and history as Britons, in the Christian context of the birth of Jesus: the event that would mark the beginning of what Steiner called 'the turning point of time'. And something of that radiance of hope in our redemption that, even now, can still glimmer when we hear the reading of that Bible text, is the radiance that permeates the action of the play: telescoping, as it does, the ancient and Renaissance worlds and demonstrating how the boundaries of earthly time dissolve when Love performs its miracles of transformation.

---

[*] *The Actor of the Future 1: Tongues of Flame.*

When we read the play with an ear for the mystery dimension of its language, we recognise in the image of the eagle on which Jupiter descends, one of the four imaginations in which astrology has clothed its understanding of the zodiacal cross that encompasses the interacting constellations of the lion, eagle, bull and human archetype (Aquarius); their vast relationships that interweave across the cosmos to contribute their potentials to our evolution.

*Figure 54 Christ in the centre is surrounded by symbols of the Four Evangelists: Matthew (human, upper left), Mark (lion, lower left), Luke (ox bull, lower right) and John (eagle, upper right)*

Likewise the esoteric level of astrology has always understood the dual aspect of the eagle constellation embodied in the fallen forces of the scorpion that would sting itself to death. And so we imagine a rehearsal process that explores:

- connecting the mysteries embodied in the constellation Scorpio with Posthumus' attempted suicide;
- how the starry beings of this constellation guide the karma of those whose destinies they influence, to deal with the mystery of death: whose sting results from the brain-bound intellect that identifies us with our bodies;
- how by penetrating through the maya of our sense perceptions, Love can redeem those fallen forces and achieve a thinking that transcends our mortal frame of reference for suffering, and soars aloft on eagle wings, into the cosmic region of the guiding powers of the universe, through whose mediation, in the final action of the play, so many threads of karma can be healed;

- what occult wisdom has always understood: that the name of Jupiter refers not just to the planetary body orbiting the earth but the planetary sphere, home to the Spirits of Wisdom (Kyriotetes), who serve the transformation of our present planet earth and human race into their next planetary cycle: the esoteric name of which is Jupiter;

- how the lion initiation, hinted through Leonatus' name, demands that Posthumus endure the refining fires of jealousy in order that his soul be purified — his astral body be transformed from the roaring predatory beast that reveals itself in Act 2, scene 5, to the noble-hearted lion in the final scene, who, passions tamed and weeping tears of gold,[48] at last is reconciled in peace with Imogen, the lamb he would have sacrificed.

Imagine an ensemble of actors, eurythmists, and eurythmic-actors, with instruments transformed in more or less degree by the practice of eurythmy and the integrated Steiner speech and Chekhov acting methodology. And then, in the light of Chekhov's words, *we are all babies on this long tremendous way,*[*] imagine a rehearsal or performance of this scene.

The actor playing Posthumus sinks exhausted into sleep and the ensemble explores how to communicate that his soul and spirit leave his body. If his eurythmic capabilities allow it, perhaps he can accomplish this himself so that the perception of the audience shifts with his transformation into the supersensible realm of sleep in which the following events takes place. Or perhaps the actor's body stays in place while eurthymists show the expansion of his soul and spirit out of it, inviting those who watch to experience both levels of reality at once. There they witness how the soul of Posthumus encounters the souls of those who had been his family on earth: his two brothers who were killed in battle, his father, who had died of grief before his son was born, his mother who had died of grief in giving birth to him. And now the audience beholds with what compassion, tenderness, outraged, bewildered grief, they welcome Posthumus and advocate on his behalf. It is a karmic community, still close to earth, unable to move on, still bound together by the unhealed wounds and questions of the destiny they share, dependent on each other for salvation.

And now their prayers rise together, beseeching that the Spirits of Wisdom (Kyriotetes) working from the planetary sphere of Jupiter, have mercy on the orphaned human soul to whom they are so intimately bound and help them understand the meaning of the pain to which they and all on earth must be subjected by the sting of death. Use our speech technique to sound from the periphery, the voices not proceeding from a central point but radiating from discarnate souls, no longer anchored in their bodies. Experiment with how eurythmy might create some sense of how they interpenetrate and weave together, to reveal the astral forms of powerful emotions experienced by human souls but no longer channelled through their earthbound personalities.

---

* *The Art of Acting,* pp. 189–191.

*Figure 55 top left: Starry being Scorpion/eagle, top right: Consonant s, bottom left: Planetary being Jupiter, bottom right: Vowel o.*

And now from higher regions, where destiny is woven, Shakespeare tells us that Jupiter, mounted on an eagle, descends. Eurythmy and Creative Speech allow us to investigate the wisdom hidden in these names. The planetary being Jupiter supported by the eagle-forces of the starry being Scorpio work together to reveal the higher understanding that alone will heal the karmic wound that plagues the hereditary stream of Leonatus. Through the activity of /s/ the beings of the constellation Scorpio have brought their healing scalpel to this group of souls who have shared the destiny of their untimely deaths. Uncomprehending of the lessons they have yet to learn, the whole family of souls is still imprisoned in the lower astral realm. Their anguish, on behalf of Posthumus, strains up in prayer, penetrating to the highest realms where the karmic consequences of our lives are weighed and the pedagogy of our further evolution is determined.

*Figure 56 Starry being Scorpio radiates through cosmic s*

And now the redeemed eagle-forces, whose harmonising love is channelled through the initiation that the constellation of the starry being, Scorpio provides, reach down through the planetary sphere of Jupiter to mediate their influence. From there the Spirits of Wisdom (Kyriotetes) who guide human beings to embrace their destiny and extract the meaning of the suffering they undergo on earth, open in our souls the vowel feeling /ɒ/(cr<u>o</u>ss) and /oʊ/(n<u>o</u>). And now in this sacred macrocosmic conversation, sound and movement weave together; the /s/ of Scorpio and /ɒ/(cr<u>o</u>ss)

/oʊ/(n<u>o</u>) of Jupiter remind us that, 'Love is the unfamiliar name behind the hands that wove the intolerable shirt of flame that human power cannot remove'.[49] And in the central mystery that Jupiter reveals to the Leonati family, /s/ and /ɒ/ and /oʊ/ together form the cr<u>oss</u> on which our mortal part must die in order to release our indestructable, immortal self.

Whom best I love I cr<u>oss</u>.

Observe the interplay of /s/ and /ɒ/(cr<u>o</u>ss) /oʊ/(n<u>o</u>) throughout the speech of Jupiter.

N<u>o</u> m<u>o</u>re, you petty <u>s</u>pirit<u>s</u> <u>o</u>f region l<u>o</u>w
<u>O</u>ffend our hearing; hush! How dare you gh<u>ost</u>s
Accu<u>s</u>e the thundererer, who<u>s</u>e b<u>o</u>lt, you kn<u>o</u>w,
<u>S</u>ky planted, batter<u>s</u> <u>a</u>ll rebelling c<u>o</u>a<u>st</u>s.

Jupiter's appearance demonstrates the paradox that when it has to wield the healing scalpel, love will often be experienced as stern by the soul as yet unpermeated by the I AM Self. Through the initiation path that Scorpio provides, the conscience-wakening words that are designed to heal, at first sound fierce to the unevolved who long only for release from pain, to have it taken from them without their lessons learned; even when mediated through the merciful embrace of Jupiter.

And as the actor/eurythmist playing Posthumus returns to his body, and wakens once again into the world of ordinary sense perception, the supersensible realm he had inhabited fades from our sight. Or perhaps it can be shown how that other world is still around him, but he no longer sees or hears it. Or perhaps it can be shown how it moves, beyond beholding, to another sphere. Posthumus is left to make sense of what he calls a dream. He finds the tablet that contains the prophecy of his redemption, but as he cannot understand the language of the mysteries, the dream fades and he remembers nothing of the wonders he experienced before he woke. His life remains as incomprehensible as the writing on the tablet he just read.

There is more for him to learn before his soul is ripe enough to grasp with earthly senses what his spirit witnessed while he slept.

This level or quality of research is the actor of the future's path into the mysteries that shape the challenges and crises of our lives. The redemptive possibilities contained in them often go unrecognised and even seem to threaten us, until we learn to see and hear with other eyes and ears. These are the faculties the actor's path specifically invites us to develop, since drama's very form and function have evolved in order to explore how karma works: whether unconsciously or, increasingly, as we consciously align with the macrocosmic healing powers that weave within our destinies.

As our organs of perception continue to evolve through practice, so too will the consciousness that gives birth to the dramas of the future. Unlike Shakespeare's plays, that were written in a time when the mystery wisdom that inspired them was seen as heresy — and needed to be clothed in images and language that preserved that deeper wisdom and could nourish audiences' souls unconsciously while being undetected — a time will come when plays will be devised and written that approach such mysteries directly. A time will come when actors trained in our Creative Speech and Chekhov acting methodology will also be proficient in eurythmy, and when enough eurythmists are proficient in the integrated speech and acting methodology. Then they will be able to convincingly perform these dramas of the future. Of course there will always be actors who are not eurythmists and eurythmists who are not actors. Each art form also functions in its own specific sphere, demanding different faculties and a different way of inhabiting the artist's instrument. However, those who are gifted in both arts can consciously develop the ability to shift from one mode of expression to the other. [*]

Once these faculties have been awakened, we will sense how to explore these levels even in dramas that offer no more evidence of their existence than our lives do when viewed only through the lens of everyday perception. Beckett's *Waiting for Godot* for example, which on the surface seems to offer no such possibilities, yielded an extraordinary harvest of discoveries to students in their fourth year of training in this methodology who were working on it as their graduation play. Yet as post-Kali Yuga human beings open to these non-material dimensions, so will the dramas of the future increasingly reflect them and in turn, become the mirrors that show us how to live our lives in participation with the other-worldly beings whose destinies are woven with our own.

---

[*] *The Actor of the Future 2, Word Made Flesh,* page 153.

In the meantime, until such plays arise, here are some more examples of scenes from existing plays that clearly offer actors and eurythmists opportunities to exercise these future faculties: the interaction of Prospero with the elemental world in Shakespeare's *Tempest*, the death of Queen Katharine in *Henry VIII*, the reception at his death of Lear's soul and spirit by Cordelia's in the final scene of Shakespeare's *King Lear*; the death of Hamlet ('and flights of angels sing thee to thy rest'); Act 4, scene 3 of Maeterlink's *The Bluebird* depicts the sphere where the souls of children of the future are preparing to be born; the final act of Thornton Wilder's *Our Town* and *Pullman Car Hiawatha*, and from his *Four Minute Plays, The Birth of the Poet* and *The Angel that troubled the Waters*; the final scenes of Marlowe's *Dr Faustus* and of Goethe's *Faust*.

Inspired by Steiner's insights, through eurythmy and Creative Speech we are ready to begin our systematic exploration of the planetary beings.

Chapter 5

# The planetary spheres: Dante's 'Paradiso' — Our High Work Masters and the vowels

In many books and lectures Steiner has elaborated on the names and functions of the nine spiritual hierarchies as they were understood and handed down within the Christian heritage. His research reveals that the centres of activity and consciousness of the seven hierarchies who most directly influence the lives of human beings are the planetary spheres connected to our sun. We can have a sense for this if we recognise how the Earth sphere is at present the centre of activity and consciousness for human beings as we evolve towards our goal to take our place among the hierarchies:

- Moon sphere — Angels or *divine messengers.*
- Mercury sphere — Archangels or *spirits of fire/folk-spirits.*
- Venus sphere — Archai or *spirits of personality/time.*
- Sun sphere — Exusiai or *spirits of form.*
- Mars sphere — Dynamis or *spirits of movement.*
- Jupiter sphere — Kyriotetes or *spirits of wisdom.*
- Saturn sphere — Thrones or *spirits of will.*

Beyond the planetary spheres lies the sphere of the fixed stars, of which the constellations of the zodiac are particularly relevant to earthly evolution. Steiner's research has confirmed that this sphere is the centre of activity and consciousness of the hierarchies known as Thrones (who mediate between the stars and Saturn sphere), the Cherubim and Seraphim. Their contribution to our human evolution and how it can expand and enrich the processes available to actors of the future will be only touched on in this present volume but will be the central focus of volume 4.

In Volume 2, *Word Made Flesh* pages 121-124, we explored why Steiner chose to base his research into the planetary beings and the vowels on the geocentric pre-Copernican conception of the cosmos. He knew that this more ancient paradigm was not just a superstition or a theory generated to explain the universe by human beings who were less intelligent than their modern scientific counterparts. Rather it was the lived experience of peoples who still perceived a universe of conscious being.

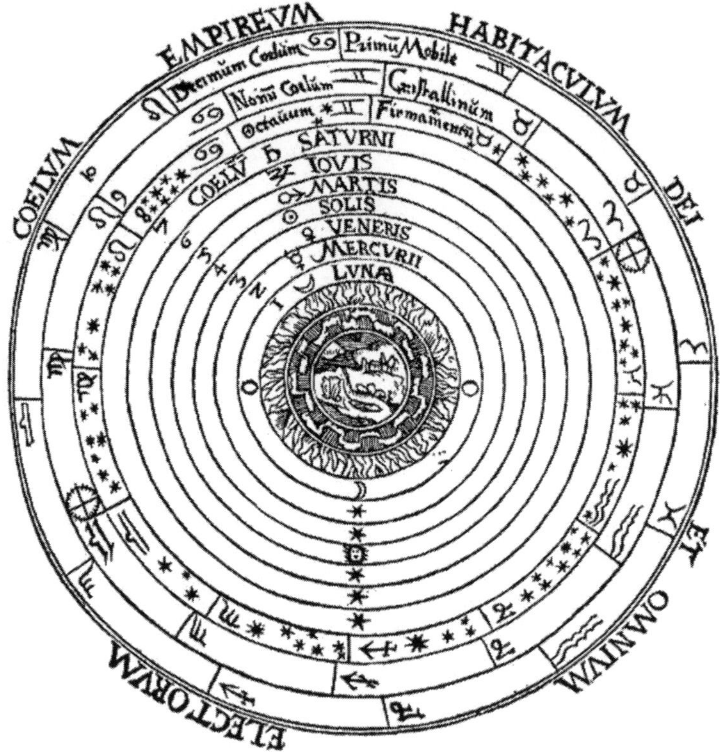


*Figure 57 The Ptolemaic view of the universe with earth at the centre.*

And it was this universe he set out to explore with his own rigorously trained spiritual-scientific organs of perception. His research has pioneered the possibilities of a future human consciousness able to transcend the materialistic scientific paradigm that posits ever vaster distances of empty space dotted with occasional conglomerates of matter, equally devoid of being.

In Western culture there is no more powerful portrayal of the seven planetary spheres as realms of consciousness of cosmic beings, than the third book of Dante's *Divina Commedia*. It was written between 1308-1320, just as the Western mind was poised between the culmination of the Mediaeval Age and the dawn of the Renaissance, when humanity would exercise its intellectual powers to make sense of a universe increasingly perceived as empty space and matter. Dante's initiation through what he experienced as planetary spheres of consciousness is recorded in the *Paradiso*. He makes it clear that his journey in each planetary sphere results from the interaction of the planetary beings with the starry beings of the zodiac. However, due to the limitations of my own research and knowledge at this point, I will focus simply on the

*Figure 58 Doré's depiction of Dante's heavenly spheres.*

planetary contribution to the evolution of his consciousness and how Steiner's intuitions help us understand that Dante's path illuminates our own.

Before arriving at this level of initiation, Dante has been guided by the poet Virgil through the *Inferno* and witnessed the suffering of those who, unrepentant and addicted to their unwise choices, continue to endure the consequences. Then, still with Virgil's guidance he has also passed through *Purgatorio* and witnessed the suffering remorseful souls endure as they purify themselves of the tendencies that led them into error (which mediaeval Christian terminology referred to as the seven deadly sins).

His learning in this sphere has advanced to the level that he is deemed worthy of the crown that is bestowed on him and signifies he has become a sovereign soul, ruler over his emotions. *

Thus he is prepared to meet again the soul and spirit being of his beloved Beatrice who since her death has continued to watch over him and now becomes his guide through higher spheres.

Throughout the *Commedia* Dante makes it clear how these two figures, Beatrice and Virgil, one from his personal biography and one from the ancient past, have inspired his artistic/spiritual journey. In doing so he helps the reader see how in the realm of soul and spirit our own immortal selves continue to be deeply interwoven with those who have been part of our development and continue to contribute to our further growth. Through Virgil's poetry Dante had experienced a meeting with his predecessor's spirit who then became his moral and artistic guide, throughout his life.[50] Through his continuing companionship, he has helped Dante understand the sacred responsibility he bears because through his poetry he will, in time, guide others just as Virgil guided him. The *Divina Commedia* is peopled with the characters and images of history, of world affairs that have impressed the soul of Dante; those with whom his own life has been woven, whether close or far, and through whose ongoing presence in his consciousness he must endeavour to make meaning of his journey. Most of the specific details of these characters and situations, so significant to him seven centuries ago, will largely be unknown and of no significance to us.

However, if we extract from these particulars the essence of what Dante's consciousness attains to in each sphere then we can build the basis of understanding the contribution made by these planetary beings not only to our own individual development but to the evolution of the soul life of the human race. This will enable us to see how the archetypes of their activity express themselves in many different aspects of experience, whether it be (as in *Word Made Flesh*) soul tendencies of individuals, or (as in the next chapter) the rhythms of each human life, or (as explored in Chapter 7) the dynamics at work in human creativity. Dante's poem is a beautiful artistic exploration of the cosmos as a 'many mansioned'[51] universe of being, abode to those of ever more advanced degrees of consciousness. These include the human souls who have refined the sensibilities available within each 'mansion' to the level that enables them to share the fruits of their experience with Dante.

Reflecting on Dante's poem in his *Four Quartets*, Eliot observes: 'The way up is the way down.' Far from the fixed and static concept of the cosmos that literal interpretation makes of the 'Inferno', 'Purgatorio' and 'Paradiso', Dante reveals an infinitely

---

* For a detailed description see *The Actor of the Future: Tongues of Flame,* pages 6-7.

mobile journey from Hell to highest bliss. As his own consciousness matures and refines he shows how access to each level depends entirely on our willingness to grow in understanding and perception. His portrayal of Paradise reveals a more mature psychology than simplistic conceptions of the mediaeval mind suggest. He reveals the soul and spirit as infinitely complex and capable of infinite development. He reveals a paradise in which souls and spirits who are still evolving in regard to certain aspects of themselves have nonetheless achieved the possibility to dwell in highest bliss and demonstrate that enlightenment can be experienced throughout the process of development. Paradise is not a final stasis, arrived at when there is nothing more to be experienced.

The lens available to Dante in his time and culture, through which to view this journey, was the Christian mediaeval understanding of the need to firstly cultivate the Christian virtues known as *faith, hope* and *love.* These would in turn infuse, through the I AM's renewing power, able now to work within those souls who make that choice, the virtues already striven for in earlier pre-Christian times and identified, by Greek philosophers like Plato, as *fortitude, justice, temperance* and *prudence.* Therefore in each sphere he will encounter souls who have attained the consciousness that qual-ifies their presence in the highest realm of the *empyrean.*<sup>*</sup> Nevertheless they appear to Dante in the planetary sphere in which the gifts, events and challenges, that shaped their lives on earth, have prepared them to bear witness to the initiation specific to that sphere. This terminology may sound out-of-date and too culturally-specific to contemporary ears. However, I hope the explorations will reveal that the wisdom embodied in these names is universal and can be recognised by anyone who under-takes initiation in our present time, whatever terminology they use or spiritual or cultural tradition they adhere to.

For example, in the first sphere of the Moon we meet the souls of those who were initially deficient in the Christian virtue *faith,* but through their struggle with incon-stancy, developed the *faith* that would in turn revitalise the pagan virtue *fortitude.* Likewise in the sphere of Mercury we meet the souls who were initially deficient in the Christian virtue *hope.* However, their lives had taught them how futile were the hopes they had invested in their personal ambitions in the realm of politics and wealth and encouraged them instead to place their hope in things eternal. This change of heart revitalised the pagan virtue *justice.* Likewise in the sphere of Venus, we meet the souls of those who were initially deficient in the Christian virtue *love,* but through their struggles had transformed their excessive natural propensity for love into its Christian counterpart. In the fourth, the Sun sphere, we meet those who, through the

---

* See endnote 73.

exercise of all three Christian virtues, developed and revitalised the pagan virtue *prudence* or *wisdom*. And finally, beyond the Sun, we meet the souls of those who, as just described, would go on to transform their weaknesses, revitalise the pagan virtues, and demonstrate maturity in each specific moral sphere. This exploration will expand our understanding of these virtues and their fallen counterparts, the vices which the mediaeval soul referred to as the seven deadly sins, beyond the confines of mediaeval dogmatism to a mature psychology; one that reaches far beyond the present mainstream paradigm. This posits our emotions as some arbitrary by-product of cellular secretions and pathways laid down in that part of our brains we share with animals in a just as arbitrary evolution.

It lies beyond the context of this present volume 3, to explore Dante's insights into the realms of Paradise that lie beyond the planetary spheres. However, we will see, within each planetary level, how a seed is planted that will develop and mature into the fruits attained by those whose practice of the virtues at the highest level maintains their presence in the highest realms of consciousness. As we explore these realms through Dante's words imbued with Steiner's insights, we shall see as well, how this mediaeval theological conception of the virtues evolves into a more contemporary understanding of the path of inner transformation and development. As well, we shall see how this provides a framework within which the actor of the future can healthily explore and excavate the vast terrain of human soul experience. Within this the range of emotions actors are accustomed to identify and access will appear as effects arising from the work of planetary beings, who pour their consciousness into the evolving human soul. Even the darkest and most challenging emotions find their place within a meaningful trajectory contingent on the human being's challenge of transforming them into their nobler counterparts. Working in this way will expand the range of emotions and feeling sensibilities available to actors and their ability to access them.

The journey through the planetary spheres described in 'Paradiso' can be experienced as an ascent, as in the first stages of our soul and spirit journey after death. This holds true both for the death of the body that concludes an incarnation or, as in Dante's case, the death that the body-bound constructed self endures as it embarks upon the conscious path to find the indestructible, immortal Self. The passage through the spheres can also be a descent, as when the human spirit, on its way towards a new incarnation, descends through each planetary sphere, gathering the substance that it needs, to form the astral and etheric sheaths it will inhabit in its life on earth.

'The way up is the way down'[52] and over many lives we will learn to make the journey in both ways, many times. However, since we are using Dante's experience through *Paradiso* as our template we will follow the ascending path as his soul and spirit work to discern and penetrate to ever more refined degrees of consciousness.

Once again our approach is phenomenological; we experience the eurythmy gestures intuited by Steiner for the planetary beings and their associated vowels as CPGs that grant access to the consciousness of beings.* We explore the micro-gestures in our mouths that enable us to speak the vowels. These two processes prepare our body of sensation to be an organ of perception through which we can discern something of the supersensible realities that Dante has struggled to articulate in human words. This will enable us to integrate his findings with the spiritual-scientific research for which Steiner found expression, not only in his books and lectures, but in the gestures of eurythmy and the pathway of Creative Speech.

As explored in volume 2, *Word Made Flesh,* each gesture, if incorporated with eurythmic consciousness, becomes a pathway of perception of the cosmic being's inner life whose task it is to generate its soul capacity within the human soul.[53] This is because eurythmic consciousness enables us to sense with I AM presence our own etheric body which then becomes an organ of perception that allows us to 'see into the life of things'.[54] In this condition of awareness, the sensations each gesture generates can be experienced as intimations of what I have called elsewhere a vaster psychology than the mental life, emotions and sensations arising from the body-bound awareness of the self, can give us any indication. Each hierarchy is on its own journey to evolve its consciousness through all the levels of the spheres, culminating in the highest sphere of Love. Each planetary sphere marks the stage that the beings who inhabit it have reached on their way towards that Love. As we penetrate the state of soul awakened by each gesture we experience a glimpse of the inner life of cosmic beings whose gift to human souls is the consciousness they have achieved in their own evolutionary journey.

The eurythmy gestures grant a glimpse of the sensibilities experienced by these beings who offer their more evolved capacities to serve our human evolution. Because they are totally aligned with the divine source of creation, their soul capacities are rooted in that source of love and light. When we experience the gestures with eurythmic consciousness, we too can learn to root ourselves in that universal source. The intimations that they generate anticipate the range and richness of the inner life that will be ours when the soul capacities bestowed on us have been developed to their highest level.

---

* Cosmic Psychological Gestures: See *The Actor of the Future 2: Word Made Flesh,* page 123.

*Figure 59 The planetary beings pour their soul capacities into the human soul*

Dante depicts the strivings of the human souls who, in their lives on earth, struggled to transform the shadow of each soul capacity into its full potential and therefore find themselves within that sphere. If we withdraw eurythmic consciousness and explore each gesture with ordinary, body-bound awareness of the self, the powerful sensations it evokes when our consciousness is cut off from the cosmos through the ego's lens, become the shadows of their nobler counterparts. These shadows are the raw material, the astral substance that our I AM must transform in this next stage of our evolution.* So it is important that we learn to recognise and cultivate each ray

---

* See *The Actor of the Future 1, Tongues of Flame,* for a detailed exploration of the evolutionary tasks and in particular the transformation of the astral body into Spirit Self.

within the higher spectrum of our inner life and identify its fallen counterpart that dominates our ego-bound experience. Our ability to alternate between eurythmic and body-bound sensation of the gestures, will allow us to directly sense the challenges and blessings for our own individual development within each sphere of consciousness. In addition it allows the actor of the future to excavate the darker aspects of the human soul within the healing context that enables us to recognise that our most challenging emotions are distortions of our highest soul potentials which it is our task to purify and bring to their fulfilment.

The eurythmic exploration of each gesture will enable us to sense the inner life of the planetary beings who bestow their sensibilities on human souls, towards which we aspire. Then if we consciously withdraw our consciousness of the etheric from the gestures and experiment with layering the tools described in Chapter 3, then we will begin to get a sense of how those higher sensibilities distort into their luciferic and their ahrimanic counterparts that manifest within our souls when we are cut off from the source of life and love. *

I was astonished to discover, as I worked, that the gestures and many of the words from Dante's text illuminate each other, sometimes a gesture guiding me to words, sometimes the words to gesture. Therefore I suggest that at some point you accompany your explorations of the full-bodied gestures and the micro-gestures in the mouth with Dante's words, speaking them at first quite quietly, as though they are your own most intimate attempts to find a name for your sensations.

Having already passed through the purifying fires of *Purgatorio*, Dante, now with Beatrice to guide him, has finally ascended to the place from which the human race began the long descent into materiality and apparent separation. He enters Eden, the earthly paradise that is a kind of antechamber to the Moon sphere, abode of angels.

*I stand in the silence with instrument attuned, available. As a hand slips into a glove and by degrees inhabits it until it feels at home, so I slip inside the eurythmy gestures Steiner has discerned for the planetary being Moon and her accompanying diphthong /aɪ/ (life). I alternate between them, allowing my body of sensation to respond, discern new consciousness begin to stir. I struggle to articulate, rightly name this will that fastens wrist to wrist, commitment to a central fixity, and then dissolves into an alternating left and right, inviting me to choose which way to go.*

---

* See Chapter 4, 'Lucifer, Ahriman and the I AM'.

## Entering Eden, antechamber to the planetary sphere of Moon

*Figure 60 Eurythmy gesture for the planetary being Moon*

*Figure 61 Diphthong /aɪ/*

It is as though my instrument, feeling for words that match what it is sensing, summons from the text those lines where Beatrice describes the fickle nature of the vows the poet made to her when, at his first meeting and in the first flush of his love, he knew her being called him to serve with his poetic gifts the Divine Creator's love that had bestowed on him his genius.

> My countenance sustained him for a space.
> I brought him with me with my youthful eyes,
> The right way ...
> [But at my death] he turned his face
> Away from me, his wishes otherwise.
> My state was raided from beauty of the flesh
> To that of soul, and virtue so increased
> In me that I became less dear, less fresh,
> Less welcome, and his questing steps soon ceased
> To come my way and went another way
> Less true, after false images of good
> Which keep no promises: nor did it pay,
> Through dreams and all the other means I could,
> To call him back, for he would not pay heed.[55]

She lovingly admonishes the poet for unfaithfulness and he responds, remorsefully:

> As soon as your face vanished, all my choice
> Was for the present day and its false bliss.

Then throughout cantos 31–33 of 'Purgatorio', Beatrice reminds him constantly that his central vow must always be to serve the love that goes beyond all earthly goals. This will prepare his consciousness to enter the planetary sphere of Moon and be enlightened further.

## Moon sphere

*Dante meets the souls of those who were initially deficient in the Christian virtue faith, but through their struggle with inconstancy, developed the faith that will in turn christen and revitalise the pagan virtue fortitude.* * *Their journey in this sphere of consciousness finds expression in the range of soul experience embodied in the diphthong /aɪ/ (life).*

---

* I use the word 'pagan' simply in the sense of 'pre-Christian'.

These are souls like Dante, who had also once professed their vows to purity and faithful service to the love of God. The circumstances of their lives, however, had forced them into marriages against their will. Hearing their stories evokes the realisation in the poet that to cultivate the virtue *faith*, the potential for which is the gift bestowed on human souls within this sphere, he must wrestle with the paradox of free will and obedience. Through verses 1-5, Beatrice responds to Dante's deepest questions:

> … God's greatest gift to man
> In all the bounty he was moved to make
> Throughout creation — the one gift the most
> Close to his goodness and the one He calls most precious
> — is free will …

And yet, as she points out, there is a paradox. For free will has to co-exist with:

> The absolute will [that] knows no yielding law:

Yet, as she warns, this opportunity for choice, which was ordained by God, does not excuse the traits of fickleness, inconstancy:

> … Feathers in every wind
> Ought not to be your model …

As we continue to explore these gestures we sense how they embody the paradox at the very centre of the mystery of human agency. With eurythmic consciousness the Moon gesture enables us to dimly sense the faithful commitment that angelic beings must feel to the central path of destiny of the precious human soul that each one is responsible to guide from one life to another. The gesture /aɪ/ (l_ife), inviting, indicating not imposing, is respectful of the individual's need to wander sometimes from the central path in order to develop independence and mature. With body-bound awareness of the self, the same gestures lead to a sense of swaying between shifting possibilities, 'distracted from distraction by distraction'[56] or a sense of being trapped, or stuck, obsessively attached to one of them.

As we alternate between eurythmic and body-bound awareness of the gestures we can sense that faith is not trust in an irrational belief that cannot be authenticated. Rather it is the steadfast will to practise faithfulness to one's own deepest impulses of being, through all the opportunities life offers. *Faith* is the most evolved expression of this planetary sensibility and lies at the other end of the spectrum to its counterpart, the deadly sin conceived of by the mediaeval soul as *sloth*. Sloth is the refusal of the spirit to take responsibility and commit to the fulfilment of its choices. Rather it allows us, through inaction, to lose ourselves in the distractions like a 'feather in the wind'. Further along the journey of initiation, faith will evolve into a higher level of the virtue of resilience or fortitude.

The micro-gestures in our mouth which channel the spoken diphthong /aɪ/ (life), move from /ɑː/ to /iː/. We must wait for the next sections to explore the paradisal love that pours itself in pure devotion from the planetary sphere of Venus and finds expression in the vowel /ɑː/ (star) and the gift of the planetary being Mercury who awakens in the soul the sense it is an independent self and finds expression in the vowel /iː/ (me).[57] For now however we can contemplate the gift of the angelic beings who mediate the soul capacities bestowed by their higher planetary counterparts, allowing them to flow into each other as they stream into our souls.

Does the cooperation of these hierarchies help us understand the mystery at work within the English pronoun I; how, when the self invokes itself within the English-speaking soul, it finds expression in the diphthong /aɪ/ (I)? Does it illuminate an aspect of the mission of the English-speaking soul that develops consciousness by being forced to wrestle with ambiguities, sort through this and that, find nuance through complexity, shifting between the left and right brain functions through which our consciousness is channelled? Perhaps in this pronoun 'I' we can begin to sense how the specific task of consciousness into which the English language channels those who speak it, is mediated by the beings of the first three planetary spheres and their cooperation.

The souls of the human beings who appear to Dante to relate their stories and describe their learning in this sphere reveal that those inhabiting this first level of the higher realms are not the insipid, static souls that sense-bound consciousness imagines as consigned to an eternity of boredom. These are mature souls who did not remain in Eden by adhering to an abstract standard of perfection and avoiding the experience of life on earth. They have made 'mistakes' but, by following the guidance offered, have learned from their experience a deeper understanding and practice of the virtue *faith*. They can share their experience with Dante in the planetary sphere of consciousness where they achieved this transformation in their souls.

Some, like Dante, had allowed life's vicissitudes to sway them from their central vows. Others, though outer circumstances made it appear they had betrayed their vows, by inwardly remaining faithful, served God's larger purposes to bring about a greater good. That all have learned their lessons in this sphere of Paradise gives Dante hope, preparing him to pass into the sphere of Mercury.

## *Mercury Sphere*

*Here he meets the souls of those who were initially deficient in the Christian virtue hope. This virtue will in turn christen and revitalise the pagan virtue justice. Their journey in this sphere of consciousness finds expression in the range of soul experience embodied in the vowel /i:/ (me).*

*Figure 62 Eurythmy gesture for the planetary being Mercury*

*Figure 63 Vowel /iː/*

Hope is the second fruit of Christian virtue and it grows from the seed that will be planted in the second sphere where the soul must be purified of personal ambition. Dante describes how, led by Beatrice and on the wings of hope, they enter the sphere of Mercury:

> …We sped like a shaft
> That strikes the mark before the cord is still
> Into the second realm…

> *Inhabiting the gesture /i:/ (m**e**) my body of sensation realigns. Shot from God's bow, I am that shaft. I can, like lightning, strike through dark, penetrating and illuminating it, or, cut off from the cosmos, driven only by my will to dominate, strike in order to control. Inhabiting the gesture Mercury with eurythmic consciousness I surrender to the cyclic round of seasons, sense its pulse, the times to rise and times to fall, times to lead and times to follow, consciously participating in the turning dance of Archangelic Beings. Without etheric consciousness, cut off from the source of love, in my mouth the micro-gesture that elicits /i:/ (m**e**), squeezed from between my lips and teeth, expresses isolated me with furrowed brow and chiselled jaw, insidiously spreads, thrusts upwards into fascist arm salute. Etheric consciousness awaken once again! Eternally at home, perfectly aligned, released from pushing, no further need to strain, to dominate, its narrow golden beam is freed and fast as light, its messages of hope speed between earth and sky.*

Dante is approached by Justinian, Emperor of the Eastern Roman Empire from 527-565 CE. Like others in this sphere, Justinian had to learn how futile are the hopes that personal ambition entertains for power or wealth or honour in this world, and instead developed hope in things eternal. This enabled him to bear political responsibility in an enlightened way and use his power to reform the Roman law and spread its justice through the empire. However, Dante does not recognise Justinian at first:

> … 'As for what you are
> However, I don't know, nor why you rank
> In this sphere, that another's beams
> Debar from mortal sight, for Mercury is blank
> Beside the blazing sun.'

The observation that for much of the year Mercury's size and position in relation to the sun means it is invisible to earthly sight becomes a metaphor that holds the mystery of the soul's ordeal in the realm of Mercury. For in this realm it must wrestle with the pride that seeks power and glory for itself. It must be humbled and learn that its true glory rests within the sun that shines not for itself but for the greater good of everyone. Only then will ambition offer up its single, isolated ray to serve the whole. Only then will power lead to justice. To illustrate this lesson, Justinian relates the epic tale of human history from which Dante learns that for law to be established peacefully the human mind must recognise that it is just. This leads him to consider the abyss between:

> Eternal Justice, and the shifting aims
> Of politics…

> [And that those who here within this sphere of Mercury] adorn this little star,
> [Are] Good spirits who did what they did to earn
> An honoured form. And when it goes so far,
> The will for fame, that it can even turn
> Honour to glory's ends, then it must mount
> More than the rays of true love, which lose force
> Accordingly. But when we make
> The count of our reward and our desert, of course,
> Part of our joy is in the way we find
> It neither less nor more. With even hand
> The Living Justice sweetens to the mind
> His judgement just because we understand
> That justice has been done, and true desire
> Can never be warped to evil.…

Justinian describes another soul who learned his lessons in this sphere, a compatriot of Dante's, Romeo,[58] who having served his ruler faithfully, humbly and without ambition for himself, was justly rewarded with both wealth and honour.

> But envy soon laid siege to Romeo's position.

Consequently he was wrongfully accused and, stripped of everything, became a beggar. However, we meet him here in Paradise because, while still on earth, he never put his trust in worldly power but lived in hope of things eternal. His ambition was to only ever serve true justice with his gifts and, like the planetary being Mercury, who brings about his soul's ordeal, he did not disdain to let his own light disappear within the greater solar rays. Nor did the changing circumstances of his outer life in any way arouse his envy, wound his pride or disturb the inner certainties in which he placed his hope. And thus through Justinian's account of Romeo we learn of the shaft of truth that pierces earth and sky and never ceases to project its ray through all the cycles of vicissitude and change:

> And if you knew the mighty heart he had,
> Begging his bread by scraps, out in the cold,
> You'd think him something more than merely sad—
> And call his smug foes stupid to be glad.
>
> …
>
> Goodness divine, which spurns all envy hence,
> Burning within, so sparkles, it displays
> All the eternal beauties. That intense
> Ignition point sends out a further blaze
> Without end, since its imprint, once embossed,
> Does not grow pale. That which comes down like rain,
> Free straight away, with not a droplet lost—
> Nothing expended that it can't regain—
> Pays no heed to the power of changing things.

In fact through this gesture we begin to sense the rhythmic cycles in which the archangelic beings radiate their contribution to the journey of the human soul. Could we accept their gifts and live in harmony with their transitions: sleeping and waking, the cycles of the seasons, rise and fall of the trends that shape communities of souls? Whatever condenses into earthly form at some point must return to the eternal plane to make way for the future that, at some point, will condense again.

Just as in the Moon sphere, the paradox of free will and divine necessity had to be explored and understood, so here in this sphere of Mercury, Beatrice leads Dante through a complex tapestry of thought to understand the paradox of how from the time of 'man's first disobedience'[59] justice and mercy could exist together in the cosmic mind. For as we learned within the sphere of Moon, the Divine Creator had created us for freedom. And so, since the separated self could not, from within its separated consciousness, free itself from the consequences of its separation, the Divine Creator must provide the remedy.

> …Adam never sought to find
> The limit to his will. It knew no rein,
> Not even for his good.

…Within his limits, man could not
Ever give satisfaction, for so low
He could not humbly stoop — no matter what
Obedience he found it fit to show —
As he had thought, by disobedience,
To rise up, and this is the reason why
Man was debarred from any competence
To render satisfaction and go high
All by himself….

We sense how justice comes about when the soul capacity of /iː/ (m_e) pierces the dark unconscious pit of human motive and shines the light of truth into what had been concealed. Yet, even as it does so, equally its beam can penetrate the heart with mercy and compassion, disarm remorse with wit. Indeed Beatrice herself, when she admonished Dante earlier for his unfaithfulness, demonstrates how these two attributes of /iː/ can work together for the good. By piercing and exposing Dante's self-justifying weaknesses, with unrelenting honesty she brings his soul to justice. Yet, so as not to weigh him down with shame but lift him to the next stage of development, her mercy and forgiveness equally ray out and pierce his heart.

…Nor was there ever known —
Nor will be….a process so sublime
And glorious in either of those ways,
Justice and mercy:…

In the sphere of Mercury we learn this mystery is only to be plumbed by human beings because of our unique position in the ladder of creation. For:

… Each
And every soul of animal and flower
Starts as a set of elements that reach
A complex balance fit to be inspired
By shining movement from the holy lights.
But your soul's life is on the instant fired
By one abrupt breath from the height of heights:
The benefaction flows straight from its source
In Him: it wants to join Him with full force
For ever after, where He reigns above …

Could there be a more inspired description of Mercury's gesture in our soul and the vowel experience of /i:/ (m_e) or the lessons to be learned within this planetary sphere?

As we alternate between eurythmic and body-bound awareness of the gestures we can sense that *justice*, the noblest expression of this planetary sensibility, lies at the other end of the spectrum to its counterpart, the deadly sin conceived of by the mediaeval soul as *pride*. Pride is the glory that the separated ego attributes to itself and would assert at the expense of other selves, resulting in injustice in the world. Justice is the state achieved when the ego finds its glory in the glory of the whole.

And so, along with Dante, we are ready to transition to the Venus sphere.

## *Venus Sphere*

*Here he meets the souls of those who were initially deficient in the Christian virtue Love. This virtue will in turn christen and revitalise the pagan virtue temperance. Their journey in this sphere of consciousness finds expression in the range of soul experience embodied in the vowel /ɑ:/ (st_a_r).*

We learn that those whose consciousness is ready for the challenge in the Venus sphere are not souls who have never loved, or have denied and suppressed their love, but those whose generous, natural powers of sympathy once led them to intemperate extremes. We have seen already in the 'Inferno', the fate of those who still remain addicted to the torments of desire. Now we encounter those who have passed through 'Purgatorio', tempered their tendency to excess and are ready to transform love's less evolved expressions, particularly *eros*, into its Christian counterpart, the virtue of *agape*.[60]

Initially, the soul of a friend whom he had loved on earth identifies himself; someone who had died while still quite young, before he could fully manifest the noble gifts that promised an outstanding contribution to the world. Instead the politics of what took place were dominated by the self-serving machinations of his brother. Dante's friend could well feel justified to wallow in resentment but his state of bliss demonstrates that he has risen far beyond such pettiness and qualifies him to address Dante's question:

> … How we come to get sweet seed
> From bitter fruit …

For in the cycles of the generations there have been noble ancestors whose children were corrupt but who in turn gave birth to noble offspring. Both Dante's friend

*Figure 64 Eurythmy gesture for planetary being Venus*

*Figure 65 Vowel /ɑː/*

and his friend's brother had a father who was generally considered to be noble and yet the brother lived entirely for his own selfish ends. At its deepest level Dante's question of how good could come from evil infers its opposite: how evil can have come from good?[61] His friend invites him to consider that the human spirit is not the product of its biological inheritance. Rather it weaves the astral garment that it needs from the stuff of stars and planets, in order to create the precise opportunities and challenges that will enable it to exercise free will at each specific stage of its development:

> The human character does not just breed:
> God gives it to us, working through the stars.
> I'll show you how this is a truth you need
> Before your eyes: your attitude debars
> Real knowledge and your back hides what is meant:

In these last three lines how can I fail to recognise the full-bodied gesture for the planetary being Venus?

> *Slipping into it, my body of sensation realigns. I sense a shift from the outgoing thrust of Mercury into a depth of inwardness and infinite receptiveness to what lives in the vast behind and, inaccessible to earthly sight, pours itself into an offering. Selfless devotion arising from plenitude of being — no hint of martyrdom — attunes my ears to hear beyond the isolated intellect's futile making-meaning-of only what the 'corporeal eye'[62] can see in front, and listen to the poet's exploration of how evil could derive from good.*

Dante's friend explains the mystery of God's diversity and how the varieties of God's creation are designed to work together for the greater whole. The problem arises when one part blocks another from expressing its uniqueness. His friend continues:

> Always, should nature meet with fortune ill
> Adapted to it, then, like seed flung down
> Away from its own soil, it can't fulfil
> Its usual expectations of success,

And if the world below could only set
Its mind on fundamental naturalness,
What men were meant to give you, you would get.
… Now what was held concealed
Behind your back you see before you …

The last two lines describe the gesture for a second time. It is too precise to be coincidence.

*With eurythmic consciousness I offer to the world before my eyes what the hand behind me sensing, stirring, gathers from the infinite, eternally renewing source, give what I receive, receive what I would give. In such abundance no call for disobedience, no lack. I remember how it was before the first Adam felt the need for more than everything. How it could be again when in maturity I freely choose to be content in Paradise, with everything.*
*I let the gesture harden, feel my senses darken as I cut off from the flow of life and then forget it is myself who makes this choice. Behind me and in front, dead, empty hands, flap restlessly, flail in a vacuum, cast about for something, anything … a vague sense of deprivation, something indeterminate gone missing. My body of sensation prompts: then take it, what the world in front of you denies! Is this how strife begins?*
*I let the gesture soften, let the greater life flow through me, fill me once again with everything. I have no need of anything.*

*I feel the vowel calling.*
*When I step into its gesture with eurythmic consciousness /ɑ:/ (st<u>a</u>r) I am a chaliced star. Cut off from the fullness, I try to make up for the lack, make myself the source of everything, become a scapegoat for the pain of others, doormat, let them walk all over me, no limit to what I am prepared to take, to give. I pour myself — no boundaries to stem the martyr tide — into the world, till there is nothing left, my offered hand is empty. Then, in hostile resignation, self-righteous indignation at unacknowledged sacrifice, arms thrust up or out defiantly at heaven or the world in /ɑ:/. Intemperance in all its forms results from this perceived unjust privation.*

As we alternate between eurythmic and body-bound awareness of the gestures, we can sense how *temperance* or moderation is the noblest expression of this planetary sensibility. It lies at the other end of the spectrum to its counterpart, the deadly sin conceived of by the mediaeval soul as intemperance or *lust*. Withdraw eurythmic consciousness from the /ɑ:/ (st<u>ar</u>) gesture, and let ourselves be drawn by Lucifer, away from earth and into levity. Uncentred, we dissolve beyond our boundaries, intemperate, stream out with longing, lose ourselves in a romantic vision of the other or let its floodtide overwhelm our banks, flow in, engulf us utterly in the delusion that the other makes me whole.

So it had been for Dante as a young and gifted poet, and Charles, his friend, crowned recently and filled with the ideals of the life ahead of him. Both, with passionate and loving hearts, were vulnerable to the new disease, already sweeping European courts. They shared the new susceptibilities, wrote poems to romantic love with its torments of desire and its challenge not to seek consummation in the satisfaction of their lust, but in the transformation of the unrequited longing into a faculty for higher love. Other souls attracted to the Venus sphere who, like Dante and his friend, had once also been too generous, affectionate, intemperate in love, now share their experience. He is surprised to find that what the world both longs for but condemns as sin, elicits here in Paradise a different response. For the source of their intemperance was that their love's rightful course on earth had been obstructed. But here, united with the source again, they have learned not to condemn their loving natures but recognise that the love in Paradise they now enjoy bears no comparison to anything experienced on earth. Here the gift of their generous and loving natures finds a truer object for its worship: love far more intense than anything their earlier, intemperate relationships supplied. One such soul is Rahab who, in spite of being labelled as a whore, or perhaps because she was a whore, as depicted in the story from the Book of Joshua,[63] now:

> Attains here, as her just reward
> Far more intensity than she once knew, and now
> She is with us and of the highest grade
> Our order grants: all other ranks must bow
> To honour her, once last but now the first …

Like Mary Magdalene who because 'she has loved much will be forgiven much' Rahab made herself a perfect channel for the unimpeded, undiverted stream of Love. What was once intemperance resulting from an overflowing heart, has now been tempered, not by suppression and obedience to the narrow laws dictated by convention, but because she has recognised the object worthy of devotion; the divine love that goes beyond those prejudices that would judge it sinful. On the path to this, one may have made mistakes, been less than conscious about how and where that love should be directed. Once again the love of Beatrice for Dante, when she met him earlier in Eden and became his guide, reminds him of the love she first awoke in him. Due to our immaturity and inexperience with handling such a mighty force, it is not surprising that it has become confused with lust, romantic flights of fantasy and notions of honour or faithfulness to cultural conventions. The possibility of tempering that the planetary being of the Venus sphere bestows on human souls is the seed that will grow into the fruit that can be offered to the world in pure devotion: it asks nothing for itself because it is rooted in the all sustaining source of Love itself.

In *La Vita Nuova* Dante articulates the effect on him of his first glimpse of Beatrice. He has beheld the divine self in the other and it makes him powerless to function in his everyday existence. Disabled, in a state of illness and obsession, he lives only to behold that presence once again. Dante has identified the template of romantic love, intuiting that it is not a fantasy but a premature perception of something human beings are unprepared initially to deal with. It will take the next stage of our evolution for that seed to mature into the ripe fruit of agape; the love with which the divine self in a human being offers itself to serve the divine self's evolution in another. Once again inhabiting the gestures with eurythmic consciousness grants me a glimpse of that future sensibility. I experience an intimation that I could be centred in a Self that is as infinite as the periphery, able to give to and receive the other in full awareness that I AM that Self.

*I sense the magnitude and bounty of a being, spring of everlasting sustenance, consciousness encompassing both forward and behind. Or cut off from the source of Love, like Dante, initially I cannot sense the fullness of the unseen realm behind or make sense of the empty hand I see before me. Whatever form intemperance assumes, whether the lust be sexual or for wealth or power, my body of sensation, unable to receive, stirs with the impulse to take and grab to stuff into the emptiness insatiable or, out of guilt, to meanly thrust and poke into a beggar's hand a sordid pittance. This is the sphere where I must learn to trust there is enough.*

*When I explore the micro-gesture in my mouth I sense my jaw slowly lower and the tongue draw down and back to let the inner chamber open wide. All resistance falls away to let the everything pour through.*

As I inhabit with eurythmic consciousness the rhythm of the cycles being stirred behind me, feel their slower, longer turning through millennia, I sense the working of the Archai who through hereditary streams direct the march of generations, the rise and fall of civilisations. I hear the words of Dante's friend as he departs the Venus sphere and vanishes to higher realms:

'… But silence.
Let the years revolve …'

Then as Dante grieves the departure of the friend that he had loved on earth, he sees that:

… the soul had turned away
Already — lamp inside that holy light —
Towards the sun that fills it, to the Good
Sufficient to all things.

He recognises the futility of grieving for the loss of someone who is now united with the source of Love itself. This causes him instead to mourn for those who lust for earthly pleasures because they have not recognised that they belong to the 'good sufficient to all things'.

Ah! souls of night,
Creatures beguiled and void of reverence, would
You turn away your hearts from such a source
Of virtue, and seek vanity instead?

Seeing the soul of his friend absorbed into this higher realm of love makes Dante aware of the transformation Charles has undergone since they had known each other on the earth.

Dante's experience causes us to re-evaluate the un-nuanced misconception of the mediaeval soul as a miserable sinner bowed down with guilt and terrified of a god whose choice to punish or forgive seems as inconsistent as it is incomprehensible. Instead we encounter souls who astonish us with the possibility that the divinity within the human being can mature to the level that it can forgive itself:

But I forgive the cause of my warm ways —
This might seem strange to you and your warm crowd —
Because it led me up into this blaze
Of love perfected.

… Here, though,
We don't repent, but rather, unlike these,
We smile to thank the Force, which, in advance,

Both ordered and forsaw. For here we find
The object of our thoughts is in this dance
Of art, this beauty, this sublime result.
We see the good by which the world above
Wheels round the one below, and we exult.

Within the Venus sphere, Dante is reminded that the crisis that led him into exile and thrust him on his path towards self-knowledge was his initial inability to accept, with absolute devotion, the task to which his gifts had summoned him. Instead of concentrating on his mission as a poet he had spent many years in political intrigue and activism. In this Venus sphere, Dante's perception has refined enough that he begins to hear what sounds forth from the next planetary sphere, the Sun. It is a hymn to the great work of art of the divine creative powers whose harmonies also find expression in the cosmic dance in which each one fulfils their role according to the gifts bestowed on them. Could Dante heed its lessons he would recognise in them, the template of the just society, towards which all legitimate political endeavour should aspire: community of the future, city of brotherly and sisterly devotion, Philadelphia.

## *Sun sphere*

*Here he meets the souls of those who, through the exercise of all three Christian virtues, faith, hope and love, had christened and revitalised the pagan virtue prudence or wisdom. Their journey finds expression in the range of soul experience embodied in the diphthong /aʊ/ (end<u>ow</u>).*

This hymnic dance reveals increasing glories as Dante's consciousness, invited by the words of Beatrice, expands to meet the consciousness of those initiated in the sphere of the Exusiai, the planetary beings of the Sun:

… Lift up your eyes with mine
And aim at that point where the sun and moon
And planets cross the equatorial line
There in the stars. Thus you'll enjoy the boon
Of taking pleasure in your Master's art,
Whose eyes are fixed upon it endlessly,
So much He loves that movement in the heart
Of one wheel through another, while we see
The day turn one way, and the way the year
Turns in the other …[64]

*Figure 66 Eurythmy gesture for the planetary being Sun*

*Figure 67 Diphthong /aʊ/*

Measuring everything that starts and ends
With light, and stamping on the world the worth
Of Heaven, nature's greatest minister,
The sun, conjoined with where spring has its birth,
As I have noted, wheeled through dawns that were
Early each time, the spiral of its drift
Towards the summer and its lengthened stay …

Building on the revelations in the Venus sphere, at the beginning of his sojourn in the Sun sphere, Dante is shown two examples of the way in which the sun projects the totality of its creative power through twelve distinctive rays, whose gifts together make it possible to manifest the whole. First he is shown the circle of the wise: twelve brilliant human minds through whom the wisdom of the universe had been revealed. Then he is shown the circle of twelve whose genius had manifested, in their individual ways, in their hearts' capacity for love. Dante beholds how the two circles of love and knowledge move in harmony within the sun's embrace.

*As I step into this gesture with eurythmic consciousness, I sense I AM the beingness within the cosmic heart. I wield the planets in my arms and mediate their intersecting levels and degrees, ordering their rhythms and their cycles in my dance of love, fountaining through veins and arteries, above, below. Left wing swings down behind to gather up the planets, whose spheres, from earth's perspective, lie between the earth and sun. Right wing swings up before me to gather up the outer planets whose spheres, from earth's perspective, lie on the far side of the sun and reach to touch the sphere of other starry beings, whose intensities move faster than material perception into the apparent stillness of their resting constellations. Thinking's radiance and fiery will converge and mingle, mediated through my pulsing solar heart, tempering each other, then, sweeping round again the orbit of the past behind, the orbit of the future up ahead, converge once more within my heart in the all-embracing Present of their interchanging streams. Cut off from the consciousness of being, my gesture hardens and rapidly descends into a frenzy of chaotic, flailing arms. Is this how Phaeton felt when he lost control of his father-sun-god's horses as he drove Apollo's chariot across the sky, and plunging helplessly towards the earth, desperately attempted to regain his mastery?*

… See the branching out,
Obliquely, of the circle where appear
Planets that answer, as they move about,
The wishes of the world.

Once again I am astonished at how the intuitions coincide of those who school their consciousness to be an organ of perception for the cosmic mysteries. How accurately Dante has described the eurythmy gesture intuited by Steiner for the diphthong /aʊ/ (<u>ou</u>t). I step inside it and imbue it with eurythmic consciousness.

*I sweep and, at the same time, feel myself swept up, fling my solar substance and in turn am flung into orbit round the centre of my solar heart, arresting each planetary aspect, momentarily in stillness, fixed precisely in its planetary angle, each aspect of my Self able to exist in singularity, and yet retaining consciousness of the totality in which I live and move and have my being. Cut off from that consciousness the gesture hardens like a traffic signal that is stuck, inflexible, compelled to control and doggedly direct the world towards its fixed intentions, unable to respond to what wants livingly to find its way.*
*I explore the micro-gesture in my mouth that shapes the diphthong /aʊ/. As an anatomical event, isolated from etheric consciousness and cut off from my soul, my mouth strains — not large enough — to encompass back to front, to grasp the whole. I am reminded how snakes detach their jaw so that their mouth can open wide enough to swallow whole their prey. I am reminded of the sin of gluttony. However, if I let etheric consciousness imbue my speaking and sense before I speak I AM that whole, then my mouth moves easily from /ɑ:/ (st<u>ar</u>) to /u:/ (tr<u>ue</u>), gathering the whole of its experience along the way and penetrating it with consciousness.*

Having reached the level of maturity within the Venus sphere where a spirit recognises its ability to forgive its own past weaknesses, we have now progressed into the sphere of consciousness of those whose self-sustaining I AM presence enabled them to exercise wise judgement, whose genius consisted in the cultivation of the virtue *prudence*. First in the circle of the wise, Thomas Aquinas, considered the greatest thinker of his time, whose intellect was honed in the scholastic order of St Dominic, reveals himself to Dante and relates the story of St Francis, the saint who most exemplified the wisdom of the heart. Then the story of St Dominic is told to Dante by the Franciscan friar Bonaventure, one of the circle of 12 who shaped their hearts as vessels for the genius of love. Both he and Thomas in their own ways, strove to integrate within themselves the polar opposites of *faith* and reason by entering so fully into the predisposition that differed from their own that they could literally step into the other's shoes and represent it from its own perspective. In doing so they demonstrate the greatest attribute of wisdom which is the integration of the heart and head. Thus are their own capacities developed to the full, enabling them not to condemn what differs from themselves but appreciate its complementary contribution to the whole.

> … Two souls, one mind.
> I, the Dominican shall speak in praise
> Of Francis, since the way those two combined
> Means lauding either one will work both ways,
> Commending each for working to one end.

Bonaventure speaks about himself, acknowledging the value of the individual within the whole:

> The angels are a choir and I one tongue.

He draws attention to the abbot Joachim, who on earth he had regarded as his enemy but in whose company he now resides, as Eliot put it in the *Four Quartets*, 'reconciled among the stars'.

> In life I quarrelled bitterly with him
> … but here we're reconciled,
> In how the bright connecting circles dance
> Of love and knowledge.
> … Each sun of glory has
> A right to shine, in one great blaze, well met.

The Franciscan's words reveal the lemniscate embodied in the gesture of the Sun. Bonaventure and Aquinas each weaves his own lemniscate between the poles of head and heart just as the planetary being Sun weaves the orbits of these two uniquely gifted individuals, into the greater lemniscate of its creative purposes. And this at a time when, on the earthly plane, so many in the Church were seeking, in the name of heresy, to obliterate what they perceived as different from themselves.

In this realm dwell the souls whose every action is imbued with wisdom, each tiny deed an opportunity to offer their entire selves to God: those who:

> … give
> A new equivalent for those two coins
> The widow gave God, and like them they live,
> For everything's the widow's mite that joins
> All we possess to heaven.[65]

Dante concludes his sojourn in this realm by understanding that:

> … we should be strict towards
> All people when they judge at too great pace,
> Like those who count the corn crop in the field
> Before it's ripe. I've seen the briar show
> Harsh through the winter and too hard to yield
> When touched, and yet when spring comes it will grow
> The rose, and on the other hand, I've known
> A ship to cross the sea for all its course
> Straight as a die, swift as a hawk alone,
> And, at the harbour's entrance, with full force,
> Crack up and drown. Let not just anyone,
> And his wife, Mrs Anyone, assume,
> Therefore, that when they witness a deed done
> They can be certain of the doer's doom
> On the divine scale. One who robs may rise,
> And one who makes an offering may sink.
> Our judgement isn't made from just our eyes,
> And least of all will it be what we think
> When we have barely taken time to blink.

The eurythmy gestures stir a consciousness of blessing and acceptance by which we recognise God's revelation in each separate form that constitutes the whole. Is this perhaps a premonition of the consciousness of the Exusiai who, in the Sun sphere far beyond the limited assessments that we make on earth, work ceaselessly to embody the divine creative impulses poured from still higher spheres in infinite varieties of form, maintaining them so long as they are needed? Just as our mouth must encompass every placement on the diphthong's journey from soft palate to the lips so does the mighty solar heart encompass each single planetary ray within its cosmic round.

As we alternate between eurythmic and body-bound awareness of the gestures we can sense that *prudence* or wisdom, the noblest expression of this planetary sensibility, lies at the other end of the spectrum to its counterpart, the deadly sin conceived of by the mediaeval soul as *gluttony*.

Thus initiated in the wisdom of the Sun, Dante is ready to move into the planetary sphere of Mars.

## Mars Sphere

*Here Dante meets the souls of those who through the practice of all three Christian virtues, had christened and revitalised the pagan virtue fortitude or courage. Their journey finds expression in the range of soul experience embodied in the vowel /ɛ/ (m<u>e</u>n), the longer form of which, in English, becomes the diphthong /eɪ/ (w<u>a</u>ke, h<u>a</u>te).*

*Figure 68 Eurythmy gesture of planetary being Mars*

*Figure 69 Diphthong /eɪ/*

Here he deepens his understanding of the nature of the world of matter that must condense and solidify continually out of the divine creative thoughts, into the forms that must be maintained until their function is fulfilled. When all that can be has been learned within the opportunities those forms provide, those same forms, in turn, must be relinquished to make way for further cycles of development, in turn requiring ever newer forms. This cyclic progressive alternation between form and movement is accomplished by the close cooperation of the Exusiai, who are active in the Sun sphere, and the Spirits of Movement, whose centre of activity is in the sphere of Mars. It is the work of these Dynamis to ensure mobility throughout creation.

The eurythmy gestures and the micro-gestures in the mouth from which the vowel /ɛ/ (m<u>e</u>n) and the English diphthong /eɪ/ (n<u>a</u>me) are formed and into which the long version of the vowel transforms itself, enable us to sense something of the shift in consciousness that Dante undergoes as he moves from the Sun sphere into the sphere of Mars. There he is granted the opportunity to learn from one of his own ancestors how, at its most evolved level in the human soul, the Mars dynamic manifests as *fortitude* or *courage*, but cut off from the source of love degenerates into aggressive competition.

*Inhabiting the gesture of the planetary being Mars eurythmically, every cell etherically attuned, wakens sensations of a being poised to strike from Heaven, intervene and split completed forms and patterns in order to release their hardened forces into movement, make way for the new. Brave heart senses need for change, confronts resistant forms. Rear up, mount stallion-steep the skies, then plunge, hooves iron shod, strike down strong, and splinter-shock, shattering resistant rock. Warrior energy, knowing its own body is a transient form, is not afraid to make a stand, to die but not back down, to speak, call out the lie. The full-bodied gesture /ɛ/ (m<u>e</u>n) and /eɪ/ (d<u>a</u>te) there at the edge where swords cross and engage, generates respect, is utterly awake. No anger or aggression just objective recognition of the self becoming conscious of itself through meeting that resistance. Withdraw etheric consciousness, however, cut off from the all renewing life, the gesture hardens, makes a hostile barrier between the self and world, battle-clash of form on form.*

*In the mouth, the cosmic gesture permeates the tissues, mus-cles, causing edge of tongue to rise up, tense, poised at the edge of teeth, its blade of truth awake, ready to respond, to differentiate, to name, call out injustice, confront the wrong. Cut off from the source of life, factional tongues, their blades thrust upwards firm against the hard-edged teeth, cross swords, clashing fixed positions. Prejudice asserts its claim to power in the war of words.*

Dante meets the soul of Cacciaguida, a crusader ancestor of his who was martyred for his faith, when he was killed in the battle for the Holy Land. He instructs his great-great-grandson in the warrior's path: courage to fight and die for what is true and good, the just employment of the martial forces. He relates the history of Florence and how, step by step, through avarice, his beloved home descended from its paradisal origins into the factional warfare between Guelphs and Ghibellines that will lead to Dante's exile.[66] Dante is appraised of this, so that in the time he still has left in his present life on earth he can use his exile to transform his wish for vengeance and instead of trying to reclaim his power, become a warrior, not with the sword but with the word.

> … let your strong, fearless voice
> So full of joy and unafraid of hurt,
> Sound forth the will to which I have no choice
> Of answer, the desire I am ordained
> To meet with my response.

Cacciaguida's words provide a template for how Dante's voice will one day reach the souls of those whose level of development will render them responsive. But Dante is terrified by the huge responsibility of his vocation and makes the excuse to Beatrice that he is a merely mortal human being in the midst of the immortals like herself and Cacciaguida. His journey through the spheres has shown him he is not morally evolved enough to undertake this task because his soul is still so easily engulfed by the intensity of his antipathies and sympathies:

> Love and intelligence, after the First
> Equality appeared to you, were led
> Each to a poise where neither was dispersed
> By the other, since the sun that lit and warmed

You both with even heat and light was so
Unbiased no imbalance can be formed.
In mortals, will and faculty don't go
Together, for their wings have not the plumes
So equally arranged. I, as you know,
Am mortal. The discrepancy assumes
In me, the form of feeling …

Cacciaguida helps him understand the fate of those who only use the energies of Mars to further earthly goals.

Then you'll see nothing strange to dwell upon
At famous families giving up the ghost,
Since cities do the same. All your affairs
Will have their death in time, like you. But this
Fact is concealed in anything time spares
For any span, and our short lives might miss
Seeing the way it ends. Just as the shores
Are covered and uncovered by the moon
Without cease from her heaven, fortune pours
Its tides on Florence, which are just as soon
Withdrawn, a flux the living eye ignores,
But it occurs…
I could name famous names. But each name means
So little now, that once meant power and wealth.
… How could they come
To nothing? Come they did …
Who now were embers once were living flames.

Beatrice urges Dante not to use his gift for poetry to add mere ornamented information to the world but to use his sojourn in the sphere of Mars to develop the courage he will need to speak the truth.

Put forth the flame of your desire, so it
May bear the mark of what lies in your head
And heart, the inner stamp that shapes to fit
The stuff that forms the sign, not just to swell
Our knowledge with your words, but to secure

The process yielding you a truth to tell
About your thirst, so that the draft so pure
May be poured out for you.

Cacciaguida predicts his great-great-grandson's exile but reminds him of Romeo's example in the sphere of Mercury, who showed that, through devotion to his calling, exile can become a pilgrimage.

Though vengeance, to prove just
The truth that sends it, will come, you will leave
All that you love the best, which is the bolt
That exile's bow shoots first. You will achieve
Full proof the bread of others tastes of salt,
And how all stairs are steep when they belong
To other men, to climb or to descend,
And what will weigh you down, however strong
Your shoulders, is the evil without end
Of all the senseless company you keep
In that sad valley into which you fall:
Ungrateful, raving even in their sleep
With fury aimed at you. Quite soon they all
Shall have red brows, not you. Their foolish deeds
Will prove their brute stupidity.

The central feature of his learning in this sphere is that Dante finds the courage to stand alone, to step back from the factional intrigue of politics and pursue his moral, spiritual transformation. He must progress from tribal consciousness towards the highest stage of moral evolution,[67] recognising:

That you
Are by yourself a party, one that needs
No other membership: that fact will do
You honour …

In his reply I feel the Mars gesture resonate throughout my instrument.

… Father, I see well
How time, that wants my destiny fulfilled,
Digs in the spurs and heads for me pell-mell

To deal the blow which falls with greatest weight
On him who heeds least …
Down through the world of endless bitterness
And on the fair hill where they purge their wrongs,
Up from the peak from which the eyes I bless
Of my dear lady lifted me to find
Light after light throughout these halls of good,
That journey forms a lesson in my mind
Which, should I tell it, would be sheer wormwood
To many …

Cacciaguida confirms to Dante the greatness of the task to which he has been called but leaves him in no doubt as to the courage he will need.

… Conscience, I'll be bound,
Shamed by its own or someone else's ways,
Indeed will find your words harsh. Still you must
Put lies aside and make your vision plain,
And let those scratch that have an itchy crust,
Since if your voice, at first taste gives them pain,
Yet it will nourish when it's taken in.
For even as the wind, this cry of yours
Will strike the highest peaks, which is to win
No little honour. This has been the cause
That you've been shown, in these wheels here, and on
The mountain, and down in the woeful pit,
Only those souls that fame has fixed upon,
In order that the story you transmit
Will capture the attention of all those
Who recognise the names …

He learns the identity of other blessed warriors who gave their lives to serve the true and good and of whose presence he became aware when first he entered the planetary sphere of Mars:

… knights
Of Christian battle whose brave names still shine
For us today …
and who occupy the cross that is rooted in eternity:

The tree that lives top down, always in fruit,
Never to shed its leaves — is home to all
Those souls whose living fame was so acute
Before they came up here, poets grew rich
In praise for praising them.

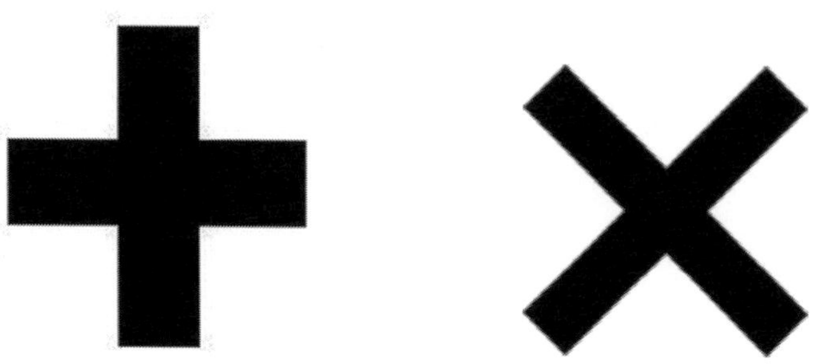

*Figure 70 Left, Greek cross; right, St Andrew's cross.*

Dante had described this cross of equal arms with great precision when he first ascended to the sphere of Mars. Known as the fixed cross or cross of the four cardinal directions, its form has always signified the laws of physical space and time, governing the world of matter. We meet its diagonal counterpart in the eurythmy gesture for the vowel /ɛ/ (m*e*n) and its long form in the English dipthong /eɪ/ (d*a*te). Contemplation of the different forms reveals the relationship of fixity and movement. The gesture of the vowel expresses that moment of perception in which the soul identifies its separation from the world. Without that detachment we could never give a name to our experience. Yet in the very act of naming it, we are in danger of fixing it and getting stuck in that description which then blocks our further insight or discovery. We can sense how the diagonal cross brings the fixed cross into movement. On the one hand, becoming conscious requires that we name our perceptions as precisely as we can, fix them as it were, long enough to build the memories that grant continuity to our experience. On the other hand, in order to mature and grow, our thinking must be mobile, able to discard old concepts and evolve new possibilities of meaning.

We can sense how both aspects of this seeming contradiction are embodied in the different crosses and as well in the eurythmy gestures: the arresting of movement as the two arms cross each other in the vowel and the gesture of the planetary being Mars who, poised to strike, then strikes with absolute precision. There is nothing arbitrary or chaotic in the movement that this being brings about within creation. For within the destruction of the old that it initiates is the movement that will lead into the future and the next name we give to what takes form: which even in the moment it is named is poised again to be un-named and brought again to movement. This flow from fixity to movement, back to fixity, then movement once again, is the living thinking to which we can aspire in contrast to the fixed thoughts that we constantly recycle and of which our everyday experience consists. Living thinking demands courage to live in the uniqueness of each moment and is accomplished in our souls by the Dynamis within the planetary sphere of Mars.

Through the Mars gesture we appreciate the words that sounded from that cross and which the poet heard when first his consciousness expanded to this sphere: *Arise* and *Vanquish*. Like Dante we can understand the challenge to transform the warlike energy of Mars from the destructive thrust and kill of battles in the outer world that serve only personal ambition, and become instead a warrior for truth. The gestures can awaken in our instrument a premonition of the consciousness of spirits who, to make the way for change, must bring creation into movement. The challenge issued to the poet in the sphere of Mars makes it clear how the Mars forces are connected to the power of speech. For words, when cut off from the cosmic source, destroy without regeneration. However, when imbued with life and love, if destroying what obstructs us from the past can be accomplished without hatred, those same words can quicken new beginnings in our souls.

As we alternate between eurythmic and body-bound awareness of the gestures we can sense that the noblest expression of this planetary sensibility, *fortitude* or *courage*, lies at the other end of the spectrum to its counterpart, the deadly sin conceived of by the mediaeval soul as *wrath*.

Dante has accepted his divine commission to communicate in words the initiation of the human soul and spirit through all the levels of existence. He has understood he must develop courage since the world that is invested in untruth may well not be receptive to his words. To transform the temptation to attack his detractors requires that he cultivate the virtue *justice*, the opportunity for which is given in the next planetary sphere. Justice will allow him to invoke his warrior energy and not become the enemy of those opposing him. It will lead him to a deeper comprehension of divinity itself which also has to face this challenge. If Dante does not understand how divine justice translates into justice on the earth how can he complete his poem worthily, dare to write about the ultimate realities when there is so much that remains a riddle? Beatrice discerns his urgent need to understand how divine love and justice can coexist with evil. Because his consciousness is ready to evolve she leads him to the planetary sphere of Jupiter where he can meet the beings whose experience can help him penetrate this mystery.

## *Jupiter sphere*

*Here he meets the souls of those who, through the practice of all three Christian virtues have christened and revitalised the pagan virtue justice. Their journey finds expression in the the range of soul experience embodied in the vowel /ɒ/ (l<u>o</u>t), /ɔ:/ (<u>awe</u>) and its other longer English form, the dipthong /oʊ/ (wh<u>o</u>le).*

*Figure 71 Eurythmy gesture for the planetary being Jupiter*

*Figure 72 Vowel /ɔ:/*

It will not be easy. He admits that he is still too susceptible to his emotions, too easily outraged at the corruption and injustice of those who hold responsibilities of state or in the Church, who should know better. Equally he can be overwhelmed with pity for those whose suffering appears unjust. How can it be just that the pope, a hypocrite who represents Christ falsely in the world, appears to flourish? Or that there are good human beings who, through no fault of their own, have never heard the name of Christ yet the Church teaches that because they are not baptised in the Christian faith they cannot be accepted into Heaven. Yet if these good souls should be condemned, the rational intellect, struggling to connect the dots within the paradigm it has constructed of material perceptions, is only able to conclude that a God could not be just or loving who governs such a world (if such a being indeed exists).

Eurythmy gestures for the planetary being Jupiter and the accompanying vowels /ɒ/ (cr_o_ss, wr_o_ng) /ɔ:/ (_a_ll) and its other longer English form, the dipthong /oʊ/ (wh_o_le), arouse in us a premonition of the sensibilities that Dante must develop in order to transform the intense antipathies and sympathies that still threaten the fulfilment of his task to be a warrior for truth. He must be able to embrace a level of reality that includes complexities beyond what the dogma of the Church is able to address. He must learn to recognise the love that transcends space and time in whatever name it calls itself and not to be deceived by sacred names, proclaimed by those who hold positions of authority without true inner substance:

… None ever rose
To this realm who did not revere the name
Of Christ, either before the doom He chose
Or after it. The tree the nails, the death:
These they believed. But some who cry Christ! Christ!
Will be less near to Him at their last breath
Than many others who do not know Christ.

*With eurythmic consciousness I move into the full-bodied gestures for the vowels /ɒ/ (cr_o_ss, wr_o_ng) and /ɔ:/ (_a_ll) and the English diphthong /oʊ/ (atone, wh_o_le). As my upper arms respond and the impulse spreads through lower arms and wrists and hands until at last the circle is complete, my heart expands to sense the source of light and love there, where I embrace infinity. The gesture of my arms is taken over by the gesture in my mouth as muscles in my tongue move down and back to form a holding space, muscles of the face and jaw lend their support to the embrace that is completed by the*

*gesture of the lips. For justice to be true it must be just for everyone. I sense how much will it takes if my embrace is to expand until it holds the space for all, so no one is excluded. At each new stage, I must embrace life's challenges, absorb, digest and get to know them. Thus do the Kyriotetes, spirits of wisdom, generate within my soul the capacity to transform judgement grounded in material perception into the spirit-conscious sensing that arises when I penetrate with love the resistance that confronts me. In doing so, as we imprint each other's memory, the world and I are changed forever.*

*Cut off from the cosmic source the circle of the gesture tightens, cordons itself off, embracing only those it finds acceptable within the kingdom of its narrow tribe.*

This is the world of factions Dante had encountered in the sphere of Mars. Its holding is a vacuous embrace that does not experience the other but puts a clamp on it, tries to control, hold on to it, fearfully clutching its object of possession. This is the gesture that produces unjust laws and societies that prop up the privileged, enabling them to hold on to and extend their grasp of power: rulers who manipulate and squeeze those that they hold, popes who exercise exclusion from the sacraments in order to control the ignorant and fearful. Exploring 'O' we understand what is required to deal justly with the world. By meeting some who were renowned for justice but whose presence in this sphere the poet questions, Dante must confront the ones he would have judged unjustly. He would exclude some that he must learn now to include—for no one he encounters in this sixth sphere of Paradise has been or is a perfect human being. He will have to grow to understand that:

> … our vision
> Is but one ray of the Mind
> That fills all things, and it is not for us
> To blink the fact that our sight's origin
> Lies far beyond the furthest we can see.
> And so the power of eyesight working in
> Your world may pierce the sheer infinity
> Of Everlasting Justice only as
> The eye into the sea, whose bottom shows

Near shore, but in the open deep it has
No bottom to be seen, though the mind knows
Depth has concealed the truth. All light must come
From clear unclouded sky. Else, darkness reigns,
The shadow of the flesh, which is the sum
Of all its sensual errors and dark stains.

The Jupiter gesture allows our body of sensation to explore this mystery.

*With etheric consciousness I sense whole worlds revolving patiently, accompany their orbits, tend their cycles as they pass in order underneath my steady gaze. I sense myself inside King David's consciousness holding his orb of royal power.[68] From my own heart of power's quiet centre, justice spreading out till everyone is gathered in my wise embrace. No need to impose control or snatch the crown. Slow revolutions mediate, from outside space and time, my fiery pulse, quieten the righteous rage, revenge-inflamed demands for injustice to be punished on an instant, virtue be rewarded. I sense the Love that chooses not to contradict its nature but, by that nature, rather to persuade the fragments in the asteroidal belt,[69] remnants of the war in heaven, not to further clash but, like the prodigal, return into its orbit.*

Dante learns that when injustice seems to triumph, it is allowed by a Divinity that does this to Itself. Goodness lets itself be vanquished so that in the long term, by its goodness, it will gather all of its creation to Itself.

For Heaven's Kingdom suffers, and will bless,
Violence of vivid love and hope on fire,
Which conquer the Divine Will not as man
May conquer man, but out of its desire
Thus to be conquered, and because its plan
Is conquest through its goodness.

Once again, Dante is reminded (and we through him) that the creative power of the universe is the Word and that until we are mature enough to understand that Word we cannot rightly judge. Our revolts at perceived injustices are immature reactions. They arise from impatience that renders us unwilling to surrender to the cycles of becoming that alone will ripen and prepare us to receive the love-permeated Word that is the fully conscious meaning of itself.

> … He that compassed all the bounds
> Of this world — and, in it, made some things bare
> To sight and others hid, so it astounds
> With its variety — could not impress
> His Power thus throughout the universe,
> Without his Word, in infinite excess,
> Remaining, and this truth we can rehearse
> By thinking of the fate of Lucifer,
> That first proud spirit, highest of the high,
> And how, before his ripeness could occur,
> He fell the day he could no longer fly,
> Because he had not waited for the light,
> The Word of God. From which it follows, all
> The lesser natures at a lower height
> Are too slight vessels for the flood we call
> The Good, which has no limits we can find
> And only by itself is measured.

The gestures for the vowels enable us to sense Love's greater purposes at work in the apparent contradictions: why should one be punished but not another? Why should the good suffer? They make us wrestle with the ambiguities until our understanding can embrace a greater whole. Functioning without this consciousness we are mere:

> … Clods of earth,
> Mud brains! Nothing can prove the Primal Will.
> Good is itself, draws from itself all worth:
> Whatever meets that mark can do no ill
> And must be just. And no good that is made
> Can draw it in because its blazing rays
> Create that good as well, and are displayed
> In all it makes, and all that meets our gaze.

Dante is shown that the answer to his questions can only be provided by the whole experience he undergoes as his consciousness expands beyond the world of time and space. In the *Inferno* he witnessed the pain of those who had succumbed to evil, some of whom, perhaps in the short terms of their lives on earth, had seemed victorious, but who inevitably found that they were trapped in their own self-generated torments. He saw that all of them, however, were free to leave *Inferno* and enter *Purgatorio* when they were ready. He learns that Paradise itself is full of those who have already made that choice. Virgil himself is somewhere on the way or he could not have guided Dante as he did. And here in this sphere of Jupiter Dante, though riddled with uncertainties and only too aware of his shortcomings, is shown a vision of eternal justice that does not condemn his mortal limitations but guides him to a place where perhaps, like those within the Venus sphere, he can offer mercy to himself. And through the slow revolving of the cosmic purposes all will be eventually embraced by the everlasting arms whose gesture demonstrates how love and justice can be one.

As we alternate between eurythmic and body-bound awareness of the gestures we can sense that the noblest expression of this planetary sensibility, *justice*, lies at the other end of the spectrum to the deadly sin conceived of by the mediaeval soul in its ahrimanic form of *greed* or *avarice* and its luciferic form of *prodigality*. Greed or avarice describes our gesture when, in order to enhance our diminished sense of self, we embrace and grasp more than we need but do so at the world's expense. On the other hand, when we extend largesse to others beyond what is wise or prudent either for themselves or us, in order to expand the diminished view they have of us and that we have of ourselves, we suffer from the 'sin' of prodigality.

There is one further ray to be explored within the spectrum of emotions and experience arising from the opportunities bestowed on human souls within the planetary sphere of Jupiter. If we recall Dante's learning in the sphere of Mercury, he was shown that true justice can only be established when laws are experienced and understood as just. Without this, what is called justice is only outer order that has to be enforced. Our exploration of the gestures reveal still further nuances within this spectrum of our soul's experience.

We could say that conscience is the consciousness within us of a moral compass against which we measure our behaviour. At one level it can simply represent the cultural norms we have internalised. However, at a deeper level conscience consists of the stirrings in our soul of what Shakespeare called 'the deity within [our] bosom'.[70] These stirrings alert us to potential or accomplished violations of the template love implants in us, against which we ourselves must ultimately measure all our actions. This awakening of conscience as the arbiter of justice in each soul marks a step in our moral evolution. It goes beyond reliance on enforced obedience to outer rules. Its power of influence depends on our ability to feel an emotion not yet identified within the range explored thus far. It is *shame*. Shame in its turn also opens out into another range of nuances. These stretch from an ahrimanic tendency towards self-retribution to the luciferic tendency towards denial or self-justified excuse.[71]

The Jupiter gesture, cut off from the source of life and love can awaken these sensations in our soul: spinning threads that spiral ever further from responsibility towards the earth into their luciferic picture of reality: or churning round and round in futile ahrimanic cycles of remorse. When we approach the full-bodied gesture for the vowel /ɒ/ (*cross, wrong*) and /ɔ:/ (*all*) and the English diphthong /oʊ/ (*atone, whole*) our body of sensation stirs with a whole spectrum of emotional response. Our soul expands with compassion to embrace those whom we may have harmed. Or, we embrace ourselves as we hide our whole body or our head in shame. Shakespeare invokes this vowel many times to express a character's remorse or shame. Each step on the path that King Lear takes towards becoming morally responsible is marked by the shame he feels for what were his unconscious deeds and finds expression in the vowel 'O'.[*] Or in the sleepwalking scene Lady Macbeth cries out her shame in three great anguished 'O's.

> … Who would have thought the old man to have had so much blood in him?…All the perfumes in Arabia will not sweeten this little hand. Oh, Oh, Oh!

Her agony is witnessed by the doctor whose initiation in the sphere of Jupiter is clearly demonstrated by the three 'O's of mercy with which his soul embraces hers and entrusts her to the justice of a higher court.

> 'God forgive us all.'

## *Saturn Sphere*

*Here he meets the souls of those who, through the practice of all three Christian virtues had christened and revitalised the pagan virtue temperance or prudence. Their journey finds expression in the range of soul experience embodied in the vowel /u:/ (truth).*

---

* See *The Actor of the Future 2, Word made Flesh*, pages 93-94.

*Figure 73 Eurythmy gesture for the planetary being Saturn*

*Figure 74 Vowel /u:/*

*As I step with eurythmic consciousness from the gesture of the planetary being Jupiter into
that of Saturn, my body of sensation realigns. Circling slows to larger orbits round the
central sun, my heart-rhythms settle into longer scales of time, allowing me to contemplate, digest, subject each step to scrutiny as I climb up and down the ladder of experience
from head towards the seat of will and back again. Sensations seeking for a name, light on
Dante's words as he becomes aware of new surroundings in the Saturn sphere:*

… No less
Than gold in sunlight flashed a ladder there,
Rising so far its top rungs fled my sight.
Descending it were splendours past compare
And so past counting I thought every light
In heaven had been poured out through the air:

*But why does Dante's heart, like mine, shrink back, draw in, contract in terror? Why
does Beatrice withhold her smile? Why so much solemnity so near the summit, and the
now in sight of, longed for glory? Why the need for warning?*

My beauty … is a fire
So brilliant that the strength your body bears
Would be, if mine were not restrained, a bough
Split by a thunderbolt …

Consciousness must be prepared if it is to cross this threshold and survive the
bliss of higher revelations. Beatrice's solemn warning is repeated when Dante
meets a soul initiated in this Saturn level of experience who helps him understand why he no longer hears the heavenly harmonies that had resounded in the
other spheres:

If you, a mortal, were touched by the sheer
Perfection of the music, then the sound
Would do to you what one look at a smile
From Beatrice would. Therefore I have come down
This sacred staircase for a little while
And just this far …

*Inhabiting the gesture /uː/ (tr<u>u</u>th) I sense as I contract, how Dante must have trembled
at this more intense awareness of himself, of how much excess must still be sheared*

*away, here in this final planetary sphere, what still must be refined before I reach the essence of pure essence of the self, the only of the all of me that will be 'sheer and clear'* enough to pass into that final starry sphere, where:*

> … love, set free, serves in this court
> For the fulfilment and the final stamp
> Of the Eternal Providence …

As he discerns, within himself, the magnitude of dross still unrefined, Dante asks this being, who has descended from still higher realms to speak with him, to identify himself. It takes courage because behind his question lurks a terrifying deeper one: is it possible to earn salvation or is the final goal predestined by an omnipotent, all-knowing deity, whose judgement will forever be incomprehensible to human understanding? The shining spirit tells him that since the highest order of the Seraphim, whose consciousness is centred in the region of the zodiac beyond the planets, do not know the answer to this question, then:

> … In the mortal world,
> When you return, make your recounting rich
> With this news, so men may no more be hurled
> Into futility by setting foot
> On such a path, to such an end. The mind
> Which shines here, smokes on earth, and therefore put
> Your thoughts to just how, down there, it may find
> The means by which it ever could achieve
> That which it can't up here.

Along with Dante we have reached a higher level of the struggle with the paradox of free will and necessity. The intimation is that there is something fundamental to the purpose of their evolution that is unique to human beings and which not only they cannot yet comprehend but even higher beings cannot grasp. Saturn is the realm of consciousness in which Dante (and ourselves) must practise patience or, in the language of the times, cultivate the virtue of *temperance*. Reason on its own cannot provide the answer to his question. Only the slow maturing of his consciousness through many aeons will prepare his understanding.

---

* From sonnet 'Carrion Comfort' by Gerard Manley Hopkins.

The soul who speaks to him reveals that in his former life on earth he was known as Peter Damien; a contemplative devoted solely to the cultivation of the spirit. He recounts how difficult it was when he was called to leave his life of contemplation, accept the post of cardinal and become involved in the Church's politics. His disgust at the corruption that he witnessed calls forth a cry of rage like thunder from all the spirits in that sphere.

> … Patience, can
> You stand all this?

Their cry shakes Dante to his core. Once again the /uː/ (*tr<u>u</u>th*) gesture generates sensations of terror at the threshold, pity too for what those souls will suffer in Inferno and, if they choose to make their way to Paradiso, must endure on their way through Purgatorio. It is a cry also to remind us that even in this lofty sphere we can be tempted to relapse into the sin of wrath. These are the flaming spirits who chose, through prayer and contemplation, to school their long and patient will not to react in rage but be:

> … fired by that heat
> That brings forth holy flowers and fruit …

to cultivate the attributes of One referred to as 'the ancient of days',[72] who dwells beyond the Fixed Stars and the Primum Mobile,[73] that mark the edge of time and space.

The next soul that he meets was on earth known as St Benedict, the founder of the first Christian order of contemplatives. When Dante asks him whether he can see him face to face, the saint replies:

> Brother, your high desire shall be fulfilled
> Above in the last sphere: for you and me,
> The endpoint of all wishes. All are stilled,
> Our long desires. They're perfect, ripe and whole.
> Up there, alone, each part is what it was
> Always, for that place turns around no pole:
> It's not in space. You see, then, by what cause
> Our ladder, going up to it, must climb
> Out of your sight … Jacob the patriarch
> Saw to the hidden top in the sublime
> And saw it packed with angels.

From his vantage point St Benedict has seen that few, if any on the earth, still value the contemplative discipline he formulated for his order:

> That high mark
> None lifts a foot to reach now, and my Rule
> Merely wastes paper …

Those still addicted to their earthly senses experience the contemplative path as one of deprivation. They cannot comprehend that earthly satisfactions hold no appeal to those who thirst and hunger for the spirit. We saw that Francis in the Sun sphere joyfully took poverty to be his bride and did not feel at all deprived because he placed no value on the riches of the earth. As we reach this highest planetary sphere the vowel gesture /u:/ (tr_u_th) enables us to sense that higher bliss is not a state of ecstasy involving loss of self. Rather it is a state of joy made more profound because it has been tempered. For the higher we ascend the ladder the more intensely must we penetrate those aspects of our destinies, our characters and the events that clothe us, that would tempt us to believe our joy depends on sensual satisfaction and thus prevent us from perceiving the miracles around us all the time. We can experience in /u:/ (tr_u_th) the sober joy that is the fruit of temperance. Such joy enables us to recognise that in this Saturn realm where 'such succour's everywhere', those rare events that seem like miracles on earth:

> … That were strange events
> Down there … [here are]
> … nothing marvellous. Common, in a sense.

Once again Beatrice addresses Dante, exhorting him to look below:

> … You're so near
> To final blessedness …
> That you must have your eyes both keen and clear,
> And so, before you go — and now you can —
> Yet further into it, look down and see
> How much already of the universe
> Is underneath your feet, put there by me,
> So that your heart be ready to disburse —
> When you meet the Host Triumphant, finally —
> Your full joy as it comes rejoicing through
> This rounded ether.

Dante's response cannot but invoke the Saturn gesture once again.

> With my sight I went
> Back down through all the seven spheres anew
> And saw the globe, the start of my ascent,
> And smiled at its pipsqueak significance.
> Whoever has his mind on other things
> Can be called just: it's scarcely worth a glance.
> I call his judgement best who never clings
> To its importance, rating it the least
> Of realms …
> All the spheres were there … without end
> The seven change position as they hold
> Their places. I could see this, and their size
> And speed, and all their distances between
> Each other. And this paltry world we prize,
> This little threshing floor where we have been
> Always so fierce, was made plain from its hills
> To river mouths, while I was wheeling there
> … They turned like mills,
> And I with them, the universe laid bare.

Dante's experience in the Saturn sphere confronts him with a question, central to the lives of most who find themselves, as Hamlet did, 'crawling between earth and heaven'. How to rightly value earth? On the one hand earth is important as the classroom in which our destiny enables us to learn through our relationships and the path of action that we take. On the other hand we need to discipline ourselves not to be enmeshed in the web of material perceptions that distract us from our task, which is to pierce through the illusion that they conjure, to the true nature of reality. This opportunity is what the meditative path provides. The age in which the poet lived generally regarded the outer and the inner paths as mutually exclusive and the latter as superior. Dante offers a more nuanced valuation. What he learns in the Saturn sphere invites us to consider whether it is — has to be — a choice of either/or? Is it not rather a necessity to find the right relationship between them as in breathing in and out? Of course there will be some, like Benedict, whose gifts lie more in one realm than the other. There will be others, like Peter Damien, who at some point will be asked to take responsibility for earthly tasks. Although it was a challenge, he learned to permeate his outer role with spiritual devotion. For the opportunities it offers for our learning Dante calls the earth 'the threshing floor' where the harvest of the long preparation to become a human being is delivered. Here in the Saturn sphere we behold the Love that subjects us on the earth to the final threshing that our 'chaff might fly' our 'grain lie sheer and clear'. [*]

Penetrated with eurythmic consciousness, the gestures for the planetary being Saturn and the vowel /u:/ (tr*uth*), generate within our instrument sensations of sustained purpose and profound solemnity. These sensations can be an intimation of what the Spirits of Will, the Thrones, experienced as they received from higher realms the divine blueprint for a new creation: the human being, whose evolution would entail unprecedented risk and levels of complexity. For Love in order to confirm Itself must know that it can still emerge triumphant and unchanged through any challenge to its nature. How out of Itself can it create what must oppose Itself and then be tempted to believe in its reality enough to be deceived by it, collude with it and even lose itself in the deception? Or will it find out how to take on the illusory existence that material reality provides, and demonstrate the path through the illusion even at its most intense? So now we understand why even higher beings cannot answer whether the salvation of the human race is predetermined. It is and it is not. It is the soul capacities bestowed on us by Saturn, as manifested in the vowel experience of /u:/ (tr*uth*) that will not allow us, as Eliot put it, to:

> … cease from exploration … [until]
> we arrive where we started
> and know the place for the first time. [†]

The gift of Saturn in our soul's /u:/ is the commitment and steadfast power to penetrate the veil of each material perception until we reach, in full waking consciousness, the Love that is our end and our beginning.

*All are predestined to be saved because Love cannot not be Love.*

*But to know ourselves, be conscious of ourselves as Love we must have the freedom to refuse to be that Love: in other words deny the essence of our being.*

*What prevents any part of Love from recognising that it is that Love is its refusal to perceive itSelf.*

*This possibility is, and must be always there, that it believes it could exist outside the everything that is itSelf.*

*But no one, not even Love itself, can know if any separated part will choose to make that journey home. That uncertainty must be the price of freedom.*

------

[*] Ibid.
[†] From T.S. Eliot, 'Little Gidding'.

*Love must learn to recognise itself within each human destiny that is lived out at each moment and which at the highest level it has chosen as the classroom for the next level of experiment.*

*That classroom has been woven from the karmic consequences of the choices made in former classrooms, so as to provide continuity for the evolving self and opportunities to grow in understanding and make amends for past mistakes.*

*But the separated self is frustrated when its wants and wishes, plans and goals, are blocked. Or, in the grip of tragic suffering, it feels it is a cruel destiny to have to wear what Eliot calls 'the intolerable shirt of flame that human power cannot remove'.*

*Thus human evolution necessitates the risk that some souls choose to stay in the inferno rather than see through their illusions and move on; that we might never choose to recognise WE ARE THAT LOVE.*

Through the gestures we can sense the immense responsibilities that weigh upon the Thrones in the Saturn sphere as they contemplate the first stage of pouring out the substance of their will: the fire from which the cosmic human being will begin the aeons-long descent into materiality and the cause and effect by which the consequences of each individual's life and actions will be woven into future lives and possibilities. The planetary gesture can awaken premonitions (or are they memories?) of the midnight hour in which each self looks down and with the help of Love and all the stars, begins to weave the substance out of which the next stage of its evolution will condense.[74]

The micro-gesture in our mouths through which we form the vowel /u:/ supports our sensing of this mystery. For our lips draw us inwardly towards the pinpoint focus of contraction that we need for any deed requiring such precision. Then, as we direct our breath through that tiny aperture, we hover on the threshold between vowel [/u:/ (tr_u_th)] and the choice to pour a stronger will into the breath and form a consonant [/w/ (_w_ound)]. As we hover, we sense our soul is on the threshold between the inner and the outer worlds. We can also choose to hover back and forth between the unvoiced breath of the aspirated /ʍ/ (_wh_en) and the movement of the breath through vocal chords which incarnates and _w_arms the voice . Exploring this spectrum between vowel and voiced and unvoiced consonant stirs perhaps a tiny intimation in our souls of the moment when the Thrones began to manifest creation of the outer world.[*] Perhaps they too hovered for a planetary instant, holding their breath with trepidation on that threshold, when the divine warmth of intention, embodied in the vowel /u:/ (tr_u_th), had been breathed in and before they would begin to breathe it out in the first makings of materiality, the element of fire embodied in the consonantal /w/.

---

[*]For a more detailed exploration of the transition from this vowel to the consonant see pages 71-73, *The Art of Speech.*

Cut off from the source of love, the gesture of the vowel does not enable us to sense that refinement to the essence of our essence. Instead we feel contracted, cut off, envious and mean, thinned into a meagre shred of self, devoid of being, fearful, melancholic and depressed. Still cut off, the Saturn gesture is solidified and stuck. Hands in desperation press and beat against the forehead and the belly, would batter through resistance, smash the unyielding, unenlightened flesh for a solution. Exploring the gesture in its unconnected form helps us sense the soul's perspective on the earth, who forgetful of the choice it made in Saturn's sphere, knows only that the 'intolerable shirt of flame' it wears and feels 'unable to remove', appears predestined by some malevolent or at the very least uncaring outside agency.

As we alternate between eurythmic and body-bound awareness of the gestures we can sense that the noblest expression of this planetary sensibility, *temperance* or *prudence*, lies at the other end of the spectrum to the deadly sin conceived of by the mediaeval soul as *envy*.

*Figure 75* Melencolia I, *Albrecht Dürer, 1514.*

Stirred up within my body of sensation, Dürer's *Melencolia* appears. Because she looks away the figure cannot see the light, most probably of Saturn, that shines above her in the heavens. This means that the planetary being works in her unconsciously, determining her melancholic temperament and tendency towards depression. The intellectual forces increasingly detached from beingness that will in later centuries give rise to the 'Enlightenment', of which this spectre in our psyche is an unintended consequence, present to us just such a jumbled world of unrelated objects as Dürer has portrayed although each holds a key that could restore the lost connectedness. And dominating all the objects is the ladder, unrelated and unoccupied, behind her. Its top and bottom steps pass from our sight, as they do in Dante's poem. But where the spheres to which his ladder leads, both up and down, are thronged with living beings, the steps here end in empty space. There is no movement through her heart to link her disconnected thoughts and will. Thus paralysed, although her eyes are open, they are focused on her pain and cannot see the opportunities for miracles around her.

## *Concluding thoughts*

As we come to the end of this stage of the soul's pilgrimage perhaps we can begin to sense how the gestures of the vowels enable us to feel how macrocosmic souls pour their astral substance into the creation of the human soul as it makes its journey on the earth.

We have seen that a vowel experience is not a simple state of consciousness but opens out into a spectrum of emotions that weave in turn within the greater range of all the vowels. Each vowel spectrum offers the evolving human soul the opportunity to not just passively receive what has been given from above but to actively engage with its dynamics, overcome its challenges and consciously transform the substance initially provided by its more evolved progenitors. We have felt, within the separated ego's body-bound experience, how this substance can degenerate into what the mediaeval soul identified as seven deadly sins. We have also felt how the I AM Self within the soul can consciously transform these degenerate emotions into their nobler counterparts and, in doing so, transform its astral body into Spirit Self, the next higher member of its constitution. [*]

It is beyond the scope of this present volume 3 to journey further than the planetary spheres. Nevertheless Dante has provided many clues to the gifts the starry beings have already woven into his experience and will explore these further as his consciousness expands to ever higher realms.

---

[*] For a more detailed introduction to the concept of the spirit self, see *The Actor of the Future 1, Tongues of Flame*, particularly Chapter 3 and pages 213-219 and 223.

Although we must wait for volume 4 to explore their work more thoroughly, music can provide us with some sense of the ever more expanding realms of bliss that lie beyond the Saturn sphere, and which Dante struggled to express in words. To name but a few: moments of unearthly ecstasy break through in the choral movement of Beethoven's *Ninth Symphony* only to disappear again and leave us longing to hear more; *Spem in Alium*,[75] the 40-part motet by Thomas Tallis, expands our souls in wave after wave of intensifying ecstasy that our bodies of sensation are barely able to sustain; the final movement of Mahler's *Symphony of a Thousand*, in which he set the last scene of Goethe's *Faust* to music, also takes us to that threshold where terror and yearning for what lies beyond each struggle for supremacy. We are challenged to stay present in such moments and not dissolve in beauty. Saturn's gift of solemn joy, bestowed through the vowel gesture /u:/ (tr*u*th) can teach us how to listen soberly, to stay conscious on that edge of bliss as it intensifies. Saturn's planetary gesture helps us gain the perspective which enables all great artists to move both up and down the levels of reality as they craft the earthly forms that can communicate their infinite experience.

Chapter 6

# The stages of life

## Infancy to old age

Throughout these books, we have explored some of the many ways in which the terms *archetypes* and *archetypal* are used to designate aspects of this methodology: Chekhov's use of *archetypes* in character creation*, the use of full-bodied movement to explore the *archetypal* qualities and gestures at work in our experience, the *archetypal* choices that determine our responses to the world along with the gestures that embody them, and finally, the *archetypal* gestures that embody the objectives of zodiacal and planetary beings.† As human beings travel on the path of life, our biographies are partly shaped by the potentials of yet another set of *archetypes*: the stages of infancy, childhood, adolescence, adulthood and growing old. Exploring these adds a further dimension to our understanding and portrayal of characters whose unique and individual biographies unfold within these archetypal stages.

Although casting actors in specific roles is usually based on the convenience of 'type', this should not limit the scope of what a training should encompass for actors whose artistic goal is to plumb the heights and breadths and depths of our humanity. We begin with observations that anyone can make.

## *Stages of life exploration 1*

1.  Discuss the leisure games that human beings play at different stages of their lives. Recall those you have played yourself or witnessed others playing. Improvise and recreate them, e.g. hopscotch, ball games, card games, What's the time Mr Wolf?, chess etc.
2.  Enjoy the qualities of character associated with each stage of life. Explore and identify them using such tools as *qualities-of-movement, tempo and dynamic, expanding and contracting, centres, qualities and sensations, PG, seven archetypal qualities of speech and gesture, vowel and consonant* etc.

## *Stages of life exploration 2—exploring tools*

1.  Observe people in the different stages of their lives. While recognising individual qualities that are unique, identify the qualities distinctive to each stage.

---

* *The Art of Acting.*

† *Actor of the Future 2—Word made Flesh.*

2. Improvise moving and speaking with these qualities.

3. Explore and identify which psycho-physical techniques allow you to consciously create those qualities: *qualities-of-movement, tempo and dynamic, expanding and contracting, centres and corresponding placements, PG, seven archetypal qualities of speech and gesture, also vowels and consonants* etc.

## Stages of life exploration 3—exploring texts

1. As you listen to this text that follows, let the images inspire your imagination. Explore each one in sound and movement (level 10–1) taking time before you move on to the next.

2. Condense your explorations to a sequence of vignettes that express through movement, consonants and vowels the qualities distinctive of each stage.

Our birth is but a sleep and a forgetting;
The soul that rises with us, our life's Star,
Hath had elsewhere its setting,
And cometh from afar:
Not in entire forgetfulness,
And not in utter nakedness,
But trailing clouds of glory do we come
From God who is our home:
Heaven lies about us in our infancy!
Shades of the prison-house begin to close
Upon the growing Boy,
But he beholds the light and whence it flows,
He sees it in his joy:
The Youth, who daily further from the east
Must travel, still is Nature's priest,
And by the vision splendid
Is on his way attended;
At length the Man perceives it die away,
And fade into the light of common day.

...

Hence in a season of calm weather
Though inland far we be,
Our souls have sight of that immortal sea
Which brought us hither,
Can in a moment travel thither

And see the Children sport upon the shore,
And hear the mighty waters rolling evermore.

…

What though the radiance which was once so bright
Be now forever taken from my sight,
Though nothing can bring back the hour
Of splendour in the grass, of glory in the flower;
We will grieve not, rather find
Strength in what remains behind;
In the primal sympathy
Which having been must always be;
In the soothing thoughts that spring
Out of human suffering;
In the faith that looks through death,
In years that bring the philosophic mind.

…

Thanks to the human heart by which we live,
Thanks to its tenderness, its joys and fears,
To me the meanest flower that blows can give
Thoughts that do often lie too deep for tears.

'Intimations of Immortality', Wordsworth

3.  Now do the same with Jaques' speech from Shakespeare's *As You Like It*. As you listen
    to the text, let the images inspire your imagination. Explore each one in sound and
    movement (level 10–1) taking time before you move on to the next.
4.  Condense your explorations to a sequence of vignettes, that express through move-
    ment, consonants and vowels the qualities distinctive of each stage. Have fun with
    the images.
5.  At a later stage, layer your work on this second text with the tools for comic style
    explored in Chapter 3.

All the world's a stage,
And all the men and women merely players;
They have their exits and their entrances,
And one man in his time plays many parts,
His acts being seven ages. At first, the infant,
Mewling and pewking in his nurse's arms.
Then the whining schoolboy, with his satchel

And shining morning face, creeping like snail
Unwillingly to school. And then the lover,
Sighing like furnace, with a woeful ballad
Made to his mistress' eyebrow. Then a soldier,
Full of strange oaths and bearded like the pard [leopard],
Jealous in honour, sudden and quick in quarrel,
Seeking the bubble reputation
Even in the cannon's mouth. And then the justice,
In fair round belly with good capon lined,
With eyes severe and beard of formal cut,
Full of wise saws and modern instances;
And so he plays his part. The sixth age shifts
Into the lean and slippered pantaloon,
With spectacles on nose and pouch on side;
His youthful hose, well saved, a world too wide
For his shrunk shank, and his big manly voice,
Turning again toward childish treble, pipes
And whistles in his sound. Last scene of all,
That ends this strange eventful history,
Is second childishness and mere oblivion,
Sans teeth, sans eyes, sans taste, sans everything.

## Stages of life exploration 4—the gates of birth and death

1. Imagine that at one end of your work space is the gate of birth. At the other is the gate of death. Between them lies the archetypal journey of a human life. Beginning at the gate of birth and ending at the gate of death, use the tools identified in *stages of life explorations 1–3* to embody the archetypal stages of that journey.
2. Weave between instinctive responses, and naturalistic and full-bodied sound and movement explorations.
3. Condense your full-bodied journey into a time frame of 2–3 minutes.
4. Divide the group in half and watch each other's work. Share your observations.

## Stages of life exploration 5—tools for the journey

1. Recreate the stages of the journey, this time focusing on qualities-of-movement: *moulding, floating, flying and radiating.*
2. Then focus on *expanding and contracting.*
3. Then focus on *tempo and dynamic.*
4. Focus on *qualities and sensations.*
5. Focus on *centres.*

6.  Focus on *objectives and PGs*.
7.  Focus on the *seven archetypal choices and their revelations in speech and gesture.* *
8.  Focus on *consonants* and *vowels*.
9.  Then consciously combine and interweave the tools.
10. Create a sequence using movement/sound and speech that consolidates which tools best express the distinctive character of each stage of the journey.

We know from our experience how a single choice attracts towards it other layers of sensation, allowing our instrument to resonate at ever richer and more complex levels. Inspired by great dramatic texts and poetry it is time to explore each archetypal stage more deeply.

## Stages of Life exploration 6—focus on each stage

*Before birth*

1.  While someone reads the following texts aloud explore the images full-bodily. Warm up with the speech and movement tools identified in *stages of life exploration 5* that most express each stage of life: tempo and dynamic, quality-of-movement, qualities and sensations, centres, objectives and psychological gesture, the seven archetypal tendencies of speech and gesture, predominant vowels and consonants.
2.  With the intimacy of your own breath, speak the texts yourself as you move full-bodily.

When I was a memory in the egg,
Of the woman I would become;
When I was a memory in the seed
Of the woman I will be;
My bodiless hollow moved
Freely through the light in a viscous
Sea. Richly surrounded was I

With the ringing of tongueless song,
And those vowels remembered Ear
As the cartilage closest to God.
And like ripe fields of spired wheat

---

* *The Actor of the Future 2: Word Made Flesh:* Chapter 2: 'Building the Bridge between Gesture, Voice and Speech'.

I attentioned upward
Towards form and heard the prismed
Glory in the Sun's white light …

> From 'When I was a memory in the egg',
> author unknown[76]

I am not yet born; O hear me! … provide me
With water to dandle me, grass to grow for me, trees to talk
to me, sky to sing to me, birds and a white light
In the back of my mind to guide me…

I am not yet born; O fill me
With strength against those who would freeze my
humanity, would dragoon me into a lethal automaton,
would make me a cog in a machine, a thing with
one face, a thing, and against all those
who would dissipate my entirety, would
blow me like thistledown hither and
thither or hither and thither
like water held in the
hands would spill me.

Let them not make me a stone and let them not spill me.
Otherwise kill me.

> 'Prayer before Birth', Louis MacNeice

## *Stages of life exploration 7*

1. Using the paintings to inspire your imagination, apply steps 1 and 2 of *stages of life exploration 6* to each of the following stages.
2. Sustaining your body of sensation, create the suggested characters or any others that occur to you.
3. Speak the texts as you explore them full-bodily and share your explorations with the group.
4. When you are ready, speak the texts, reducing the level of outer movement (10–1).
5. Share your observations.

# Infancy and childhood

*Figure 76 Thomas Cole,* The voyage of life: childhood

How like an angel came I down!

How bright are all things here!

When first among his works I did appear,

O how their glory did me crown.

The world resembled His eternity

In which my soul did walk,

And everything that I did see

Did with me talk.

The skies in their magnificence,

The lively, lovely air,

O how divine! How soft, how sweet, how fair ...

I felt a vigour in my sense

That was all spirit, I within did flow

With seas of life like wine.

I nothing in the world did know

Save 'twas divine.

Thomas Traherne,<br>seventeenth-century metaphysical poet

Now as I was young and easy under the apple boughs

About the lilting house and happy as the grass was green,

The night above the dingle starry,

Time let me hail and climb

Golden in the heydays of his eyes,

And honoured among wagons I was prince of the apple towns

And once below a time I lordly had the trees and leaves

Trail with daisies and barley

Down the rivers of the windfall light

...

All the sun long it was running, it was lovely, the hay

Fields high as the house, the tunes from the chimneys, it was air

And playing, lovely and watery

And fire green as grass ...

'Fern Hill', Dylan Thomas

Hubert de Burgh has been ordered to blind and kill the king's nephew Arthur. In the text that follows, the young boy begs for mercy.

*Arthur*: Must you with hot irons burn out both mine eyes?

… Have you the heart? When your head did but ache,

I knit my handerkerchief about your brows,—

The best I had …

Do and if you will.

If heaven be pleased that you must use me ill,

Why then you must. Will you put out mine eyes?

These eyes that never did nor never shall

So much as frown on you?

*King John*, Act 4, scene 1, Shakespeare

# Adolescence

*Figure 77 Thomas Cole,* The voyage of life: youth

*Romeo*: Her eyes in Heaven,

Would through the airy region stream so bright,

That birds would sing and think it were not night…

See how she leans her cheek upon her hand?

O that I were a glove upon that hand,

That I might touch that cheek …

She speaks:—

O speak again, bright angel! For thou art

As glorious to this night, being o'er my head,

As is the winged messenger of heaven

Unto the white upturned wondering eyes

Of mortals that fall back to gaze on him

When he bestrides the lazy pacing clouds

And sails upon the bosom of the air.

*Juliet*: O Romeo, Romeo! Wherefore art thou Romeo?

Deny thy father and refuse thy name;

Or if thou wilt not, be but sworn my love

And I'll no longer be a Capulet.

…

Thou knowest the mask of night is on my face,

Else would a maiden blush bepaint my cheek

For that which thou hast heard me speak tonight …

Goodnight! Goodnight! Parting is such sweet sorrow

That I shall say goodnight till it be morrow.

*Romeo and Juliet*, Shakespeare

*Alan*: Stay Equus. No one said Go! … That's it. He's good. Equus the Godslave, Faithful and True. Into my hands he commends himself—naked in his chinkle—chankle … Here we go. The king rides out on Equus, mightiest of horses. Only I can ride him. He lets me turn him this way and that. His neck comes out of my body. It lifts in the dark. Equus, my God-slave … Now the king commands you. Tonight, we ride against them all … The hosts of Hoover, the hosts of Philco. The hosts of Pifco. The House of Remington and all its tribe! The hosts of Jodphur. The Hosts of Bowler and Gymkhana. All those who show him off for their vanity. Tie rosettes on his head for their vanity. Come on Equus. Let's get them! Trot … Come on now—show them! Canter … And Equus the mighty rose against All! His enemies scatter, his enemies fall! Turn! Trample them, trample them. Trample them, Trample them, Turn!

*Equus*, Peter Schaffer

*Hughie*: I can't stand waste. Waste of lives, waste of men. That whole thing—Anzac—Gallipoli—was a waste. Certainly nothing to glorify. God! There's been another war since then! Dozens of wars everywhere, thousands of lousy little victories and defeats to forget. But they go on and on about this one year after year as though it really was something ... Don't laugh at me! This time last year I watched him getting worse and worse. I thought I won't go. I won't observe it any more. But I did. When it came to the point I did. Well that was the last time. This time I'm going to celebrate Anzac Day my way, with my feelings, my photos from my camera, on paper, in print. Even if it rubbishes absolutely and completely all I've been brought up on, that's what I'm going to do.

*The One Day of the Year*, Alan Seymour

*Irina*: I woke up this morning, I got up, I washed—and suddenly I felt everything in this world was clear to me—I felt I knew how life had to be lived. I can see it all. A human being has to labour, whoever he happens to be, he has to toil in the sweat of his face; that's the only way he can find the sense and purpose of his life, his happiness, his delight. How fine to be a worker who rises at first light and breaks stones on the road, or a shepherd, or a teacher, or an engine driver on the railway ... Lord! Never mind being human even—better to be an ox, better to be a simple horse, just so long as you work—anything rather than a young lady who rises at noon, then drinks her coffee in bed, then takes two hours to dress ... that's terrible! In hot weather sometimes you long to drink. That's how I have begun to long for work. And if I don't start getting up early and working then shut your heart against me!

*The Three Sisters*, Anton Chekhov

## Adult and midlife

*Figure 78 Thomas Cole*, The voyage of life: manhood

Midway life's journey I was made aware

That I had strayed into a dark forest,

And the right path appeared not anywhere.

Ah, tongue cannot describe how it oppressed,

This wood so harsh, dismal and wild, that fear

At thought of it strikes now into my breast.

So bitter it is, death is scarce bitterer.

Opening lines of Canto 1 from Dante's 'Inferno'.


For what wears out the life of mortal men?

'Tis that from change to change their being rolls;

'Tis that repeated shocks, again, again,

Exhaust the energy of strongest souls

And numb the elastic powers.

Till having used our nerves with bliss and teen,

And tired upon a thousand schemes our wit,

To the just pausing Genius we remit

Our worn-out life, and are — what we have been ...

Who fluctuate idly, without term or scope,

Who strive, nor know for what we strive,

And each half lives a hundred different lives; ...

Light half believers of our casual creeds,

Who never deeply felt, nor clearly willed,

Whose insight never has borne fruit in deeds,

Whose vague resolves never have been fulfilled;

For whom each year we see

Breeds new beginnings, disappointments new;

Who hesitate and falter life away,

And lose tomorrow the ground won today ...

We wish the long unhappy dream would end,

And waive all claim to bliss, and try to bear;

With close lipped patience for our only friend,

Sad patience, too near neighbour to despair …

'The Scholar Gypsy', Mathew Arnold

*Hamlet:* I have of late, but wherefore I know not, lost all my mirth, foregone all custom of exercises and indeed it goes so heavily with my disposition that this goodly frame the earth seems to me a sterile promontary. This most excellent canopy the air, look you, this brave o'er hanging firmament,this majestical roof, fretted with golden fire, why it appeareth no other thing to me than a foul and pestilent congregation of vapours. What a piece of work is a man! How noble in reason, how infinite in faculties, in form and moving how express and admirable, in action how like an angel, in apprehension, how like a god! And yet to me what is this quintessence of dust?

*Hamlet,* Act 2, scene 2, Shakespeare

*Olga:* I'm at school each day, then I give lessons for the rest of the afternoon, and I end up with a perpetual headache, I end up thinking the kind of thoughts I'd have if I were an old woman already. And in fact these last four years since I've been teaching I have felt as if day by day, drop by drop, my youth and strength were going out of me. And the only thing that gets stronger, is one single dream ... to go to Moscow. To sell up the house, to finish with everything here, and off to Moscow ... The band plays so bravely — you feel you want to live! Merciful God! Time will pass and we shall depart forever ... The band plays so bravely, so joyfully — another moment, you feel, and we shall know why we live and why we suffer ... If only we could know, if only we could know! ... If only we could know! If only we could know!

*The Three Sisters,* Anton Chekhov

*Andrey:* Oh where is it all gone? What has become of my past, when I was young, gay and clever, when my dreams and thoughts were exquisite, when my present and my past were lighted up by hope? Why, on the very threshold of life do we become dull, grey, uninteresting, lazy, indifferent, useless, unhappy? ... Our town has been going on for two hundred years, there are a hundred thousand people living in it, and there is not one who is not like the rest, not one saint in the past, or the present, not one man of learning, not one artist, not one man in the least remarkable who could inspire envy or a passionate desire to imitate him ... They only eat, drink and sleep, and not to be bored to stupefaction they vary their lives by nasty gossip, vodka, cards, litigation; and the wives deceive their husbands, and the husbands tell lies and pretend they see and hear nothing, and an overwhelmingly vulgar influence weighs upon the children, and the divine spark is quenched in them and they become the same sort of pitiful, dead creatures, all exactly alike, as their fathers and mothers.

*The Three Sisters,* Anton Chekhov

*Macbeth:* Tomorrow and tomorrow and tomorrow
Creeps in this petty pace from day to day
To the last syllable of recorded time;
And all our yesterdays have lighted fools

The way to dusty death. Out! Out brief candle!
Life's but a walking shadow, a poor player
That struts and frets his hour upon the stage
And then is heard no more. It is a tale
Told by an idiot, full of sound and fury,
Signifying nothing.

## *Old Age*

*Figure 79 Thomas Cole,* The voyage of life: old age

### *Stages of life exploration 8—approaching death*

Explore the following texts as suggested earlier but include these suggestions:

1. At one end of the space create a boundary that represents the *gate of death*. Warm up full-bodily with the tools identified in your adult/midlife explorations. From this starting point, move towards the 'gate' exploring each of these perspectives in turn.

   • You expect obliteration of your consciousness; when you reach the gate you will cease to exist.

   • You expect that when you reach it you will pass through it into a new and beautiful existence (Heaven).

   • You expect that when you reach it you will pass through it into a terrifying state (Hell).

   • You expect that when you reach it your soul and spirit will continue to evolve.

   • Not convinced of any one of these, but entertaining all of them as possibilities, you move between them.

2. Consolidate each journey in a PG that embodies that experience.

3. Explore which of these feels most aligned with the characters that follow and layer that PG with your other choices for that character.

4. Explore which tools allow you to explore some of the other differences in older characters, e.g.: even as some find their bodies more challenging, they experience their mind is loosening and 'floating off': *moulding* in relation to the body, *floating* in the inner world. While others who also struggle with the body's challenges maintain an inner fire and youthful vigour: *moulding* in relation to the body, *radiating/flying* in the inner world.

*Firs:* Locked. They've gone. They've forgotten about me. Well, never mind. I'll just sit here for a bit ... And I dare say he hasn't put his winter coat on, he's gone off in his Autumn coat. (*sighs anxiously*) I never looked to see. When will these young people learn? (*mutters something*) My life's gone by and it's just as if I never lived at all. (*lies down*) I'll lie down for a bit, then ... No strength have you? Nothing left. Nothing ... Oh you ... silly billy ... (*lies motionless*).

*The Cherry Orchard*, Anton Chekhov


*Maria Josefa:* I know it's a lamb. But can't a lamb be a baby? It's better to have a lamb than not to have anything ... Everything's very dark. Just because I have white hair you think I can't have babies, but I can ... babies and babies and babies. This baby will have white hair, and I'll have this baby and another and this one other; and with all of us with snow white hair we'll be like the waves—one then another and another. Then we'll all sit down and all of us will have white heads, and we'll be seafoam. Nothing but mourning shrouds here ...

When my neighbour had a baby I'd carry her some chocolate and later she'd bring me some and so on ... always and always and always.

*The House of Bernarda Alba*, Lorca


*Wacka:* Nothin' to tell. It was just — Oh, I d'know ... Nobody seen the whole thing that day. All you seen was what y'was doin' y'self. And then y'couldn't hardly see more than a few feet ahead of yer ... It was the terrain. Y'never seen such hills in y'er life. They musta thought we was bloody mountain goats to send us up'm ... When we landed on the beach it was still dark. The current'd carried us down a bit far, everything was disorganised. Well — we had to get up them 'ills just the same. Y'didn't know where the old Turk was or how many of'm was up top, but y'knew they was sitting up there like Jackie waitin' to pick y'all off as y'climbed ... It was the feelin' of not gettin' anywhere that was the worst ... All round yer ... Noise, crikey ... Y'd never know who'd come over the next rise at yer, burst of gunfire or bloody Turk. Then when the sun came up y'could see y'r mates ... bodies ... corpses every-where ... blood and everything ... Sometimes y'd be runnin' and y'd hear a noise and it'd be yourself sorta screamin'. Y'd have y'r bayonet out and when they came at y' ... Y'couldn't stop and help y'r mates, that was the worst ... y'had to keep pushin' on ... We got together again, some'ow. Some of us. Soon we was all dug in, up and down them hills. We stayed there in the stinkin' heat with the stinkin' flies 'n the bully beef 'n' dysntery and sometimes the Turk trenches not ten yards away — we stayed there nine months. Then we pulled out, whole bang lot of us. When we went in there we was nobody. When we come out we was famous. Anzacs. Ballyhoo. Photos in the papers. Famous. Not worth a crumpet. Sorry ... Didn't mean t'bash y'r ear ...

*The One Day of the Year*, Alan Seymour


*William Ricketts (speaking at the age of ninety-four)*: I belong to no one. I belong nowhere, but I belong ... My spirit has been given a task and nothing in the world will prevent me from completing my work.[77]

*Forest of Love*, a documentary


*The Countess Rosmarin (of uncertain older age)*:
And when the last Thursday comes,
Which may be this one, I should like to be present.
So many years of meeting deserve to end
In a rare parting. It's quite true, the world
Being uncertain, I may spoil it all
By being here again next Thursday. But I'd rather
Go out, after the style of a night-light,

In a series of apologetic returns,

Than leave without ceremony, which would be surely

Ungracious to an earth which has entertained me.

…

There was more to come, so I imagine,

But then [my days] were interrupted.

I wish I could go on singing.

I am very much in love with something;

What it may be I can't remember;

It will come to me.

That was a roundabout drive in the snow,

Owing to my eccentric sense of direction.

The Dark is Light Enough, Christopher Fry.

Shakespeare's *King Lear* offers a detailed exploration of an old man in his eighties. Here are just a few examples of the many different moods and qualities he demonstrates.

*Still trying to control:*

Nothing will come of nothing, speak again.

*Enraged at loss of control:*

Let it be so! Thy truth then be thy dower! ….

Come not between the dragon and his wrath …

Darkness and Devils! Saddle my horses! Degenerate bastard, I'll not trouble thee. Yet have I left a daughter.

*Self-pitying:*

You see me here you gods a poor old man, as full of grief as age.

*Remorseful:*

I did her wrong.

*Mad:*

Ha! Goneril with a white beard! They flattered me like a dog, and told me I had the white hairs in my beard ere the black ones were there. To say 'ay' and 'no' to everything that I said. 'Aye' and 'no' too was no good divinity. When the rain came to wet me once and the wind to make me chatter; when the thunder would not peace at my bidding; there I found 'em, there I smelt 'em out.

*Wise:*

> … Come let's away to prison:
> We two alone will sing like birds in the cage.
> When thou dost ask me blessing, I'll kneel down
> And ask of thee forgiveness: …

*Fragile:*

> Where have I been, where am I? … I will not swear these are my hands.

## Stages of life exploration 9—all the stages

The following process provides the opportunity for five actors to rotate through a set of characters, warming up each archetype between, until each one has played each character. Based on the nativity described in the Gospel of St Luke, three shepherds follow the angel's tidings, and come to worship at the birth of Jesus in the stable. Many mediaeval plays of the Nativity portrayed the shepherds as representing youth or late childhood, middle and old age. In addition the Mary of this Gospel was traditionally viewed as very young. On this basis then, we can arrange the characters according to these archetypes and without regard to gender:

- The newborn infant (non-speaking).
- The teenage mother.
- The child shepherd.
- The middle-aged shepherd.
- The old shepherd.

1. All actors prepare all characters. Choose simple other *archetypes* (e.g. mother, shepherd etc.) to layer with the archetype of age (e.g. infant, adolescent etc.).
2. Improvise events that lead up to to the meeting in the stable; for example, the shepherds watch their flocks and are woken by the singing of the angels etc. Allow time for this extensive preparation.
3. Learn the lines of this verse from the poem 'The Shepherds Hymn' by Richard Crashaw. Explore how each character would move and, except for the infant, speak.

> Welcome! All wonders in one sight!
> Eternity shut in a span!
> Summer in winter, day in night,
> Heaven in earth and God in Man;
> Great little one! whose all embracing birth
> Lifts earth to heaven, stoops heaven to earth.

4. Cast the first configuration of characters and actors. Prepare your character by warming up around the central space.

5. When everyone is ready to connect (mother seated on a stool, baby settled at her feet) the shepherds enter and approach, kneel and sense when to give their gifts, exchange lines with the child and mother as well as with each other, then depart. Speak on impulse, weaving lines or phrases in whatever order, or repeating them, to make a whole.

6. Release your character and move on to the next. Prepare and meet etc. until each actor has played all the roles.

7. Share your observations.

8. Apply this archetypal preparation to any of the mediaeval shepherds' plays. In the English tradition choose a passage from *The Second Shepherds' Play* from the Wakefield Cycle or the *Shepherds' and Kings' Play* from the Coventry Cycle.

9. Adapt the whole exploration to the visit of the kings by changing the archetype of *shepherd* to the archetype of *king*. Explore this archetype and integrate it with the archetypal stages.

# Our High Work Masters : the stages of life and the planetary beings

Lord, what fools these mortals be!

So Puck exclaimed in Shakespeare's *A Midsummer Night's Dream*, witnessing the comedy of human characters convinced only of their body-bound perceptions and blind to the other beings who participate in their reality. Actors will increasingly confront this threshold — choosing either to work within the paradigm of consciousness that dominates our present mainstream culture or to cultivate the faculties that will allow us to perceive and then express the greater mysteries at work within our lives.

Those who make the second choice are fortunate that through the evolving Steiner/Chekhov methodology, we are delivered from fantasy and speculation. Instead we are provided with the opportunity to further cultivate our budding organ of supersensible perception by exploring Steiner's observations that the seven-year cycles that unfold in our biographies are also an expression of the planetary beings. As described in Chapter 2, in the exploration of the *Foundation Stone Meditation*, and again in Chapter 5, these planetary beings he equated with the spiritual hierarchies as they were known in Christian esotericism.[*] As always, Steiner shares his observations from different perspectives according to the context. His initial research has been taken up by many who have each developed it in different ways.[78]

The following meditative explorations are based on the chart provided in the book by George and Gisela O'Neil and Florin Lowndes whose work to understand the stages of a human life has been inspired by Steiner's insights.[79] From birth to age 63, we explore the potential bestowed on us by each of the planetary beings starting from the Moon sphere which is closest to the earth and expanding out to include the Saturn sphere. Then, since conditions in our present time allow increasing numbers of the human race to live into their seventies and eighties and beyond, we will explore the potential for still further growth and evolution that is bestowed on us.

> Thus the grand life-movement begun with the moment of birth is, after 63, returning upon itself in a majestic spiral form, marking a new birth on a higher level with the beginning of the 64th year... If, indeed, one is able to become inwardly renewed, reborn after a 63 year pregnancy, then it appears as if the course of his later years recapitulates at a higher level (on the movement of the spiral [shown] above) the early years on the left side of the Life-Chart. If so, then although he is free of the influence of the planetary spheres he has, so to speak, already passed through, he nevertheless may avail himself of their beneficial forces when he passes over them again, this time over two spheres at once.
>
> *The Human Life*, George and Gisela O'Neill and Florin Lowndes.

---

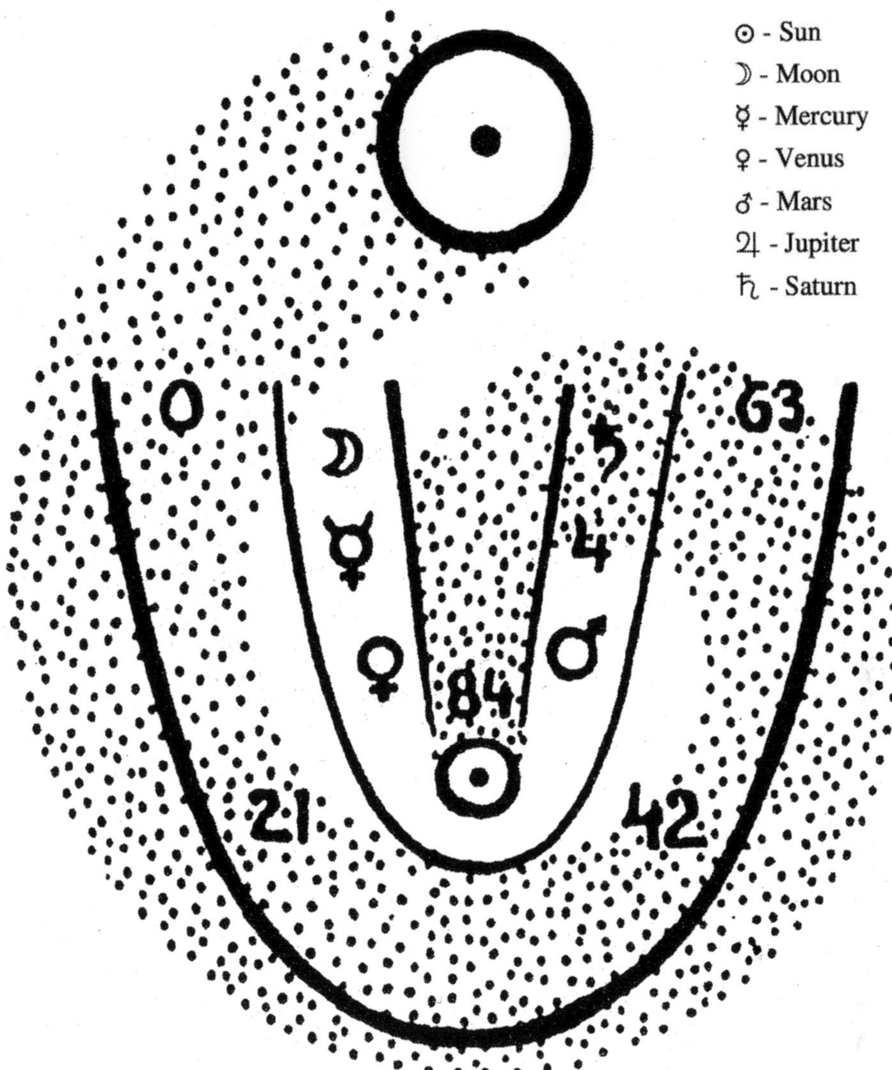



*Figure 80 Cycles of the human life*

Prepared by *Stages of life explorations 1–8,* we stand with instrument attuned. Once again, we slip inside the planetary gestures with their accompanying vowels. As our body of sensation resonates, we feel them reconfiguring our inwardness, stirring intimations of the purposes, challenges and gifts the macrocosmic bearers of the soul bestow on human beings, through each seven-year cycle of our lives. The meditative passages that follow are my stream of consciousness attempts to render from their own perspective my discernings of those beings' purposes for human souls.

## *0–7 Planetary being Moon—Sphere of the Angels—/aɪ/(life)*

*Into your still undefined, hardly-here-yet misty milkiness, I wind your threads of destiny, Beloved, entwine and bind them into your silken soft not yet too solid flesh. /aɪ/ And though you cry to find the gate of birth so firmly shut behind you — too late to change your mind — I am here to help you find your way. Come! Incline along this path! Through your perceptions recognise your guide /aɪ/.*

*Figure 81 top right: Planetary being Moon, bottom left: Diphthong /aɪ/*

## *7–14 Planetary being Mercury—Sphere of Archangels—/i:/(m<u>e</u>)*

*I fl<u>i</u>ng my lightn<u>i</u>ng <u>i</u>nto, f<u>i</u>ll each arter<u>y</u> w<u>i</u>th brighter sap. Life surg<u>i</u>ng through your st<u>i</u>ll soft pudge, Beloved, no cell of you <u>i</u>s fr<u>ee</u> from my intens<u>i</u>ty. Tighten<u>i</u>ng the perfect tension of your selfhood str<u>i</u>ng I draw you <u>i</u>nto verti-cal<u>i</u>ty. P<u>i</u>tch perfect, I rel<u>ea</u>se your spr<u>i</u>ngtime energ<u>y</u> of m<u>e</u>, prepar<u>i</u>ng you to channel your immens<u>i</u>ty /i:/.*

*Figure 82 top right: Planetary being Mercury, Vowel /i:/*

## *14–21 Planetary being Venus—Sphere of the Archai—/ɑ:/ (st<u>a</u>r)*

*All your k<u>a</u>rma has prepared, I stir from f<u>a</u>r in deepest everywhere, to st<u>a</u>rt you on your p<u>a</u>th. Have you begun to w<u>o</u>nder who you <u>a</u>re? Open your <u>a</u>rms, Beloved! I c<u>a</u>rve a p<u>a</u>thway to your h<u>ea</u>rt! Receive abundance from my proffered p<u>a</u>lm /ɑ:/.*

*Figure 83 top right: Planetary being Venus, bottom left: Vowel /ɑ:/*

### 21–42 Planetary being Sun—Sphere of the Exusiai/ Spirits of Form /aʊ/(out)

*Preparation n<u>o</u>w complete, <u>out</u> of this gr<u>ou</u>nd you fl<u>o</u>wer. I call you into singularity of being from the all ar<u>ou</u>nd, Beloved, your distinctive tone all<u>o</u>w to s<u>ou</u>nd, res<u>ou</u>nd. Setting out n<u>o</u>w on your own to test your p<u>o</u>wer, at the world's edges h<u>o</u>w your waves reb<u>ou</u>nd and resonate, and then again, reb<u>ou</u>nd /aʊ/.*

*Figure 84 top right: Planetary being Sun, bottom left: Diphthong /aʊ/*

## 42–49 Planetary being Mars—Sphere of the Dynamis/Spirits of Movement—/ɛ/(m_e_n) /eɪ/(d_a_te)

*Ag_ai_n, ag_ai_n, Beloved, with precision driven _e_dge of bl_a_de, I seek your cleavage pl_a_ne, watch your brightness f_a_de, your f_e_lt for the first time weariness, forge_tt_ing why you c_a_me: the hugeness of your span Odysseus, you g_a_ve-it-all-you-had, w_a_sted, washed up on the rocks, a nobody exhausted on the sand. Hard to n_a_me as love what had to crack you open in this w_a_y, watch you try ag_ai_n, ag_ai_n, appear to show no pity for your p_ai_n, that your br_a_ve heart might w_a_ken sober in the light of d_a_y /ɛ/ /eɪ/.*

*Figure 85 top right: Planetary being Mars, bottom left: Dipthong /eɪ/*

## *49–56 Planetary being Jupiter—Sphere of the Kyriotetes/ Spirits of Wisdom /ɔː/(awe)*

*Beh__old__ s__o__ many br__o__ken bits of you, Beloved! I sh__ow__ you how to gather, s__or__t and dr__aw__ the nothing-l__o__st-for-ever-__a__ll into your __o__rbit, to rev__o__lve around your s__o__lar s__ou__rce once m__o__re /ɔː/.*

*Figure 86 top right: Planetary being Jupiter, bottom left: Vowel /ɔː/*

## *56–63 Planetary being Saturn—Sphere of the Thrones/Spirits of Will /u:/(tr<u>u</u>th)*

*Sift them thr<u>ough</u>, Beloved, no hurry <u>to</u>, however many cycles it c<u>ou</u>ld take to r<u>u</u>minate. Nothing t<u>oo</u> insignificant, t<u>oo</u> f<u>oo</u>lish, wasted, trivial or lost but must be penetrated thr<u>ough</u>, until, each precious drop of tr<u>u</u>th distilled, your cup is f<u>u</u>ll! /u:/*

*Figure 87 top right: Planetary being Saturn, bottom left: Vowel /u:/*

## *63–70 recapitulating Saturn/u:/(thr<u>ough</u>) and Moon/aɪ/(l<u>i</u>fe)*

*Do you ch<u>oo</u>se to die so s<u>oo</u>n, Beloved, or to d<u>o</u> death consciously, take time to sift the tr<u>u</u>th and work it thr<u>ough</u>? C<u>ou</u>ldn't hurry even if y<u>ou</u> wanted t<u>o</u>. Body, thr<u>ough</u> its own resistance, p<u>u</u>lls y<u>ou</u> slowly thr<u>ough</u> the birth canal towards the light, gate behind y<u>ou</u> this time, closing gently t<u>o</u> /u:/.*

*Den<u>i</u>al of the ebbing t<u>i</u>de, resist-ing its resistance makes it hard to d<u>ie</u>. Terr<u>i</u>f<u>ie</u>d, incl<u>i</u>ning this way, that — can't recogn<u>i</u>se yourself in failing body, m<u>i</u>nd — have one f<u>i</u>nal, fut<u>i</u>le tr<u>y</u> at l<u>i</u>fe.*

*No going back now to a t<u>i</u>me def<u>i</u>ned b<u>y</u> deeds, accomplish-ments or strife. Let the midw<u>i</u>fe g<u>ui</u>de you back, Beloved, to the other s<u>i</u>de. What was bound, unb<u>i</u>nd. All the threads you wove, unw<u>i</u>nd. What was unk<u>i</u>nd, tr<u>y</u> again to put it r<u>i</u>ght. For one last t<u>i</u>me al<u>i</u>gn yourself before you d<u>ie</u> /aɪ/.*

### *70–77 recapitulating Jupiter /ɔ:/ (<u>awe</u>) /oʊ/ (<u>o</u>nly) and Mercury/ɪ/ (<u>i</u>n) /i:/(m<u>e</u>) /oʊ/*

<u>O</u>nly when you kn<u>o</u>w the glory, h<u>o</u>lding
<u>a</u>ll that fruited from the seeds you s<u>o</u>wed,
Beloved, <u>a</u>ll the fruits that you have
gr<u>o</u>wn, <u>o</u>nly then inv<u>o</u>ke the blessing of
the harvest /ɔ:/

    '… ripeness is <u>a</u>ll'.[80]

<u>See</u> y<u>o</u>urself, Beloved, w<u>i</u>s-
dom tempered going h<u>o</u>me.
Your golden b<u>ea</u>m, rel<u>ea</u>s-
ing as it gr<u>ee</u>ts, is gr<u>ee</u>ted by
the world beyond. S<u>i</u>gnall<u>i</u>ng
a new beginn<u>i</u>ng /ɪ/, /i:/ (s<u>ee</u>).

## *77–84 recapitulating Mars /ɛ/(m_e_n) /eɪ/(d_a_te) and Venus/ʌ/ (w_o_nder)/ɑ:/ (st_a_r)*

*D_ea_th! The thud of /d/ procl_ai_ms the body's _e_nd. The breath exhaled in /th/, the soul's release and spirits passage home ag_ai_n. In between the vowel that s_e_vers, cuts the thr_ea_d /ɛ/ (d_ea_th): splitting any atoms that rem_ai_n, that would pers_ua_de your spirit to resist my bl_a_de.*

*… 'do not go g_e_ntly, r_a_ge, r_a_ge ag_ai_nst the dying of the light'.[81] Bl_a_me the world, bl_a_me _e_verything, OR _e_lse, Beloved, ch_a_nge that anger to the _fl_ame that battles with d_e_ception, in the 'm_e_ntal fight'.*

*Open your _a_rms. Receive what death was always holding in her p_a_lm. S_e_nse how all along she was your fri_e_nd. Unb_a_r your body's l_a_st resistance and surrender to the truth of who you _a_re. Tread c_a_lmly. Death is j_u_st the way we take to reach a st_a_r /ɑ:/.[82]*

Observe in these three pairs of recapitulating cycles how the vowels belonging to each planetary being converse, absorbing something of each other's character.

When the text does not reveal the precise age of a character, these archetypes may help us to intuit one. Often, however, the dramatist informs us or provides a clue. We are told for instance that Juliet's *not yet 14*, Alan Strang in *Equus* is 16, Prior in *Angels in America* is 30, Kent in *King Lear* 48, King Lear ' fourscore and upward', Gayev in *The Cherry Orchard,* 51. From clues the gravedigger provides we determine Hamlet must be 30. Without indications as precise as these, based on all the evidence, we make an estimate. The young Arthur from *King John* and other child-to-youthful characters in Shakespeare's plays display the qualities that Mercury bestows.[83] This would place them in the years between 7–14. When we move on into adolescence and beyond, these characters whose age we know provide the opportunity to explore the rich dimensions that the planetary beings bring. Here are some examples of characters whose ages, if not specifically identified, are indicated.

*Venus: 14-21*
Juliet — 14
Alan Strang from *Equus* — 16
St Joan (known to have been burnt at the stake at age 19) in the many dramatic versions of her story

*Sun: 21-42*
Mozart from *Amadeus* — spans the years from 25-35
Hamlet—30
Hedda Gabler—29
Prior Walter from *Angels in America* — 30
Proctor from *The Crucible* — middle thirties
The daughters from *The House of Bernarda Alba*

*Mars: 42-49*
Kent from *King Lear* — 48
George from *Who's Afraid of Virginia Woolf?* — 46
May in Beckett's *Footfalls* — in her 40s

*Jupiter: 49-56*
Gayev from *The Cherry Orchard* — 51
Martha from *Who's Afraid of Virginia Woolf?* — 52
Winnie from Beckett's *Happy Days* — in her 50s

*Saturn: 56-63*
Winnie from *Happy Days* — in her 50s [*]
Bernarda from *The House of Bernarda Alba* — 60
Willy Loman from *The Death of a Salesman* — 63
Pizarro from *The Royal Hunt of the Sun* — over 60

*Saturn and Moon recapitulation: 63-70*
Krapp from Beckett's *Krapp's Last Tape* — 69
Vladimir and Estragon from *Waiting for Godot* [†]
Woman in Beckett's *Not I* — coming up to 70

*Jupiter and Mercury recapitulation: 70-77*
Rebecca Nurse from *The Crucible* — 72
Vladimir and Estragon from *Waiting for Godot*

*Mars and Venus recapitulation: 77-84*
Maria Josefa from *The House of Bernada Alba*
King Lear — 80s
Firs from *The Cherry Orchard* — 87

Ibsen's Peer Gynt and Goethe's Faust both travel from youth to age, providing opportunities to explore how the planetary rhythms illuminate their journeys.

Such a list invites us to explore how to integrate the gifts of the planetary beings with our other choices and enrich our understanding not only of the characters we play but of the deeper mysteries at work in our biographies. And thus, through the actor's task of character creation, our instrument continues to evolve into an organ of perception for the High Work Masters who help to shape our lives.

---

[*] When the character's age is not mentioned directly, I have placed the character in both possible age groups.

[†] As above.

Chapter 7

# Archetypes of the artistic process—the creative tension between opposites

This chapter extends the exploration of those artistic principles that Chekhov called the *Four Brothers.*[*] Perhaps we have experienced performers who have developed a reliable technique, even possibly a brilliant craft, but who do not move us because they cannot either access or release the depth of inwardness a work requires. Or others who are embarrassingly 'naked'; who pour out their intensity and raw emotion with no vessel to contain and give it form. As artists we seek through our technique not to extinguish the impulses released from our unconscious heights and depths but to form and channel them. At one extreme, without that firm vessel of technique, raw intensity can simply spend itself. At the other, without emotional intensity to fill it, even the most perfect vessel is an empty shell. We will try to build a bridge between these two extremes.

Whatever the medium, what moves us in a great work of art depends on the artist's ability to balance the interplay of three sets of polarities. These have been named in different ways by others and throughout the ages but for now I simply call them: *form and energy, subjective and objective,* and *masculine and feminine.* We will explore each set in turn and, I think, discover that although each overlaps the other two in some respects, their distinctive nuances are all essential to the process of creation.

## Form and energy—Apollo and Dionysus

The Ancient Greeks experienced the opposing principles of *form* and *energy* as divine creative powers that were each as necessary to our lives as to artistic practice. Mount Parnassus, where the twin peaks still rise above the Delphic ruins, was where their complementary sacred presences could be especially invoked. Two shrines were consecrated: one to the god of light, Apollo and one to his darker brother, Dionysus.

---

[*] See *The Art of Acting,* Chapter 5: the sense of ease, form, beauty and the whole.

## *Dionysus — energy, passion, freedom, chaos, ecstacy*

One of the most potent explorations of the role played by Dionysus in Greek experience was undertaken by Euripides in his tragedy, *The Bacchae*. In this excerpt the chorus celebrates the god's gifts of abandonment and energy.

On, On! Run, dance. Delirious, possessed!
Dionysus comes to his own …
 … Soon the whole land will dance
When the god with ecstatic shout
Leads his companies out
To the mountain's mounting height
Swarming with riotous bands
Of Theban women leaving
Their spinning and their weaving
Stung with the maddening trance of Dionysus …
The celebrant, wrapped in his sacred fawn skin,
Flings himself on the ground surrendered
While the swift footed company streams on;
There he hunts for blood and rapturously
Eats the raw flesh of the slaughtered goat …
Possessed, ecstatic, he leads their happy cries;
The earth flows with milk, flows with wine,
Flows with nectar of bees …
The celebrant runs entranced, whirling the torch …
And with shouts he rouses the scattered bands,
Sets their feet dancing,
As he shakes his delicate locks to the wild wind …

How well the Greeks knew this pole of their experience: its gifts and the dangers of its excess. And how well the Romans, whose culture superseded theirs, experienced them too. For nearly two millennia, the Christian Church bent all its efforts to suppress them in the cultures over which it exercised authority. It would be nearly 2500 years after Euripides before the energies of Dionysus, pushed down by successive cultures into the subconscious realm, would once again erupt into the open in artistic form. In 1913, at the world premiere in Paris of *The Rite of Spring*, Stravinsky's music and Diaghalev's choreography shocked the European public and incited them to riot. In his poem, 'Kubla Khan', Coleridge explores the paradox that the artist's state of inspiration is akin to possession and can be just as terrifying as it is transporting.

> Could I revive within me,
> Her symphony and song,
> To such a deep delight 'twould win me,
> That with music loud and long,
> I would build that dome in air,
> That sunny dome! those caves of ice!
> And all who heard should see them there,
> And all should cry, Beware! Beware!
> His flashing eyes, his floating hair!
> Weave a circle round him thrice
> And close your eyes with holy dread,
> For he on honey-dew hath fed,
> And drunk the milk of Paradise.

Is there a legitimate place for these awesome energies which can so easily intensify into an orgy of abandonment? In the face of the power they unleash are cultures destined to alternate forever between suppression and abandonment? Or are there tools that artists can rely upon to bring those poles into creative dialogue?

Given the influence of Artaud's ideas* on the theatre practice of the last 100 years, the tragedy of his life prompts a fundamental question for the art of acting: is there a way to invoke and be inspired by Dionysus *but not be destroyed* by him? Our whole integrated Chekhov acting/Steiner speech technique offers such a way: inspiring courage to plunge completely into what the character or play demands, because we have the skills to ride the waves and steer our way with conscious clarity of what we do.

This first exploration allows us to be swept up by those energies and, at the same time, use our body of sensation as an organ of perception that allows us to explore them consciously.

### Dionysus exploration 1

1. Listen to music that arouses the energy of Dionysus: from the classical repertoire perhaps Stravinsky's *Rite of Spring* or Carl Orff's *Carmina Burana* and any of the numerous examples from the contemporary 'pop' music culture.

---

* See, *The Art of Speech,* pp. 5–10, and *The Alchemical Actor* by Dr Jane Gilmer.

2. Move to the music and observe the sensations it arouses. Identify them as precisely as you can and what it is in the music that arouses them.

3. Identify which psycho-physical tools are likely to allow you to invoke them consciously.

*Here is my attempt — Flying ... radiating ... expansion ... centre outside my body ... fast tempo ... psychological gestures for objectives like: I want to hurl myself off the edge or I want to lose myself ... floating... let myself be hurled by ocean waves, swept by a tsunami, imaginary centre in a tiger heart, not human, or a heart on fire.*
*All these swirl and surface, then dissolve and swirl again within my body of sensation; sometimes singly or in different combinations. And somewhere in the midst, a need to feel the earth, gravity, will centre driving down, stamping into it, superhuman power tearing roots of tree-trunks from the earth, wrenching earth itself from her orbit, heaving earth to sky, I hear myself cry out, a god ecstatic. PG expressing my objective: I want to smash all boundaries, transcend all limitations.*

In this way I awaken consciousness within abandonment; identifying useful tools, surrendering to each precise intensity while I retain awareness of my *actor's centre*, channel the energy through *consonants (rolled r, h, p, k,)* permeate my breath and speech with their elemental power and pour my soul into the expanded surface of the *diphthongs* /aʊ/ (<u>ou</u>t) /aɪ/ (l<u>i</u>fe) /ɔɪ/ (j<u>oy</u>).

Although the character may be lost in their sensation, how not to lose my centred actor self?

## *Dionysus exploration 2—partner work*

1. A, use the tools identified above and any others you find helpful to achieve a full-bodied Dionysian abandonment. B, prepare yourself to meet A's energy full-bodily, with the objective to control it.

2. Engage each other for a given length of time (30 seconds is probably enough). This will set a boundary to your exertions, allowing you to totally invest your energy because you know when you can stop.

3. Without physical contact, recreate the energy and dynamics of your interaction.

4. Reverse roles and repeat steps 1 and 2.

5. Create a solo movement sequence in which you integrate both roles within yourself. Explore the spectrum of control: at one end, total abandonment to energy, at the other such control that you extinguish it, between these two extremes a satisfying balance of control and energy.

6. Identify the tools implicit in B's role in step 1. *Body of sensation stirs, recognising, for example: radiating compressed into moulding ... energy of stormy floods calmed into*

*legato waters ... stick inflexible, unbending tight control ... will centre in my belly pierced by clear rays from my head penetrating, stilling, ordering, integrating thought and action ... PG expressing my objective: I want to penetrate, investigate, control your energy by understanding it.*

7. With your partner again, A and B decide on your role and prepare it with the tools you have identified. Engage with each other. Your goal is not to dominate your partner but explore how to integrate your roles.

8. Reverse roles and repeat the process.

9. On your own again, recreate each role and bring them both to a satisfying balance in yourself.

## Apollo — control and order, form and reason/thought

In contrast to the trance-like possession by unconscious forces inspired in his followers by Dionysus, the Greeks also worshipped the awake control and daylight consciousness bestowed by Apollo, Sun God, Lord of the Lyre and the Silver Bow.

O golden lyre, by Apollo and the Muses violet crowned
Alike beloved; so soon as thy quivering prelude rings, ...
Even the warrior lightning, with his spears of quenchless flame,
Thou stillest — even the eagle of Zeus thou makest tame ...
The very God of War
Forgets his savage spear thrusts and dreams in peace an hour —
In the Muses deep of bosom, and Apollo, lies such power ...

'A lyric', Pindar of Thebes, 518–438 BCE

For the Ancient Greeks, Apollo was the divinity inspiring Orpheus, whose lyre could tame savage beasts, ordering and harmonising chaos. He released the silver arrows of his reason straight into the heart of any conflict. In *The Eumenides* of Aeschylus, Apollo summoned the Athenian elders to decide if Orestes was guilty of the crime of matricide. This first jury set a precedent; justice would subsequently be achieved by reason and debate, not driven by the savage furies or the instinct for revenge.

Apollo encouraged those who sought guidance from the oracle at Delphi to awaken their intelligence. By inspiring his priestesses to deliver their responses in the form of riddles needing to be solved, he encouraged the growing independence of the human race who would otherwise remain unconscious and dependent on the guidance of the gods. At Delphi, his wisdom was embodied in the words: *Nothing in excess. Know thyself!*

Through the ages these two opposing principles have wrestled for supremacy. Artists strive to find their way in the battle — between the apparent coldness of the technique inspired by Apollo and the energy, intensity and spontaneity inspired by Dionysus. The story of Orpheus and Eurydice illuminates the artist's struggle to integrate the conscious and unconscious realms so they can work together to communicate the mystery of *why we are here and why we suffer.*

When Eurydice died, Orpheus, pupil of Apollo, lost his muse. Bereft, he followed her into the Realm of Shades: Pluto's kingdom of the underworld. To tame the savage beasts who waited at the entrance to destroy him but whose help he needed on the way, he played his lyre. Like Caliban, the terrifying shapes that inhabit the unconscious world also longed for beauty and could be persuaded to yield up their mysteries when they experienced its power. Through Orpheus we witness how the conscious mind longs for the inspiration it has lost and to be creative once again. Courageously it enters the unconscious realm, risking all for love of what is hidden there. At length he finds his muse again and begs that she be able to return with him. Pluto pities him and allows Eurydice to follow her beloved Orpheus back to the world of daylight consciousness, provided he does not look back to see if she is following. At the last moment he loses faith and turns around, only to see her disappear into the Realm of Shades. Again bereft, Orpheus wanders the world until the savage Maenads, ecstatic followers of Dionysus, come upon him in the desert of his grief and dismember him.

In the creative process it is tempting to look back to what inspired us in the past and try to hold on to it, repeat what worked for us before. We delve into our underworld, attempting to control and recreate past inspiration, not trusting that if we let go of it we could move forward into something new. We mourn that our creativity deserts us. Looking back is no solution. Now there is nowhere to turn, no inspiration flows. Like Orpheus, despairingly, we wander in the upper regions, the barren desert of our intellect, trying to construct out of our technique something that will pass for creation, but all the time we know it does not work.

If only we had not looked back, the unconscious energies would have followed our conscious mind up into the light of day and united with it to create something altogether new and unforeseen. But fear has made us unavailable. Our creative energy becomes destructive. It pursues us, tearing us to pieces. If only we had trusted. If only we had not tried to fix and make secure what by its very nature must be unpredictable, not able to be summoned on demand. Our technique must invite and woo the unconscious mind to follow it into the light of day, but not try to control it.

According to the legend, the dismembered head of Orpheus was flung into a river still continuing to call the name of his beloved — Eurydice. So does our technique, cut off from the heart, the source of inspiration, mourn the loss of that which gave it life and purpose.

## *Apollo/Dionysus exploration 1*

1. Choose a speech by a Shakespeare character you have already worked on.
2. Warm up your character choices and express the content of the speech in your own words. Do this several times until you are confident you have extracted the intensity and every nuance of meaning and experience contained in the material: no matter how long or unwieldy your version of the speech becomes.
3. Now pour all that intensity and meaning back into Shakespeare's language.
4. Share both versions with a partner and/or audience.
5. Share your observations. What is different for the actor when expressed each way? What for the audience?

## *Apollo/Dionysus exploration 2*

1. Try *Apollo/Dionysus exploration 1* with poems that have strong forms and rhythms and with which you are familiar. Identify how the form and rhythm affect communication of the content.
2. Try *Apollo/Dionysus exploration 1* with a sonnet you know well. Identify how the sonnet form affects communication of the content.
3. Write a sonnet that expresses an intense experience of yours.
4. Explore the emotional depth in Romeo and Juliet's first meeting. Use psycho-physical tools to express that depth in movement and your own sounds and words.
5. Now explore how the sonnet form, in which Shakespeare has expressed this meeting, affects your experience as actor and as audience.

## *Apollo/Dionysus exploration 3*

1. Choose an artwork that you love in a medium in which you have no skill. Immerse yourself in it, explore it with your psycho-physical tools until you have a sense of what the artist wanted to communicate.
2. Now try to express that experience without the skill to do so. For example, you love a particular Beethoven sonata, or Mozart aria. You feel in your whole being what the composer wanted to express. You try to sing it but your voice cracks or can't reach the notes. You try to express it on the violin or piano but cannot play them. You feel in your whole being what van Gogh wanted to express when he painted the *Starry Night* or the *Potato Eaters* but you cannot paint. You try but have no skill with brush or colours. You feel in your whole being what Michelangelo wanted to express when he carved the *David* or *Pieta*. You try to carve a piece of marble but it cracks and shatters.
3. Share your reflections.

### *Apollo/Dionysus exploration 4*

Alan Strang's monologue from *Equus*, as it builds, could tempt an actor to indulge in a Dionysian frenzy and therefore provides a perfect opportunity to try to balance the Dionysian pole with the Apollonian.[*]

1. Prepare the character choices for Alan suggested in Chapter 1 and integrate them with the steps in *Apollo/Dionysus exploration 1*.
2. Work through the monologue paying careful attention to the tools required to structure it.[†]
3. Observe your experience while focused on these technical requirements.
4. As the vessel you are building becomes increasingly secure, release the character's emotion until intensity and form are balanced.
5. Experiment with degrees of imbalance: so much form that you strangle the intensity, so much intensity that you obliterate the form and, finally, aim for maximum intensity crafted in a 'perfect' form.
6. Sustain maximum intensity and try the whole monologue again without regard for any of the conscious choices you have made for crafting character or structure. Consciously allow yourself to go to the Dionysian extreme so you know how it feels when 'the horse bolts' or 'the train runs out of your control'.
7. Once again channel that intensity into the form.
8. Share your experiments and exchange your observations with a partner or audience. Does the experience differ for the actor and the audience?

## *Improvisation*

For centuries the great composers and comedians have been brilliant improvisers. The success of the Commedia dell'Arte, for example. depended on the actors' ability to improvise. In our own time, improvisation has become an artform in its own right, giving rise to performance styles that do not take their starting point from pre-existing texts: Theatre Sports, Devised and Playback theatre, all depend on improvising.

At first glance, improvising seems by definition to be entirely the domain of Dionysus; we are free to play, free to do just what we like, to be totally available and present in the NOW. Yet, paradoxically, it is adherence to agreed rules or principles that releases our spontaneity, allowing us to be in the moment, unconstrained by what we did before, or judgements of failure or success or 'good' or 'bad'.

---

[*] You'll find the text in Chapter 1.

[†] Described in Chapter 1.

To be fruitfully spontaneous, the conscious mind must provide a framework within which the unconscious feels invited to attend and when its impulses announce themselves, we can recognize and welcome them, quieten the judgements that would silence them, and be prepared to follow them. Say: 'Yes, let's! *

## *Creative paradigms*

Although conceived in different forms throughout the ages, most cultures until recently, ascribed creation to a divine creative being or multiplicity of beings. These origin accounts reflect the tendencies that wrestle with each other in the microcosm of our human creativity. We can see how each one manifests more or less of the form or freedom archetype. 'Enlightenment' thinking, with its Graeco-Latin roots planted in a culture still imbued with Hebrew-Christian values, regarded God as a patriarchal being who created and controls a rigid universe that runs like clockwork with meticulous precision. Evolutionary thinking sees creation as an event that takes place over vast trajectories of time in which genetic processes, improvising in response to changing circumstance, result in forms of ever more complexity. Such a view of creation does not, for some, require the presence or consciousness of a creator. For others however it does not preclude it. Still others imagine that those final forms arrived, finished and perfected, through one single and original creative act. In our modern age, many conceive of a creator or creators who improvise on an infinite scale within the constraints of the laws that science is progressively uncovering. Others conceive of a universe of chance governed by arbitrary whim and increasingly, since creation is conceived of as taking place with no creator, struggle to make sense 'how anything' so totally devoid of plan or pattern or any consciousness at all, can possibly relate to anything.

Improvising is increasingly regarded as an ultimate artistic goal in what have been traditionally thought of as 'the arts' as well as life itself. From this perspective, even the great masterpieces of the past record what their creators originally improvised according to the laws dictated by their medium. Artists who perform such completed works must be able to trace back to the source, through the evidence bequeathed in text or manuscript, and either reconstruct that first creative act or reconfigure it within the present context. The greatest performers are not afraid to invoke Dionysus, lord of chaos, who grants them freedom, energy and passion, because Apollo, lord of form, shows them how to build a vessel that can channel and control their spontaneity.

---

* *The Art of Acting*, page 18.

## Subjective and objective

We sense when an actor or their work is too subjective and too personal, or too objective and not personal enough. The latter leaves us unmoved while the former makes of us unwitting voyeurs sensing that the actor's and our own boundaries have been violated without us having granted our permission. These polarities are a related nuance of the struggle to find balance between form and energy. Technique is like a safety net. Our grasp of the objective laws that govern working in our chosen medium allows us to transform our raw experience into something we can offer to another in a way that nourishes and also leaves them free, just as we do not serve a hungry human being with the raw ingredients that make a loaf of bread but first transform them into food they can digest.

The intensity and urgency that pressures artists to communicate what they feel has been revealed to them can generate frustration with the time it takes to build their craft. A lengthy process interferes with spontaneity. Why should we not simply pour out our subjective impulses without delay? Yet it is a paradox that the lack of an objective vessel or technique in which to clothe our subjectivity becomes its own restraint. For although it is often a necessary and exhilarating stage in our creative process to simply 'put it out there', what is a relief to us does not necessarily communicate successfully to others. Subjecting the personal ever and again to the objective requirements of our medium allows what is universal in it to reveal itself. This not only deepens our experience but allows it to communicate to others. On the other hand, those who are attracted to the practice of technique in order to avoid the exploration and exposure of their vulnerable depths will also struggle to communicate.

If it is our goal to integrate these opposites, we must recognize them as extreme ends of a continuum within which we learn to be at home and to negotiate and balance the degrees of interaction that determine the shifting boundaries between them. The great texts that have stood the test of time have been bequeathed by dramatists and poets who have done this work. Actors who interpret them, without themselves engaging in that struggle, will not be able to reveal all the dimensions of experience condensed into those words.

The entire content of these books consists of opportunities to cultivate our instrument to be an organ of perception that allows us to move freely through the spectrum. First, the explorations generate subjective richness of sensation, then teach us to discern in it the laws and principles by which the macrocosmic soul and spirit permeates our microcosmic souls and finally, to explore those laws and principles in such a way that they reveal themselves through our subjective souls. For example, exploring the epic, lyric and dramatic styles, as described in Chapter 6 of *The Art of Speech* and again in this book's Chapter 2, trains us to recognise and comfortably inhabit all degrees and nuances arising from the interaction of these two polarities.

The epic style requires us to transform our own responses to what happens in order to describe events objectively so that the audience may have their own experience. We could call this the striving for subjective objectivity. The lyric style requires us to enter so deeply into our personal responses that our own soul becomes a vessel for the universal human soul. We could call this the striving for objective subjectivity. Dramatic style requires that we enter another character's experience so that we portray it, not from our perspective but from its own subjective point of view. At the same time we must penetrate that character's experience in such a way that its thread can be woven in the fabric of the drama as a whole and reveal the objective laws at work even in the lives of characters who do not recognise or understand them.

It is a longer, more demanding path for actors who recognise this call to move beyond their talent. Not everyone can face its challenges. The work to achieve objective form is often felt as 'death' to the subjective soul. The resistance we meet as we struggle to transform our habit-body on the way to make our instrument transparent, can tempt us to accept the easy path. Why should we wait to express ourselves until our instrument is free of our subjective mannerisms and able to reveal the spiritual activity of consonants and vowels, for example?

As Chekhov expressed it, the purpose of technique is to release our *artistic individuality;* the creative genius that lives in each of us. It is illusion to think because we have poured out what lives inside us in a naïve, unexamined way, that we even know ourselves what we experience let alone communicate it to another. But it is equally deluded to think we can arrive at art that moves an audience if we hold ourselves aloof from the subjective, afraid to be too personal. Recognising when we have transgressed that boundary in either way can be a blessing that informs us of the further work we need to do. The artistic path requires us to know our tendencies and boundaries so that we can move back and forth in search of balance. If we follow the road less travelled, we arrive at riches beyond what the subjective self can, on its own, deliver. It has been one purpose of these books to reconnect technique to the everlasting spring which is its source, allowing it to stream as direct sensation into our subjective souls and thereby resurrect it from the graveyard of abstraction.

## Masculine and feminine

It seems to me that the controversies generated by the complexity surrounding gender roles that manifests at every level of contemporary culture — historical, political, economic, psychological, domestic, biological, sexual, anatomical — obscure the universal principles at work within these levels. Traditional Chinese culture referred to them as yin and yang. I will call them *feminine and masculine* to distinguish these archetypal principles from male and female gender issues. Masculine and feminine each play their part in the creative process and in themselves are neither negative nor positive, superior, inferior, nor more or less important than each other.[*] Artistry demands that we work with both, sometimes in equal balance, sometimes consciously allowing one to dominate. Distinguishing these archetypes from *gender*, allows us to explore the necessary contribution made by each to the creative process.

Most cultures have been and continue to be shaped by the significance they attach to them. It manifests in attitudes to male and female bodies, relationships, institutions and cultural conventions. Till recently, these archetypes have broadly been identified with male and female gender. Now, however, it is recognised increasingly that what I call the masculine principle or archetype may equally be active in someone with a female body or the feminine within a male.[†] As always in life, richness arises from the complex ways in which the archetypes become specific as they manifest and interact in differing degrees and forms, sometimes subtle, sometimes more extreme. It is when these complex interactions manifest unconsciously or are forced into poles identified with rigidly heteronormative male or female gender roles that we end up in the minefield I alluded to.

---

[*] The differentiation between gender and these archetypes is a major theme in *The Actor of the Future 1:Tongues of Flame.*

[†] See *The Actor of the Future 1: Tongues of Flame.*

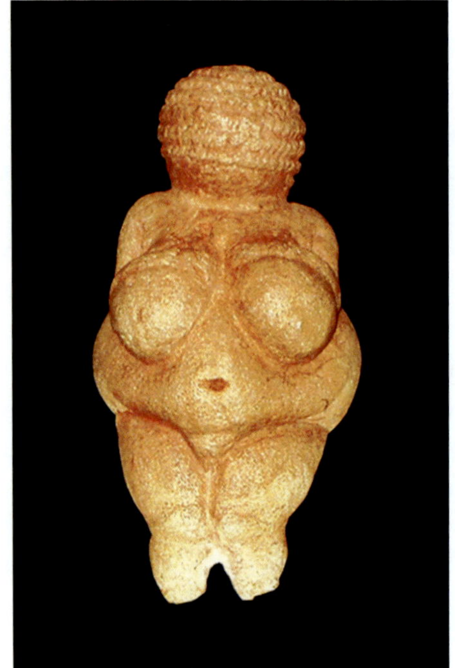

*Figure 88 Venus of Willendorf*                    *Figure 89 Priapus of Ephesus*

Heteronormative male and female forms[84] appear as extreme ends of a continuum that our present age is only just beginning to acknowledge. For my purpose in this context I will define male or female gender as the differentiation into outer form of the masculine or feminine archetype. Throughout the ages 'male' and 'female' attributes were sacramentalised in rites that celebrated the fertility of human beings, plants and animals and their capacity to reproduce themselves. The aspects of the female body so sacramentalised were its roundness, its nature as receptacle, as vessel for interiority designed to hold the egg, receive the male seed in order to be fructified, and nurture new life in its protective sheath. The aspect of the male body that was sacramentalised was the phallus, designed to thrust its seed into the world and fertilise the egg in the receptacle.

If we now extract the *principles of form* from their anatomical expressions, we may recognise their psychic counterparts. The 'feminine' gesture of inwardness, receptiveness, surrender, creates a vessel within which the unique imprints of our memory and intuitions from the future are stored and nurtured from within. The 'masculine' gesture wills to penetrate and know the outer world, to imprint its intention on the world. The feminine capacity to listen and be sensitive allows that unconscious knowing deep within to be penetrated by impressions from the world outside which fertilise those intuitions. From the merging of masculine and feminine, creative impulses arise and are nurtured in the womb of our imagination, until they are ready to be born.

An act of creation must include both principles: surrender, willingness to receive and nurture inspirations and the capacity to act and manifest them in the world. If we function one-sidedly in the receiving pole, although our inner life may be intense and rich, we cannot communicate it to the world. If we function one-sidedly in the active pole, lacking inwardness and sensitivity, we will impose our impulse on the world.

Artistry is generated in relationship. That means listening. Absorbing *from* the world to which we would contribute our creation, then creating what speaks meaningfully *to* the world. So art becomes true conversation. This integration of the masculine and feminine archetypes in the creator is embodied beautifully in the two sculptures from Chartres Cathedral which depict God imagining and then creating Adam.

*Figure 90 Chartres Cathedral, left: The Creator conceives the creation of the human being ,*
*right: The Creator creates the human being.*

Leonardo's portrait of the face of Christ also reveals this mystery.

*Figure 91*

In the Grail mythology these two principles are represented in the chalice and the lance. The lance was the masculine tool with which Longinus pierced the side of Christ; at that moment Christ's body was a chalice that received that thrust. Through this act, the greater chalice of the earth received Christ's fructifying blood and the transubstantiation of the planet could begin. For human consciousness not yet evolved enough to comprehend this mystery its wisdom was preserved in the legend of the Holy Grail. It told how Joseph of Arimathea caught the sacred blood in a cup and consecrated his hereditary stream to guard and serve its impulse for the future. Then as human consciousness matured, ever deeper layers of this metaphor could be revealed.

The lance that pierced the side of Christ reminds us how a great work of art can pierce and break us open. Yet if the lance that is aimed at us is not to work destructively it must have first been dipped in the chalice of the heart. If the lance of the artist is to pierce with healing power, it must be driven by the will to penetrate but its action must have been prepared in love. When we are struck by such a blow we are not harmed but awakened to a deeper sense of our humanity. Life flows into us through such awakening.

Within the safety net that healthy art provides, the soul is purified; the powerful emotions which often work destructively in life are safely exercised. Thus, in what

Aristotle called *catharsis*, the terror that the downfall of Oedipus elicits in the audience is balanced by pity and compassion.

Some who sense that there is more to the genius of Shakespeare and his mission in the world than an accident of genes, are convinced that the truth of his identity might be concealed behind the Mystery significance connected with his name. One version of the myth that describes Athena's birth tells how she had to shake her spear in order to be born from her father Zeus's head. Thus she was called Pallas Athena which means 'spearshaker': one who shakes her spear at ignorance. Another connection to this name is the picture of the archangel Michael brandishing his spear at the dragon of untruth. Whatever our position regarding the identity of the one who wrote the plays we cannot fail to recognise that Shakespeare's words possess the power to shake our consciousness awake and pierce and heal us in the way described above.

In *The Actor of the Future 1* we have already seen that the human larynx has the form of a chalice. When we were still students at the London School of Speech Formation, my friend and colleague Geoffrey Norris,[85] shared with me his insight that a chalice is embodied in our whole speech-anatomy.* The figure that follows shows my illustrator's exploration of his insight.

---

* Also see the frontispiece for an image of the larynx as a chalice.

*Figure 92 The Chalice of Speech*

In *The Art of Acting* we saw that the spear-thrower's gesture reveals how masculine and feminine work together in the act of speaking.[86] First, by reaching back into the listening space, I prepare myself to be a vessel that receives an impulse. Then I project what I receive into the space.*

---

* *The Art of Acting*, pp. 132–4.

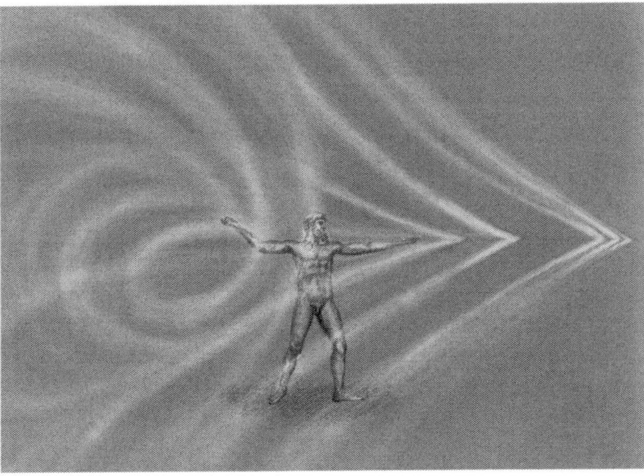

*Figure 93 The spear thrower*

## *Archetype or stereotype*

Archetype[*] becomes stereotype when its identifying features are divested of beingness and reduced to outer attributes. These then become the single lens through which a complex being is viewed. Thus a man in whom the masculine stereotype predominates may be labelled by himself or others as a 'macho' or an 'alpha male', while one in whom the feminine is dominant may be labelled by himself or others as effeminate or a 'queen'. A woman in whom the feminine stereotype predominates may be labelled by herself or others as a 'dumb blonde' or 'helpless female' while one in whom the masculine is dominant may be labelled by herself or others as 'butch'. Perhaps imprisoning the infinite dimensions of ourselves or others in the straitjacket of a *type* (female, male or any other) is a necessary stage along the journey to become a human being. Distinguishing these stereotypical attributes may also help us clarify the archetypes from which their shallow counterparts have been extracted and allow us to explore their greater depth of being. This will enable us to:

- move freely through the gender spectrum of our cultural experience;
- explore how the archetypes relate to our artistic tendencies and how to consciously invoke them to expand our range;
- integrate their layers with more complex characters;
- build characters who identify themselves with the stereotypes.

## *Masculine/feminine exploration 1—stereotype*

1. Explore full-bodily the attributes identified as 'feminine'.
2. Exaggerate them to the level of stereotype and caricature.

------

[*] *The Art of Acting*, Chapter 3.

3. Repeat steps 1 and 2 with attributes identified as 'masculine'.

4. Share your work and observations with a partner or group.

## *Masculine/feminine exploration 2—distinguishing archetype from stereotype*

Improvisation: a group of refugees has plotted their escape from a political regime where they are under constant threat. You approach the border authority with false passports and assumed identities that include a change of gender. You must convince the official that you are who you claim to be. Any hint of caricature will arouse suspicion.

1. Take time to build a picture of your character, giving them a name and biography that enables you to answer questions confidently.

2. Create your character by layering your observations from *masculine/feminine exploration 1* with your other choices.

3. Improvise the situation.

4. Share your observations in the group. What allowed you to convince officials of your gender? How did you avoid caricature or stereotype?

## *Masculine/feminine exploration 3*

1. Explore freely and with full-bodied movement/accompanying voice and speech, the attributes you have identified as masculine and feminine.

2. Observe whether you regard any of them as, in themselves, *good/bad, positive/negative, superior/inferior*.

3. While you move, pay attention to your body-of-sensations. Which psycho-physical tools do they remind you of? Identifying these will allow you to consciously create the attributes. Here are some suggestions:

*Masculine*

    *Centres/speech placements for thinking and will.*

    *Radiating directed to the outer world.*

    *Moulding—willingness to engage with the resistance of matter.*

    *Fast tempo and staccato dynamic.*

    *Psychological gestures for objectives such as, 'I want to penetrate/conquer the outer world' etc.*

    *Revelations of speech and gesture: pointing, flinging out a limb, stepping back on own ground.*

    *Qualities and sensations: single-minded, ambitious, confidently, powerfully, driven.*

    *Greek Gymnastics: Javelin.*

    *Incorporating an object: stick.*

*Feminine*

    *Centres/speech placements for feeling and will.*

    *Floating and flying focused inward.*

    *Slow tempo and legato dynamic.*

    *Greek Gymnastics: discus.*

    *Giving and Receiving.*

    *Psychological gestures for objectives such as, 'I want to nurture, feel my inner world' etc.*

    *Revelations of speech and gesture: holding on to self, questioning, reaching to touch.*

    *Qualities and sensations: compassionately, thoughtfully.*

    *Incorporating an object: veil.*

4. When you have explored each tool, move in and out of them until the layers that compose each archetype fuse into one full-bodied movement/voice and speech sequence.
5. Move through each sequence and explore which vowels and consonants are most aligned with it.
6. Working full-bodily, explore these phrases from Gerard Manley Hopkins's sonnet, 'Hurrahing in Harvest':

    *Masculine:* Majestic as a stallion stalwart.

    *Feminine:* … very violet sweet.

## Masculine/feminine exploration 4

1. Explore in movement how to integrate both sets of attributes: masculine outgoing strength with feminine depth of inwardness.
2. Take any psycho-physical tool such as *staccato/legato, expanding/contracting* or speech exercise such as *reforging gales* or *in the vast …*
   - Warm up with your masculine sequence then explore the speech exercise.
   - Warm up with your feminine sequence then explore the speech exercise.
3. Integrate both sets of attributes, then explore the speech exercise.
4. Share your observations.

## Masculine/feminine exploration 5

Working full-bodily use the steps of *masculine/feminine exploration 4* to investigate the images in D H Lawrence's poem, 'Song of a Man who has Come Through'.

    Not I, Not I, but the wind that blows through me!

    A fine wind is blowing the new direction of Time.

    If only I let it bear me, if only it carry me!

If only I am sensitive, subtle, oh, delicate, a winged gift!

If only, most lovely of all, I yield myself and am borrowed

By the fine, fine wind that takes its course through the chaos of the world

Like a fine, an exquisite chisel, a wedge-blade inserted;

If only I am keen and hard like the sheer tip of a wedge

Driven by invisible blows,

The rock will split, we shall come at the wonder, we shall find the Hesperides.


Oh, for the wonder that bubbles into my soul,

I would be a good fountain, a good well-head,

Would blur no whisper, spoil no expression.


What is that knocking?

What is that knocking at the door in the night?

It is somebody wants to do us harm.


No, No, it is the three strange angels.

Admit them, admit them.

## *Masculine/feminine exploration 6*

Observe whether you tend more towards one or the other archetype in your artistic work. Use the tools you have discovered to consciously expand your range.

## *Masculine/feminine exploration 7*

Now we are ready to explore how the archetype becomes distorted into what is sometimes called the *negative masculine* or *negative feminine*.

1. Create a PG expressing the objective: *I want to control or dominate.*
2. Layer this into your full-bodied masculine sequence.
3. Create a PG expressing the objective: *I want to demonstrate my helplessness so you will rescue me.*
4. Layer this into your full-bodied feminine sequence.

## *Masculine/feminine exploration 8*

Here are some characters to explore in the context of these archetypes.

- In *The Bacchae*, Euripides depicts Dionysus as androgynous.
- Shakespeare creates a number of female characters — Portia, Viola, Imogen, Rosalind — whose path of initiation requires them to disguise themselves as men in order to awaken the masculine pole of their experience.

- Cordelia in *King Lear*, while displaying all the attributes of the feminine archetype, also confidently leads the French forces when her husband is summoned back to France.
- Francis Flute in *A Midsummer Night's Dream* is an adolescent — 'I have a beard coming' — who reluctantly accepts the role of Thisbe, the heroine in the Duke's wedding play.
- In *The Tempest*, Prospero's journey begins with the masculine lust for power and control and ends with the feminine compassion and humility that embraces all parts of himself and others. He must achieve the 'chemical wedding' and unite both aspects in himself.
- The Macbeths allow us to explore the negative aspects of the archetypes. Here are a few examples:
    - Although he is courageous in battle, she sees him as weak; 'too full o' the milk of human kindness'.
    - He says: 'I dare do all that may become a man, who dares do more is none.' She says: 'If you were a man you would do it' — kill the king and take the crown.
    - He sees her as more masculine: 'Bring forth men children only.'
    - She recognises that if she is to get what she wants she must behave 'like a man' and crush the feminine aspects of her nature. 'Unsex me here.'
- In Ibsen's *The Dolls House*, both Nora and Torvald are challenged to transform their negative stereotypes.
- In a completely different way, Tennesee Williams presents the negative stereotypes in Stanley and Blanche in *A Streetcar Named Desire*.
- *Angels in America* by Tony Kushner provides rich opportunities to explore the complexities that arise from the interplay of stereotypes with gender and with archetypes. There is also an Angel who manifests an androgynous integration of both archetypes, suggestive of our future evolution.
- Many plays explore the character of Joan of Arc — the warrior woman.
    - Shakespeare's, *Henry VI part 1*.
    - Shaw's, *St Joan*.
    - Maxwell Anderson's, *Joan of Lorriane*.
    - Brecht's, *St Joan of the Stockyards*.
    - Anouilh's, *The Lark*.
- *The Good Woman of Sechzuan* by Berthold Brecht.[*] In order to access her masculine attributes the female central character impersonates her male cousin.
- In Peter Brook's *Mahabharata*, the warrior prince Arjuna spends time in a female body.

---

[*] *The Actor of the Future 1: Tongues of Flame*, pp. 75–76.

## Our High Work Masters

Different streams of cultural consciousness have given their own names to all of these creative archetypes. As we have seen, the Ancient Greeks attributed their qualities to gods or goddesses. Contemporary mainstream consciousness prefers to see them as forces generated by our physiology: the by-products of brain activity or cellular secretions. Yet if we strive for an art of acting which has its source in supersensible reality, these polarities can be no exception. Indeed, to take the step from recognising qualities to an encounter with the beings who reveal their nature through those qualities is simply one more opportunity to explore the path of spiritual cognition as identified by Steiner. As we were reminded in the Introduction, this requires that we develop clarity of thought and observation with which to penetrate our deepening perceptions as we move through Imagination, Inspiration and Intuition.

The renewed understanding of the planets through Steiner's work, once again allows us to explore what would otherwise be abstract qualities as attributes of *beingness*. I stress once again that the following connections I have made between these qualities, the planetary beings and the hierarchies are not definitive. They are intended as suggestions to inspire your own explorations: how the eurythmy gestures intuited by Steiner function as Cosmic Psychological Gestures (CPGs) that evoke precise sensations, allowing us to get to know the beings who inspire our own creative processes. Indeed if we human beings are the great work of art that is still in progress, created by macrocosmic artists to recognise and consciously participate in our creation, how else could it be?

As with all potentials, when experienced unconsciously they can manifest in ways that may initially inspire but can also plague, torment and undermine the artist's life and creativity. However, from that moment when our I AM presence wakens from within, signalling the start of our conscious participation in our own creation, each potential can subsequently be ennobled. It is these multiple perspectives that I have striven to articulate. Our artistic practice is both what enables us to exercise each attribute and in turn to be enriched by it. The work that follows is the first suggestion of a pathway on which artists/actors may discern how the forces that can otherwise possess them may be transformed by consciously cooperating with the planetary beings who bestow them. As explored in detail in *The Actor of the Future 2—Word Made Flesh*, it is the vowels and the soul-states they embody that enable us to recognise their work in us.

Once again I have composed the meditations that follow in order to convey something like the stream of consciousness released by embodying the planetary gestures and the vowels. However, in this case I have expressed the multiple perspectives they release into our body of sensation; how the planetary being itself speaks into us and the responses it calls forth within our higher I AM Self as well as the untransformed distortions in our soul. They are written to be spoken out aloud by the reader, and are woven from the vowels appropriate to each. As discussed in Chapter 5, as well as in *The Art of Speech* and *Word Made Flesh,* variations in the spelling and pronunciation of each vowel or diphthong in the English language grant access, not to a single aspect but rather to a spectrum of experience that emanates from its activity. It is this spectrum I have chosen to explore which includes, but is not confined to, the precise sensations of the vowels phonetically associated with the placements in the mouth. Their phonetic symbols are provided to indicate the vowel/s around which each intended spectrum manifests.

*I stand with instrument attuned, my body of sensation scans the field of energies, sweeps the skies in search of the consciousness that is each vowel's source, sensing its way into the gestures that align our souls with it and provide a pathway to the deeper revelations of its being. I want to know you, giver of these gifts.*

## First pair of creative opposites—Dionysian and Apollonian poles

### *1. Dionysian pole: manifestations—passion/energy/freedom/chaos*

*Suggested planetary sphere: Mercury, centre of activity of the Archangels*

Their activity within our souls generates the psychophysical sensation expressed in the vowels /ɪ/ (s<u>i</u>p) and /iː/ (m<u>e</u>)

Archangels speak:
> I <u>incre</u>ase the tension <u>in</u> the altar of your mouth and throat,
> tighten<u>i</u>ng and tun<u>i</u>ng lar<u>y</u>nx str<u>i</u>ngs,
> flatten<u>i</u>ng tongue against hard palate roof and edge of t<u>ee</u>th,
> l<u>i</u>ps sideways squ<u>ee</u>ze
> unt<u>i</u>l your <u>i</u> nd<u>i</u>v<u>i</u>dual<u>i</u>t<u>y</u>
> <u>i</u>s th<u>i</u>n enough to sl<u>i</u>p betw<u>ee</u>n,
> rel<u>ea</u>se its narrow b<u>ea</u>m of sound
> and r<u>i</u>ng out fr<u>ee</u>.

> Each mortal thing does one thing and the same:
> Deals out that being indoors each one dwells;
> Selves — goes itself; *myself* it speaks and spells,
> Crying Whát I dó is me: for that I came.
>
> As Kingfishers Catch Fire…Gerard Manley Hopkins

He must increase but I must decrease.

John 3:30.

*Figure 94 Planetary being Mercury*

*Figure 95 Vowel /i:/*

## *Gestures of the planetary being Mercury and vowel /ɪ/ (s<u>i</u>p) /i:/ (me):*

Mercury speaks:

*Through long held back, explod<u>i</u>ng spr<u>i</u>ng, <u>e</u>ternall<u>y</u> return<u>i</u>ng gold from buds and bulbs, ben<u>ea</u>th which sp<u>e</u>ars p<u>i</u>erce upright gr<u>ee</u>n, rep<u>ea</u>tedly prepared through w<u>i</u>nter's fr<u>ee</u>ze, w<u>e</u> offer you, Beloved, cycl<u>i</u>c m<u>y</u>ster<u>ie</u>s of self red<u>ee</u>med, t<u>ea</u>ch you how to sp<u>ea</u>k, how through mother tongue, a language str<u>ea</u>ms that others share: cycles of yourself <u>e</u>volv<u>e</u> with<u>i</u>n <u>e</u>volv-<u>i</u>ng contexts of commun<u>i</u>t<u>y</u>, ind<u>i</u>v<u>i</u>dual<u>i</u>t<u>y</u> evolv<u>i</u>ng through the centur<u>ie</u>s.*

*The human soul responds*

The artist's curse:

*Suddenl<u>y</u>, your voltage through m<u>e</u>, fl<u>i</u>ngs me to <u>i</u>nf<u>i</u>n<u>i</u>t<u>y</u>. Glanc<u>i</u>ng off I r<u>ee</u>l from r<u>i</u>m to r<u>i</u>m and f<u>ee</u>l how faster than the earth I sw<u>i</u>ng around the sun on sandalled w<u>i</u>ng while slower*

*planets labour. Compelled to w<u>i</u>n, d<u>i</u>splay the glor<u>y</u> of my b<u>e</u>ing, obl<u>i</u>vious to others' m<u>i</u>sery, br<u>i</u>lliant, yet isolated at the f<u>i</u>n<u>i</u>sh line, crucif<u>i</u>xion now beg<u>i</u>ns. 'I must d<u>e</u>cr<u>ea</u>se.' Excruc<u>i</u>at<u>i</u>ng on th<u>i</u>s cross, gr<u>ie</u>f crying <u>i</u>n the w<u>i</u>lderness, w<u>i</u>nce as I am squ<u>ee</u>zed, refined to th<u>i</u>n and th<u>i</u>nner, through t<u>ee</u>th prised into narrow spl<u>i</u>t; the <u>e</u>go's dr<u>ea</u>m rec<u>e</u>des.*

The artist's gift, the I AM:

*'H<u>e</u> must <u>i</u>ncr<u>ea</u>se.' R<u>i</u>sen and red<u>ee</u>med, I br<u>i</u>ng the energ<u>y</u> of M<u>E</u> to serve the n<u>ee</u>ds of other p<u>eo</u>ple, the ensemble, rel<u>ea</u>se my g<u>i</u>fts to set theirs fr<u>ee</u>, exp<u>e</u>rience divin<u>i</u>t<u>y</u> with<u>i</u>n our W<u>E</u> /i:/.*

## 2. Apollonian pole: Manifestations—control and order, form and reason/thought

*Suggested planetary sphere: Jupiter, centre of activity of the Spirits of Wisdom (Kyriotetes)*[87]

Their activity within our souls generates the psycho-physical sensation expressed in the vowels /ɒ/ (of) /ɔ:/ (form) and the English diphthong /oʊ/ (grow, home)

Spirits of Wisdom speak:

*I form the altar of your mouth and throat to be a home where you may hold and order what you know, and spin the straw of knowledge into gold.*

*Figure 96 Planetary being Jupiter*

*Figure 97 Vowel /ɔ:/*

# *Gestures of the planetary being Jupiter and vowel /ɒ/ (of) /ɔ:/ (form) /oʊ/ (grow, home):*

Jupiter speaks:

*Not on your own! I cannot let you, mothlike, bold, throw yourself, Beloved, into the solar cauldron and immolate your precious soul. Or without direction let you go from so much this to — lost in labyrinths of — so much that. And so I throw my net, wide enough to catch*

*your eternally in search of never-enough experience and reel you in. I am a match for you and hold you as you struggle to be free, winding in your bright — more thin and faster threads, escaping to the edges of the light. Orbiting round and round my central will we wrestle and revolve, I feel your energy condense into a something still-not-solid-yet, for I know your fear of being fixed forever, trapped, imprisoned in an anything — so I loose my hold enough to let you swim a little free, pursue another inspiration. Respectful of your energy and goal I reel you in again, to once more orbit round my central will, my forming principle.*

*The human soul responds:*

*The artist's curse:*

*Fearful inspiration's door will close or worse, explode and force me from my comfort zone, I impose control, hold onto what I know, choke further exploration, foregoing process in pursuit of product, stifle what wants to grow and go beyond where I have gone before.*

*The artist's gift, the I AM:*

*Gesture of /ɔ:/ /oʊ/ — I invoke your force, Beloved. Show me how to hold sensation long enough to know what I am sensing. Arms and lips enfold, not squash and not impose yet find a form to clothe sensation in, and still be able to evolve. Neither form nor impulse on its own can make a whole. Then let them not be foes at war but honour both. For out of our resistance, slowly drawing closer, impulse is finally absorbed into my form and consciousness is born; wildness honed by wisdom, form that throbs a-glow. Form into freedom, impulse into form, into freedom, into form — evolving on and on.*

# Second pair of creative opposites—subjective and objective poles

## *1. Subjective pole*

*Suggested planetary sphere: the Moon, centre of activity of the Angels*

Their activity within our souls generates the psycho-physical sensation expressed in the diphthong /aɪ/(m_y_).

The Angels speak:
*_I_ al_i_gn the altar of your mouth and throat to gl_i_de from parad_i_sal Venus w_o_nder /a:/ (st_a_r) to self-identit_y_ of Mercur_y_ expressed in /i:/ (m_e_).*

*Figure 98 Planetary being Moon*

*Figure 99 Diphthong /aɪ/*

# *Gesture of the planetary being Moon and diphthong/aɪ/*

Moon speaks:

*It is time, Beloved, to confine infinity, not try to manage everything at once, explore one tiny finite life. Glance /ɑ:/ this way, see where I lead /i:/. Can your senses recognise the signs that I provide to find your way? I guide you through the eternal birth canal, then seal the entrance tight, shut out the light that you may bind perception, through your own thinking's might, into continuity of mind.*

*The human soul responds:*

*The artist's curse: Frightened, feeling I will die if I decide to be precise, the gates will close behind me, each finite choice will bind me, I fly commitment, just want to feel alive, eternally inspired, ride forever on the tide of my emotions, slide from one sensation to another, feeling my experience inside. Or else, frightened of sensation's slippery slopes, I bind them into abstract concepts, lock them tight!*

*The artist's gift, the I AM: Glide from paradisal /ɑ:/ so far back in the throat, towards the condensing, tensing, sense of me in middle of my mouth /i:/. Arms glide too from side to side, try this and that: diphthong /aɪ/.*

*Have I, looking elsewhere, missed the signs, expecting something else, some shine more brilliant, spectacular; not trusting, unaware how angels guide me through more humble sights and sounds, align me with eternity? My experience is mine. Strive to pay attention, refine my senses to divine the world and find in it my I. I am the world; the world is I.*

## *2. Objective pole*

*Suggested planetary sphere — Saturn, centre of activity of the
Thrones/Spirits of will*

Their activity within our souls generates the psycho-physical sensation expressed in the vowels: /ʊ/ (t<u>oo</u>k) /u:/ (tr<u>ue</u>)

The Spirits of Will speak:

*I p<u>u</u>ll the altar of your mouth and throat int<u>o</u> a pinpoint t<u>oo</u>l thr<u>ou</u>gh which your soul can p<u>u</u>sh thr<u>ou</u>gh its experience to pr<u>o</u>ve it tr<u>ue</u>.*

*Figure 100 Planetary being Saturn*

*Figure 101 Vowel /u:/*

# *Gesture of the planetary being Saturn and the vowel /ʊ/ (t<u>oo</u>k /u:/ (d<u>o</u> pr<u>o</u>ve tr<u>ue</u>)*

Saturn speaks:

*M<u>o</u>ve slowly now, Beloved, for I would prise your m<u>oo</u>n-closed fists, scr<u>e</u>wed fast to finite self-hood, l<u>oo</u>se. L<u>oo</u>k how your hands unfurl and slide across each other like sensitive tectonic plates, create a canopy, a shifting shelter, shading eyes to scan above, below, within, per<u>u</u>se. I w<u>ou</u>ld sch<u>oo</u>l you thr<u>ou</u>gh my slower r<u>ou</u>te around the sun to find the passage thr<u>ou</u>gh your heart and, as you m<u>o</u>ve from will to thinking, thinking back again to will, again, again, sense if what you d<u>o</u> f<u>u</u>lfils world purposes.*

*The human soul responds — /ʊ/ (took)/u:/ (do prove true)*

The artist's curse:

*Lips contract, concentrate my essence to a t<u>oo</u>l of terrifying scru-tiny. Fear stops my heart. Love's corridor is blocked! Demanding pr<u>oo</u>f before I start, of what I can only pr<u>o</u>ve is tr<u>ue</u> by d<u>o</u>ing it, f<u>u</u>tile intellect, isolated in its tower, with no experience to process, churns round upon itself, gets in the way, maintains control, gen-erating countless reasons not to d<u>o</u>; complexities of text, of char-acter, their impact on my own, the need to get it right, all make me unavailable, unable to respond, be present for my partner or the scene, afraid to m<u>o</u>ve. Paralysis! Thought and will unable to comm<u>u</u>nicate, stuck in my head, abstract r<u>u</u>les prod<u>u</u>ce a with-ered fr<u>ui</u>t?*

The artist's gift, the I AM:

*Prepared to l<u>oo</u>k a f<u>oo</u>l, not knowing what I d<u>o</u>, I m<u>o</u>ve on impulse: the mystery of will. Now weave the threads of my experience with threads of light, sensing as they intertwine within my heart, does their pattern match the bl<u>ue</u>print that it passes thr<u>ou</u>gh? Then down again into the dark, digest another belly f<u>u</u>ll, up into the light again, till what is personal is woven through with threads of the eternal on this consecrated l<u>oo</u>m. The fr<u>ui</u>t is bea<u>u</u>tiful and g<u>oo</u>d and tr<u>ue</u>.*

## Third pair of creative opposites—masculine and feminine poles

### *1. Masculine pole*

*Suggested planetary sphere — Mars, centre of activity of the Dynamis/Spirits of Movement*

Their activity within our souls generates the psycho-physical sensation expressed in the vowel /ɛ/ (m<u>e</u>n) and English dipthong /eɪ/ (d<u>a</u>te)

The Spirits of Movement speak:

> *I sh<u>a</u>pe the altar of your mouth and throat to m<u>a</u>ke a keen-<u>e</u>dged bl<u>a</u>de.*

*Figure 102 Planetary being Mars*

*Figure 103 Diphthong /eɪ/*

## *Gesture of the planetary being Mars and the vowel /ɛ/ (m**e**n) diphthong /eɪ/ (cre**ate**):*

Mars speaks

*I m**a**ke you br**a**ve, Beloved, to penetr**a**te the world with clear int**e**ntion, then f**a**ce objectively what you cre**a**te, ass**e**ss its imperf**e**ctions, **e**xperi**e**nce dissatisfaction rear up on your w**a**y with **e**lem**e**ntal force, procl**ai**m n**e**c**e**ssity to ch**a**nge, to br**ea**k its satisfactory till th**e**n, but now imperfect, superseded sh**a**pe. Precision poised, no h**e**sit**a**tion, no conc**e**ssion to weak s**e**ntiment or fear of p**ai**n, of hurting, being hurt. Not afr**ai**d to wield the bl**a**de.*

*The human soul responds — /ɛ/ (men) /eɪ/ (create)*

*The artist's curse:*

*On fire, imagin**a**tion cannot w**ai**t until the soil is r**ea**dy and prep**a**ration is complete. Imp**a**tient, I thrust too hard. Recognition comes too l**a**te. The seed is w**a**sted, cannot germin**a**te. What I cre**a**ted f**ai**ls! The s**e**lf defl**a**tes. The internal critic, n**e**ver satisfied, h**a**tes what I have m**a**de. Heartless and d**ea**f to pity's s**e**lf-preserving cries, I demolish it in r**a**ge, rear and plunge ag**ai**n, ag**ai**n, rel**e**ntless savage r**ai**n from sky to earth and back ag**ai**n! Smash, like Michelangelo the stubborn unresponsive stone![88] No l**e**ss mercil**e**ss to s**e**lf than others' p**ai**n!*

*The artist's gift, the I AM:*

*My cre**a**tion now exists outside me, s**e**par**a**ted from mys**e**lf. Ass**e**ss obj**e**ctively! Does it expr**e**ss what I int**e**nded to cre**a**te? Does any st**ai**n rem**ai**n to blur perf**e**ction? No need to react aggr**e**ssively. Warlike Mars has also been evolving to another st**a**ge. R**e**cognise what needs to ch**a**nge. Do not be afr**ai**d to let my words **e**valu**a**te, diss**e**ct, inv**e**stigate, l**a**y bare, anatomise, criticise constructively, d**e**t**e**ct a new world in the broken r**e**mnants of the m**e**ntal fight and, redefining love, initi**a**te the n**e**xt step on the w**a**y.*

## *2. Feminine pole*

*Suggested planetary sphere—Venus, centre of activity of the Archai*

Their activity within our souls generates the psycho-physical sensation expressed in the vowels: /ʌ/ (c<u>u</u>p) and /ɑː/ (st<u>a</u>r)

The Archai speak:
  *I c<u>a</u>rve the altar of your mouth and throat to open unimpeded the p<u>a</u>thway to the v<u>a</u>st inner s<u>a</u>nctum of your h<u>ea</u>rt.*

Figure 104 Planetary being Venus

Figure 105 Vowel /ɑ:/

# *Gesture of the planetary being Venus and the vowel /ʌ/ (cup) /ɑ:/ (star):*

Venus speaks:

*Left palm trawling in the underdepths I plumb the far and farther inwardness of hearkening skies. As from the past's dark well I stir, cultures arch and cycle through my arms. From their depths I summon eggs of memory of all humanity has been and will become. I grant them to you. Guard them, Beloved, in the womb of your imaginative heart. Await the bridegroom Mars to plant in them his stallion seed. It will rearrange your particles and start you on the pathway to become a star.*

*The human soul responds — /ʌ/ (cup) /ɑ:/ (star):*

*The artist's curse*

*Ah! I am too sensitive, too porous, have no boundaries, no skin. Without a hardened crust I cannot stop the world's substance flooding me, bar its largeness from engulfing me, its traffic passing through me or keep its suffering apart from mine. I don't know when to say, 'Enough!' Call out, 'Stop, pull back!' Blundering, aghast, can't distinguish self from other, I wear a mask to stop myself from disappearing, being torn asunder.*

*The artist's gift, the I AM:*
*What my left arm receives, my right arm gives. Your gesture in my mouth, offers no defence, erects no barrier, nothing to hinder passage to and from the rose's heart within. Inspiration passes through me from the world, from others. I receive it consciously into my heart and make it new within. I sense how much to offer to my partner, to the audience, my character, and yet, the breathing membrane of my boundaries intact, remain apart. An artist's task is to be both gardener and garden, harvester and harvest. I am become a cup of sun. 'O Lady we receive but what we give.'[89]*

## *The wild woman*

Another important archetype to be explored within this context is the *wild woman*. Kate from *The Taming of the Shrew* and Martha from *Who's Afraid of Virginia Woolf?* are good examples. To view both characters through the lens of this set of polarities enriches the dimensions we can bring to them. The separation of the masculine and feminine from gender and gender-role helps us understand that Kate and Martha are confused about the way these archetypes express themselves in their rejection of the gender-roles they are expected to fulfil. The stallion energy of Mars rears up unconsciously in each of them, causing them to plunge destructively, tread their male opponents underfoot, and thus assert their dominance. Before it can be mastered from within, each must meet a warrior whose strength is equal to their own but, tempered in unsentimental love, elicits the respect that alone inspires surrender to the Venus archetype to which each one unconsciously aspires. These dynamics are pictured in the Greek myth of Theseus who defeats the female warrior tribe of Amazons, subsequently marrying their queen, Hippolyta.

It is a simplistic feminist reading to interpret Kate's eventual surrender to Petruchio as acceptance of the male's traditional subjugation of the female. In the light of Shakespeare's complex understanding of the human being and his portrayal of her character — no matter how much her resistance to the passive role to which her culture would assign her may be justified — we cannot think that there is anything to recommend in Kate's display of wild rebellion. She is yearning for a partner who can match her stallion energy and also recognise that her untamed chaos is a waste of her potential.

If Shakespeare had written only this one play we might condemn the ending as a disappointing acquiescence to the relative status of the gender roles accepted until recently, and that still persists despite the fundamental shift now taking place. But we know from the whole body of his work that he could never have intended such a reading. It was not possible for Shakespeare to explore everything about relationships in one set of characters or interactions. Paulina in *The Winter's Tale* demonstrates how Katherine's Mars-energy can be transformed: it empowers Paulina to defend the truth no less fiercely than Kate defends her right to self-determination. Again and again we see the stallion in Paulina rear up at lies and self-deception, then strike down with merciless precision. It is clear that Shakespeare does not equate maturity with gender for we see him, in Paulina's case, reverse Petruchio's role in educating Kate. When Leontes' self-obsession is shattered by the deaths of his wife and son, it is Paulina he accepts to be the hierophant who will guide him to maturity.

And so we arrive at the I AM spirit self, who, having learned to mediate and order these polarities within the kingdom of their soul, is able to transform the world around. Characters like Imogen, Cordelia, Paulina and Marina and, eventually, Prospero, demonstrate how human beings can evolve to be 'the lords and owners of their faces' of whom Shakespeare speaks in sonnet 94. Their rich *subjective* passion and intensity is consecrated to the evolution of our human consciousness towards *objective* Love, the actor/human being of the future.

## *Holding the Centre*

*Suggested planetary sphere: the Sun, centre of activity of the Spirits of Form/Exusiai*

Their activity within our souls generates the psycho-physical sensation expressed in the diphthong: /aʊ/ (ar<u>ou</u>nd)

The Spirits of Form speak:

> *I end<u>ow</u> the altar of your m<u>ou</u>th and throat, with p<u>ow</u>er to open vast and grasp far for-*
> *ward future Venus ah! then reaching back towards far-distant Saturn past ooh!, bending*
> *time ar<u>ou</u>nd its final must-have-always-been-there-from-beginning future s<u>ou</u>nd.*

*Figure 106 Planetary being Sun*

*Figure 107 Diphthong /aʊ/*

# *Gesture of the planetary being Sun: diphthong /aʊ/*

The Sun speaks:

*Heart androgynous aflame: above, below, in front, behind, both arms scan the infinitely outward skies, manly sweep six[90] dancing planets into orbit round my self-sustaining, anchored in my infinitely-inward feminine centre of their dance; choreography encompassing their intersecting rhythms, sounding cycles, gifts of everything, each in its exactly necessary bound. I AM the surrounding centre of the whole. Unless the seed contains already the founding blueprint of the plant, how could it condense divinity through root and stem and leaf to flower? I AM your central star, Beloved. Unless I housed already your divine human blueprint, in my cosmic fount of fire, how could the mystery profound of you find outer form? I fling my planetary organs into orbit all around, orchestrate creation's crown to flower in the complex being of a human 'thou'.*

*The human soul responds:*

*The artist's curse:*
*/aʊ/ my mouth, surrounds, devours, now swallows whole your flaming round. Unable to digest your power, ungrounded and without foundation, I proudly swell above the crowd in search of vain renown. Or else, responsible for everything and everyone, I try to do too much, encompass everything, be everything to everyone and drown!*

*The artist's gift, the I AM:*

*Digesting it, I AM the starry centre of my own creator self, a human sun; governing the planets, mediating their polarities, weaving their potentials from within the microcosmic universe, myself, I know my boundaries, have found what it is mine to do. No less profound, this bounding of the boundless. I love my characters enough to light each one's specific path, illuminate each journey, through knowing my creations Know Myself and in my actor's centre stand my ground.*

*Figure 108 Circle of planetary beings with vowels*

Each polarity within its pair speaks to its opposite. They dance in dialogue. Moving through them, round the circle other conversations stir, weaving the greater dance, back and forth, between, across, around, each contributing their gift within the whole: consummate artistry.

**Chapter 8**

# New planets, new sensibilities and the actor of the future

We have explored some of the archetypes at work in human creativity. We have seen their possible connection with the macrocosmic creativity of the beings associated with the classical conception of our solar system. In *The Actor of the Future 2: Word Made Flesh* * we asked whether the increased complexity of soul that is a feature of our currently evolving consciousness,[91] might be considered as the work of the planetary beings Uranus, Neptune and Pluto, whose bodies at the farthest reaches of our solar system, have been more recently identified. We asked as well whether it is their activity within our souls that finds expression in the diphthong /ɔɪ/ (j<u>oy</u>) and in the umlauted vowels (ö and ü) which do not appear, however, in their pure form in standard English usage. Along with these we now include the umlauted vowel ä and will explore its possible connection to the still more recently discovered planetoid that scientists have designated Chiron.

I can still confirm the insights arising from my explorations into the umlauted vowels ö and ü as described in volume 2. However, as a result of further exploration into the planetary beings, my experience of which vowel is the expression of which planetary being, has evolved. Therefore I withdraw my suggestions in *Word Made Flesh* that the vowel experience of ö might express the activity within our souls of the planetary being Uranus and the vowel experience of ü, the planetary being Neptune. My latest explorations would suggest that these connections be reversed.[92]

What distinguishes all three umlauted vowels is that the placement in the mouth required to channel each of them requires the fusion of two very different placements. Each fusion generates a complex body of sensation through which the vowel is channelled that exactly matches what is generated in our souls as they are carved by our currently evolving, increasingly more complex consciousness. These vowels will act as portals through which we can enter the spectrum of creative impulses that have exploded since the end of Kali Yuga with increased intensity, and allow us to explore how they relate to the influences of these 'newer' planets.[93]

---

* See pp. 143–153.

On the one hand, our souls are ever more released from the binary, traditional divisions into good/bad, hero/villain, black/white, male/female etc. On the other, they feel lost in the confusing, often contradictory, more subtle nuances of meaning and experience that no longer fit the dualistic paradigm. However, through each cycle of this often-agonising struggle, our souls are refined to ever higher levels of discernment: of the future sensibilities these planetary beings would bestow on us. These future sensibilities can be observed in the revolution that has taken place in all the arts since the end of Kali Yuga; and in particular, the art that is the subject of this book.*

As discussed in *The Actor of the Future 1*, the art of acting stands at the threshold of its next evolutionary leap. If it remains on this side of the still broadly acceptable, dualistic body/soul division of the human paradigm, gifted actors will undoubtedly continue to evolve the skills with which they can already so impressively reveal the unconscious depths that drive the body-bound persona. However, such a path of acting cannot encompass the dimensions of the human being that exist beyond the earthbound personality. In this case, we must continue to rely on technological advances to manifest our fantasies or even our perceptions of what lies beyond. However, by their very nature, the resulting images can only keep us trapped in the maya of material appearances. Actors will only take the step towards an *acting of the future* if they cultivate the faculties that allow them to discern and manifest those supersensible dimensions and in doing so, expand the paradigm of what is human.

Till then, although it may have streamed through them unconsciously, we can still appreciate the 'consummate artistry' demonstrated by our greatest mainstream actors which represents the zenith of the possible within that mainstream paradigm.

Steiner left no indications for the CPGs (cosmic psychological gestures)† expressing the objectives of the planetary beings whose bodies move beyond the Saturn sphere. Therefore we will continue to explore connections we have made already between the gestures of the vowels, the sensations that they generate and what

---

* For an exploration of theatre experimentation in the twentieth century see 'The Century of Research' in *The Actor of the Future 1: Tongues of Flame*.

† See *The Actor of the Future 2: Word Made Flesh*, page 123 for a detailed explanation of this term which I evolved from Chekhov's term 'psychological gesture.' Chekhov called a gesture 'psychological' when it embodied and released the inner life of a character. In my experience the eurythmy gestures discerned through Steiner's research enable us to sense into the inner life of beings. Therefore, I have borrowed Chekhov's term and added the word 'cosmic' to convey the sense that eurythmy gestures are a pathway into the psychology of macrocosmic beings.

both Steiner's spiritual-scientific research (and those who have based their work on this) and the research of other psychologically mature astrologers,[94] tell us of the macrocosmic beings of these more recently discovered planets.[*] We have seen how the micro-gestures in our mouths that make it possible to speak the vowels ö and ü [and their English counterparts /ɜ/ (h<u>ea</u>rd), /ju/ (imb<u>ue</u>) /uɪ/ (s<u>wee</u>t)] as well as the diphthong /ɔɪ/ (j<u>oy</u>) generate sensations that confirm what mature research indicates may be bestowed by the beings, Uranus, Neptune and Pluto. These micro-gestures in our mouths and their full-bodied counterparts (eurythmy gestures for the vowels) allow us to discern and express the impulses that work within our souls to crack the old forms open, release new sensibilities, and demand new skills to excavate and manifest them. On this basis, we can explore how the pathways of consciousness channelled by these vowels connect as well to a new artistic paradigm for which actors (indeed, practitioners of all the arts) have been searching since the end of Kali Yuga.

While doing so I could not help but notice how these pathways of consciousness connect with the processes of transformation related to the elements of earth, water, air and fire and called by alchemists the Magnum Opus. In *The Alchemical Actor* my colleague, Dr Jane Gilmer, has framed her exploration of Steiner's, Chekhov's and Artaud's visions for an acting of the future in the context of these processes.[95] The suggested connections between them and the vowels are overwhelmingly confirmed by our psycho-physical experience, as will be shown. Indeed it was the strength of this experience that led me to reverse the first connections I had made in volume 2 between Uranus (ö) and Neptune (ü). To expand the path of research to include the new dimension opened up by Gilmer's work only confirms our deepening sense that the alchemical journey that actors of the future (and indeed all human beings) must embark upon is inspired by the planetary beings we are now considering. Indeed, that it is their activity within our souls that activates the transformation processes, the necessity of which confronts the collective psyche of the human race in the alembic[96] of the planet as a whole. As discussed in *The Actor of the Future 2: Word Made Flesh* the fact that these planets have been only recently identified does not mean they have not been previously present or active in our evolution. However, it signifies a new cycle of their influence that human beings are increasingly aware of them and can consciously work with the potentials they bestow on our development.

Since the stages of this work of transformation are cyclic and proceed ever and again through the same necessities, though on ever higher levels, and through differing

---

[*] *The Actor of the Future 2: Word Made Flesh*, pp. 143–153.

degrees and interactions of their processes, they do not follow in a strict linear progression in which each stage can be discreetly separated from the rest.[97] I present my suggestions therefore in the order that these 'newer' planets have revealed themselves to our perception.

We can observe that each of the suggested vowels in this sequence embodies a complex spectrum of experience that finds expression in the English language as a diphthong (which articulates the vowel movement from one state of soul to another thus enabling us to identify their separate elements) or the pure vowels (ä, ö and ü) that result from a fusion or integration of their complex elements.

It is possible that these two states of diphthong and more complex pure vowel are expressions of the processes identified by alchemists as *separatio* and *coniunctio*. We must ask whether languages that feature ö and ü and (as we examine later) ä, intimate perhaps the future state of consciousness that is identified alchemically as the marriage or *coniunctio* of opposites? This will have been achieved when through our conscious work to penetrate our thinking with our will, we develop the capacity to penetrate in turn the world of our illusory material perceptions and overcome the dualistic paradigm. Is the English language, with its tendency to turn all vowels into diphthongs, a vessel for our present stage of consciousness that must slide between the options, hover on the edge between the states the soul must pass through on its pathway back to wholeness?* Diphthongs simply will not let us leap across the *separatio* before our souls have felt their way through the uncertainties, nor think our intimations of that future state mean we have arrived at conscious unity.

---

* See *The Actor of the Future 4: One More Time* (upcoming 2024) for a detailed exploration of the present stage of human consciousness.

## Our High Work Masters

### *New sensibilities: Sensitivity to what requires refinement, blurs transparency, discernment of imperfection, what is out of tune.*

*Suggested alchemical process is centrally concerned with the fire element or state of warmth* — **calcinatio.**

*Suggested planetary sphere* — *Uranus.*
The activity of this planetary being generates the psycho-physical sensation expressed in the placement of the pure vowel ü, the nearest to which, in the English-speaking soul, are the placements of the diphthongs /ju/ (imb<u>ue</u>) and /uɪ/ (s<u>wee</u>t)

*Uranus speaks:*

> I imb<u>ue</u> the altar of your mouth <u>wi</u>th the <u>wi</u>ll to end<u>u</u>re excr<u>u</u>ciating friction as <u>you</u> fuse the energies of Merc<u>u</u>ry and Saturn in your soul, in order to artic<u>u</u>late the f<u>u</u>ture.

Children born in this hour spend all their lives in a sharper longing for the perfection that awaits them.

'The Angel that Troubled the Waters', Thornton Wilder


The only hope or else despair
Lies in the choice of pyre or pyre —
To be redeemed from fire by fire.

Who then devised the torment? Love.
Love is the unfamiliar Name
Behind the hands that wove
The intolerable shirt of flame
Which human power cannot remove.

*Four Quartets*: 'Little Gidding', T.S. Eliot


Oh, for the wonder that bubbles into my soul,
I would be a good fountain, a good well-head,
Would blur no whisper, spoil no expression.

'Song of a Man Who has Come Through', D.H. Lawrence

## *Suggested alchemical process — calcinatio*

In traditional alchemy the process by which fire consumed the gross substance or dross and burned away impurities, until only a fine ash was left behind, was called the *calcinatio*. In psycho-spiritual alchemy this ordeal is experienced as burning away our soul impurities or moral imperfections. Recognition that we have betrayed the 'deity in our bosom' is felt as burning shame. Conscience rubs our soul against the spirit's measure of its own perfection. This friction generates the fire, the spark of spirit flame which in Greek mythology was brought to earth by Prometheus in order to ignite our human journey towards selfhood.[98] Being burned in this way wakens an excruciating sense of what is imperfect in the work of art we are creating, whether it be external to ourselves or our own moral being. The spark ignites, consuming all that is consumable; this, as esoteric wisdom has always recognised, is only ever the maya of appearances. Nevertheless, the same spectrum of sensation from discomfort, through to agony as the soul is purified, finally emerging from the flames as an instrument of fine discernment, is generated in our mouth when we consciously experience the placement or micro-gesture of the pure vowel ü.

To form the pure vowel ü inside the mouth two gestures wrestle with each other. One moves the tension forward lowering the tongue and causing lips to strain towards the tiniest contraction that still creates a passage for the breath, /ʊ/ (t<u>oo</u>k) /u:/ (sh<u>oe</u>). At the same time the gesture that would tense the tongue to flatten up against the hard palate just behind the teeth, forcing the lips to split sideways in order to release the /ɪ/ (s<u>i</u>p) /i:/ (m<u>e</u>), resists it. The two conflicting gestures fuse. It is as though the lightning flash of Mercury /ɪ/ (s<u>i</u>p) /i:/ (m<u>e</u>) strikes against the resistant flint of Saturn /ʊ/ (t<u>oo</u>k) /u:/ (sh<u>oe</u>); the slow resistance that the planetary being Saturn activates within us as we engage with the density of karma, the leaden weight of all we have brought with us to transform. The sparks arising from this friction ignite the tinder and generate the purifying flames. In the pure vowel ü, it is as though Uranus brings about the *coniunctio* or integration of these two opposing states within our soul. Prometheus has brought the fire. Now we must learn to manage it.

In the English language we do not experience the coniunctio of ü. In the English diphthongs which approximate most nearly, we experience the shift of balance as we slide back and forth: in /ju/ (imb<u>ue</u>) from Mercury to Saturn and in /uɪ/ (s<u>wee</u>t) from Saturn to Mercury. This allows us to experience the process of *calcinatio* as a spectrum or continuum in which we can become aware that we have not yet achieved coniunctio but are still in a process of managing our transformation consciously, learning to control the fire, to sustain our presence in the flames.

The soul can resist the process (expressed in such words as <u>wi</u>nce, f<u>u</u>rious, ref<u>u</u>se) or it can accept the burning that refines it to a higher level of vibration (expressed in such words as <u>wi</u>lling, f<u>u</u>ture, b<u>eau</u>ty).

The eurythmy gesture for ü, the vowel through which, perhaps, Uranus finds expression in our human speech, generates within our full-bodied instrument the tension we experience within our soul between that aspect of itself that is striving upwards to the light and the aspect that resists and drags it down. That tension acts as a kind of tuning fork against which we can sense what is out of tune, imperfect, in what we are creating.

*Figure 109 Eurythmy gesture for pure vowel ü, nearest to English diphthongs /ju/ (imb<u>ue</u>) and /uɪ/ (sw<u>ee</u>t)*

## *Planetary being Uranus speaks—/ju/ (imb**ue**) /uɪ/ (sw**ee**t)*

*Are you mat**u**re enough, Beloved, to end**u**re your spirit's p**u**rifying flame? Kno**wi**ng what I do, kno**wi**ng it is time, into your conf**u**sion I radiate my macrocosmic certainties, stretching **you** bet**wee**n extremes, offering the opport**u**nity to finer t**u**ne your instrument towards transparency! Your gross imp**u**rities must be red**u**ced to ash, only then allo**wi**ng **you** on phoenix **wi**ngs to rise an**ew** and ass**u**me your destiny, O h**u**man being, in f**u**ture be**au**ty, utterly cons**u**med.*

*The human soul responds*

*The artist's curse:*

*Perfectionism! T**wi**sted on the rack bet**wee**n some obsc**u**re, el**u**ding always, disappearing, distant vi**ew** of p**u**rity, and the hideous m**u**tation, over-shado**wi**ng myself, l**u**ring, **wi**lling me towards the sp**ew**ed forth ever n**ew**er revelations from unconscious depths, f**u**tile to esch**ew**, too ast**u**te, too finely t**u**ned to ignore the agony of imperfection, even if I **wi**shed, f**u**rious at my st**u**pidity, unable to end**u**re the excruciating flame.*

*The artist's gift, The I AM:*

*Terrifying M**u**se, I feel you **wi**nce **wi**thin my soul, alerting me to what is out of t**u**ne. Tied to the stake, I **wi**thstand the agony, kno**wi**ng that what f**ue**ls the fire are my ill**u**sions. Thus burned away, my ill**u**minated self emerges p**u**rified. I am the flame that is cons**u**mer and cons**u**med.*

## *New sensibilities: surrender to the unknown and uncertainty, questioning of old values and authority.*

*Suggested alchemical processes are those concerned with the watery element or liquid state —* **solutio**

*Suggested planetary sphere — Neptune.*

The activity of this planetary being generates the psycho-physical sensation expressed in the placement of the pure vowel ö /œ/ the nearest to which, in the English-speaking soul, is the placement of the neutral vowel or schwa /ə/ (above, the man) and its longer form, /ɜ/ (heard).

*Neptune speaks:*

*I work to shape the altar of your mouth and throat into an organ that serves your search for learning how to merge the conflicted energies of Mars and Jupiter.*

There is no end, but addition: the trailing
Consequence of further days and hours
While emotion takes to itself the emotionless
Years of living among the breakage
Of what was believed in as the most reliable —
And therefore the fittest for renunciation.

…

'O voyagers, O seamen,
You who come to port, and you whose bodies
Will suffer the trial and judgement of the sea,
Or whatever event, this is your real destination.'
So Krishna, as when he admonished Arjuna
On the field of battle. Not fare well,
But fare forward, voyagers.

…

Old men ought to be explorers
Here and there does not matter
We must be still and still moving
Into another intensity
For a further union, a deeper communion
Through the dark cold and the empty desolation,
The wave cry, the wind cry, the vast waters
Of the petrel and the porpoise. In my end is my beginning.

*Four Quartets*, 'The Dry Salvages', T.S. Eliot

## *Alchemical process* — solutio

In traditional alchemy the process of dissolving or *solutio* was associated with the element of water and the liquid state. In psycho-spiritual alchemy it signifies the soul's ordeal as the familiar forms of material perception, even the way it sees itself, on which its confidence in its identity was based, dissolve, until it learns to surrender to the limbic space of in between, uncertainty, unknowing. The swan was totemic of this state. Out of the water and not at home on earth, as the soul feels when confronted with the unfamiliar, the swan staggers clumsily. Then as the soul surrenders to its new environment of ever shifting states, at home in the tide of questioning, like the swan in its element, it glides majestic on the waters of discovery. This spectrum of experience is clearly embodied in the placement or micro-gesture in the mouth of the pure vowel ö.

In the micro-gesture of the pure vowel ö /œ/, the tensions in the inner structure of the mouth and lips maintain the outer shape of /ɒ/ (d<u>o</u>t) and /ɔ:/ (<u>awe</u> or f<u>a</u>ll). At the same time, conflicting tensions in the inner structure of the mouth and lips strain against this, to create the resistant edge of /ɛ/ (m<u>e</u>n).* It is as though the fiery thrust of Mars /e/, generated by Uranus through the friction of Mercury and Saturn, as described before, is quenched in the unifying form of Jupiter's embrace /o/. And through the merging of their different conditions, the primal fire condenses to the liquid state, of which water in its liquid form is only one expression. It is easy to relate the fiery energy of Mars to the liquid state if we picture the molten rock and metals in the outer core or mantles of the earth[99] and all the planets closer to the sun and which from time to time spew forth from the crust's embrace, along with the gaseous vapours from which the element of water will finally be formed. We see how lava, just as water does, searches, feeling its way forward† over every detail of the landscape it traverses, questioning if you like, as it takes into account the resistance offered, and filling every hollow, carving others on its quest to find the path that it must take. In doing so it intimately gets to know the landscape it becomes a part of. In the same way we are led to a more intimate connection with the landscape of our lives, both inwardly as well as outwardly, as we feel our way uncertainly around and forward through the hindrances it places in our way. Is this perhaps the gift bestowed on us by the planetary being Neptune?

---

* The English language does not contain this vowel placement in its longer form but turns it into the diphthong /eɪ/ (d<u>a</u>te).

† We cannot help but sense the connection between this gesture and the gesture Steiner called 'feeling forward in the face of hindrances' in the Speech and Drama course. There he refers to it as one of the 6 revelations of speech. It is explored in detail in *The Actor of the Future 2: Word Made Flesh* pp. 31–34.

In the pure vowel ö /œ/, the conflicted gesture in the mouth embodies the continually-coming-into-being, as the liquid state responds to the resistance on its path, and the embrace that allows it to continue to evolve. Perhaps the coniunctio implicit in the ö intimates a future state of oneness that will be achieved when the parts of consciousness arising out of separation and the need to question that they generate are integrated once again. The conflicted placement of this vowel arouses in my body of sensation a spectrum of creative tensions within which my soul confronts discomfort, then finally embraces it, remaining totally awake to a continuity that continually forms itself out of its ongoing dissolution.

In this case however, the English language does not, as in the case of ü, create a diphthong by moving from one component vowel to another. Rather it negotiates a path between them. Thus in the conciliating fashion of the English-speaking soul, it avoids the extreme discomfort that arises when the two component vowels fuse in ö. Rather, it is content to ride in the uncertainty and ambiguity that the placement of the neutral vowel or schwa /ə/ (above) and its long form /ɜ/ (heard) express. We observe it in the stammer or stutter that expresses hesitation. 'Er!' is how we manifest uncertainty. Its interruption to our certain flow of words and thoughts that punctuates our discourse in some degree or other, can be perceived as weakness. We can be grateful though for Neptune's gift that allows us to search anew for what we mean and not continue to confidently mouth outdated, though perhaps once valid, thoughts or unexamined dogma or opinion. When the Mars energy predominates it manifests in the staccato dynamic of a glottal stop, a sensation of being winded in more or less degree. When the Jupiter energy predominates, the soul embraces its uncertainty, expressing this in the more legato vowel /ɜ/ (heard).

The eurythmy gesture for ö, the vowel through which, if we have discerned correctly, Neptune finds expression in our human speech, generates within our full-bodied instrument, the tension we experience within our soul when we prise something open in order to explore what lies within.

*Figure 110 Eurythmy gesture for /ɜ/ (h<u>ear</u>d)*

### *Planetary being Neptune speaks — /ɜ/ (he<u>ar</u>d)*

*Beloved, have you h<u>ear</u>d my call? Can you keep your n<u>er</u>ve as the c<u>er</u>tainties of centuries, all to which the past re<u>ferr</u>ed, dissolve? As I prise open old beliefs, st<u>ir</u> outworn philosophies, aesthetics, dismantle old techniques you will tremble on the v<u>er</u>ge of life's absu<u>r</u>dity. Through p<u>er</u>petual unc<u>er</u>tainty, I s<u>er</u>ve your s<u>ear</u>ch for freedom, b<u>ur</u>st what keeps it shackled, timid, bound, too frightened to em<u>er</u>ge. Do you th<u>ir</u>st enough to jo<u>ur</u>ney f<u>ur</u>ther?*

*The human soul responds:*

*The artist's c<u>ur</u>se*

*Self-doubt, ambiguity, fear of taking risks, paralysis of creativity. As th<u>e</u> w<u>or</u>ld moves forw<u>ar</u>d <u>ear</u>th shakes und<u>er</u> me, no long<u>er</u> firm. Pert<u>ur</u>bed, I doubt the relevance of past exp<u>er</u>i<u>e</u>nce, what w<u>or</u>ked till now. Naked without the old techniques to stand <u>u</u>pon or hide behind, old tal<u>ent</u> fails, p<u>er</u>cep<u>tio</u>n bl<u>ur</u>s. N<u>er</u>v<u>ou</u>sly, I stumbl<u>e</u>, unc<u>er</u>tain I am on the track of any sembl<u>a</u>nce f<u>ur</u>ther than humiliating unsuccess; y<u>ear</u>n to feel myself an artist once again. Well-made plays writt<u>e</u>n to a formul<u>a</u> no long<u>er</u> s<u>er</u>ve; texts that bear witn<u>e</u>ss to a simpl<u>er</u> w<u>or</u>ld of values, clear<u>er</u> sense <u>of</u> right or wrong, <u>of</u> darkness plumbed — once held in an ord<u>er</u>ed univ<u>er</u>se — now appear perv<u>er</u>se, must f<u>ir</u>st be deconstruct<u>ed</u>, simpl<u>er</u> charact<u>er</u>s rev<u>er</u>t to complex lay<u>er</u>s of postmod<u>er</u>n, fragment<u>ed</u> not easy to det<u>er</u>m<u>i</u>ne anti-selves … <u>Er</u>! I n<u>ur</u>se the h<u>ur</u>t of questioning the w<u>or</u>th of — ev<u>en</u> does my art<u>i</u>st self exist — or of my w<u>or</u>k.*

*The artist's gift — the I AM:*

*As I l<u>ear</u>n to ride the s<u>ur</u>ge, I find that I pref<u>er</u> new ways to w<u>or</u>k, disc<u>er</u>ning in unc<u>er</u>tainty a different kind of c<u>er</u>tainty em<u>er</u>ge. 'Direct<u>or</u>s' that — 'block' — th<u>e</u> — play — reh<u>ear</u>sals, t<u>ur</u>n into w<u>or</u>kshops, willingness to live on the creative v<u>er</u>ge, be et<u>er</u>nally a l<u>ear</u>ner, welcome chaos, excavate it, discov<u>er</u> process that releases growing edge disc<u>er</u>nments, try not to confirm too <u>ear</u>ly or pres<u>er</u>ve, be willing to def<u>er</u> f<u>ir</u>st, <u>ear</u>ly judgements of 'p<u>er</u>fect' or 'success'.*

## *New sensibilities: Death of the earthbound personality or egoistic self and resurrection of the higher Self*

*Suggested alchemical processes are centrally concerned with the earth element or solid state* — coagulatio *and* putrefactio

*Suggested planetary sphere* — *Pluto:*

The activity of this planetary being generates the psycho-physical sensations expressed in the placements of the diphthong /ɔɪ/ (j<u>oy</u>).

*Pluto speaks:*

*I twist the altar of your mouth and throat into a tightened c<u>oi</u>l, through which your v<u>oi</u>ce, delivering death's sting, springs up again in j<u>oy</u>.*

In my beginning is my end. In succession
Houses rise and fall, crumble, are extended,
Are removed, destroyed, restored, or in their place
Is an open field, or a factory, or a by-pass.
Old stone to new building, old timber to new fires,
Old fires to ashes, and ashes to the earth
Which is already flesh, fur and faeces,
Bone of man and beast, cornstalk and leaf.
Houses live and die: there is a time for building
And a time for living and generation
And a time for the wind to break the loosened pane
And to shake the wainscot where the field mouse trots
And to shake the tattered arras woven with a silent motto.
…

I said to my soul, be still, and wait without hope
For hope would be hope for the wrong thing; wait without love
For love would be love of the wrong thing; there is yet faith
But the faith and the love and the hope are all in the waiting.
Wait without thought, for you are not ready for thought:
So the darkness shall be the light, and the stillness the dancing.
Whisper of running streams, and winter lightning,
The wild thyme unseen and the wild strawberry,
The laughter in the garden, echoed ecstacy
Not lost, but requiring, pointing to the agony
Of death and birth.

*Four Quartets*, 'Burnt Coker', T.S. Eliot

## *Suggested alchemical processes*—coagulatio *and* putrefactio

In traditional alchemy *putrefactio* or *mortificatio* describe the processes in which the hitherto serviceable form/s or corruptible body/ies into which the creative spirit had condensed and crystallised its work (coagulatio) must disintegrate, decay or be actively dismantled or destroyed in order to release the indestructible and still evolving being into its next cycle of becoming. In psycho-spiritual alchemy the soul that has invested its substance to create that form identifies with it and suffers its destruction as its own death, undergoing the ordeal that mystics through the ages called 'the dark night of the soul'. It is a necessary stage of learning that is only possible because the spirit risks condensing so far into matter that it loses consciousness of its existence (death). It must experience its own apparent nothingness in order to discover how to wrest its reality from death. Having once confirmed its existence to itself at this level, though it faces continuing ordeals and further challenges, it will be forever unassailable.

> So when this corruptible shall have put on incorruption, and this mortal shall have put on immortality, then shall be brought to pass the saying that is written, Death where is thy sting, grave where is thy victory?

> 1 Corinthians, 15:54

Our capacity to sense this spiritual journey is expressed in the micro-gestures in the mouth which enable the soul to move from the ɔ:/ (<u>awe</u>) to the /i:/ (m<u>e</u>) resulting in the dipthong /ɔɪ/ (j<u>oy</u>). This complex journey encompasses the dynamic impulse that arises when the energy of Dionysus/Mercury, embodied in the gesture /i:/ (m<u>e</u>), pierces through the form bestowed by Jupiter/Apollo in the gesture /ɔ:/ (<u>awe</u>), in order to emerge in resurrection spring.* Whether the diphthong tends towards the darkness of the soul's ordeal (embodied in words like v<u>oi</u>d, destr<u>oy</u>) or the release of the spirit into light (embodied in words like j<u>oy</u>) will depend on where the soul is situated in its journey.

---

* Refer to the exploration of the opposing tensions of Dionysus and Apollo and their connection to the planetary beings Mercury and Jupiter, in Chapter 7.

*Figure 111 Eurythmy gesture for /ɔɪ/ (j<u>oy</u>)*

### *Planetary being Pluto speaks—/ɔɪ/ (joy)*

*Are you ready to consign all for which you t**oi**led to the grave? Death to past achievements, fantasies of brilliance, eg**oi**sm's brittle glitter, celebrity's quick shake of shining f**oi**l! Do not rec**oi**l, Beloved! Nothing that is real can be destr**oy**ed. To crush the fruit seems cruel, yet from it springs the consecrated **oi**l. The corpse desp**oi**led, the severed, putrefying head, its hollow garg**oy**le eyes through which blind maggots crawl; it is the s**oi**l from which the living thoughts can spring.*

*The human soul responds:*

*The artist's curse:*

*Rec**oi**ling from the slightest critical remark, delivering death's p**oi**son sting, too desperately embr**oi**led in its writhe and wring, its mocking n**oi**se, to make the ch**oi**ce to hear the positive or sober v**oi**ce. In death's dark c**oi**ls I spiral down into the blackened v**oi**d of what's the p**oi**nt — depression! Or catching a compliment, spiral up again on an effusive word, a flattery, into elation's transitory j**oy** — convinced it is a work of genius, I am a genius — riding manic high, consumed in flames that signal the inevitable, disapp**oi**nting final fizzle back into the v**oi**d.*

*The artist's gift — the I AM:*
*For this was I app**oi**nted l**oy**al servant of your r**oy**al genius, Creator of the Universe. P**oi**sed at the graveside, the an**oi**nted one accepts your criticism j**oy**fully, Beloved, willing to die to the eg**oi**stic self, bore down into imperfection, deconstructing, not afraid to sp**oi**l it further, j**oi**n it in the grave: gainfully employed in Pluto's dark domain, until my eyes adjusting, p**oi**nt the pathway out.*

## *Further intimations of the future: the wounded healer*

If it is not *the* first, *Titus Andronicus* is certainly one of Shakespeare's earliest creations. In it he depicts a world bereft of mercy or forgiveness in which the instinct for revenge determines all interactions and events. In it he sounds the first notes of the theme that is central to his whole creative life: how can revenge be transformed into forgiveness? In the Roman Empire in the reign of Saturninus, Titus Andronicus is a patriot who sacrifices everything for Rome. Though he acts in accordance with his understanding of the rule of justice, his inability to render mercy to the captive Gothic Queen, Tamora, sets in motion a tale of retribution and such mindless cruelty it is as though the demons of revenge themselves unleash their fury in the world. Titus is obsessed with justice and acts according to its rules, expecting to be treated on its terms. Instead, at every point, he finds only retribution and betrayal. At length, driven mad by pain, he writes letters to the gods — Saturn, Apollo (Sun), Mercury, Mars, Artemis (Moon), Jupiter (Jove), and Pluto — demanding justice. He attaches them to arrows and orders his attendants to shoot them at the heavens. Their pleas for justice are unheeded, the arrows fall to earth, and the feast of horrors is resumed.

It is a brilliant theatrical conceit: a many-levelled metaphor that illustrates the dilemma of the Kali Yuga human being cut off from the beingness of stars and planets. Any superstitious hopes that those unresponsive bodies occupying empty space might hear our prayers are dashed as our pleas for justice fall upon deaf ears, provoking outrage and a final cynical rejection that casts us back upon our isolated selves.

At the other end of his creative journey in *The Tempest*, Shakespeare shows how Prospero finally transforms his will for power. He prepares to return to his dukedom and serve the people that he once abandoned in his lust for the knowledge that would deliver him that power. Having recognised a power greater than the power to impose his will, he rejects the 'rough magic' of his art and surrenders to a different kind of magic: the audience's mercy. In another brilliant theatrical conceit, Shakespeare reverses the image of the unconscious human being shooting arrows at an unresponsive cosmos. Having seen at last that the darkness he condemned and is in need of mercy lies within himself, Prospero finds the 'deity in [his] bosom' and is subsequently able to forgive those who had wronged him. Through his own healing transformation, he discovers that the new pathway to the mercy of the gods must be sought within the microcosm of himself; only through our human agency can we reconnect maturely with the macrocosm and thereby bring salvation to the earth.

The r<u>a</u>rer action is in virtue than in vengeance.

His final deed is to throw himself, with all his faults, upon the mercy of the audience and offer them the opportunity that he was given: to forgive.

> And my ending is desp<u>air</u>
> Unless I be relieved by pr<u>ayer</u>
> Which pierces so that it assaults
> Mercy itself and frees all faults.
> As you from crimes would pardoned be
> Let your indulgence set me free.

Like the metaphor of Titus shooting arrows at an empty heaven, this one speaks to us on many levels. One must be to actors who, being dedicated to the evolution of our art towards the future, are also dedicated to the evolution of ourselves, since one cannot succeed without the other. Like Prospero, we can only place ourselves and our attempts in all humility before the audience and beseech the audience that as they pray for mercy for themselves, so they may be merciful to us.

We have already met the English diphthong/ɛə/ (r<u>a</u>rer, desp<u>air</u>, pr<u>ayer</u>) that spreads its gentle blessing, delicate as air, through Prospero's redemptive words, when we explored the indication Steiner gives to actors in relationship to weeping. In Chapter 3 of *Word Made Flesh* we could sense how the micro-gesture in the mouth that forms the pure vowel (as in German) ä, is nearest to the English diphthong /ɛə/(d<u>are</u>). We could sense also how it perfectly embodies that spectrum of experience that moves between *resistance* to the pain our wounds inflict and *surrender* when we finally allow ourselves to accept and feel the pain. We have seen how, in order to protect ourselves from feeling pain, we hold our breath, but in doing so, we dampen *all* our feelings. However, if we surrender to it and allow ourselves to feel it, the breath that we had held releases, allowing us to feel our other feelings once again as well.[100] This grants the wisdom and compassion that allow the soul, matured by its experience, to channel it in healing service.

In 1977 another body in the heavens was identified, orbiting between the planets Saturn and Uranus. It was assigned the name of *Chiron* after the centaur in Greek mythology from whose story Jung identified the 'wounded healer' archetype. Astrologers who work with the transpersonal dimension of psychology immediately sensed in the psychic field that attracted scientists (whether consciously or not) to choose that name, the presence of the new healing paradigm that had begun to surface in the consciousness of human beings at that time. Its central intuition is that only we can heal who have ourselves been wounded and through our own pain can understand the suffering of others. Like Prospero, only through acceptance of our woundedness, transforming the instinct to blame and seek revenge, can we release the blessings it bestows on us and bring release to others.

We have discussed many times how each of the English vowels have a tendency to move within a spectrum of placement that turns them into diphthongs. This reflects the mobile state of consciousness that, at its noblest, is the gift of the English-speaking soul, whose destiny it is to keep absorbing other languages and accents, along with the states of soul that they embody. My own research leads me to suggest that the micro-gesture of the German pure vowel ä (nearest in English to the diphthong /ɛə/) contains the dynamics of experience suggestive of this wounded healer archetype. For our wounds to be consecrated and become the sacred portals through which healing can flow into the world, we must first have been released from their power over us. This can only happen by acknowledging and not resisting them: letting ourselves experience their pain in order to explore and understand the lessons suffering would teach us. Only then can we transcend it and receive the blessings that our woundedness bestows. This is only possible when we allow the divinity within, our I AM self, to be active in our souls.

This archetype appears already in Sophocles' depiction of the character of Oedipus.[101] In *Oedipus Tyrannus*, after initially resisting, Oedipus surrenders to the agony of recognising the unwitting crimes he has committed in his attempt to flee his destiny. He finally accepts his primal wound: rejection by his parents at his birth. Then, in *Oedipus at Colonus*, through his years of atonement, we witness him achieve the enlightenment enabling him to die a 'wondrous' death, which it was prophesied would bless the community in which his body is entombed.

We find this spectrum of sensation encompassing the journey from resistance to surrender and release embodied in the micro-gesture of the English diphthong /ɛə/ (despair, prayer). Could this vowel be the vocal expression of this archetype within our souls? And, as astrologers suggest, might the being of the Chiron planetoid be the macrocosmic bearer of this archetype?

## *New sensibilities: Surrender to the wounding in order to penetrate the pain, transcend it and in the process develop empathy for others and the power to heal.*

*Suggested alchemical processes are centrally connected to the airy element or gaseous state —* **evaporatio** *and* **distillatio.**

*Suggested planetary sphere — Chiron*
The activity of this planetary being generates the psycho-physical sensations expressed in the placement of the pure vowel (as in the German ä) which is nearest in English to the placements of the diphthong /ɛə/ (d<u>are</u>).

*Chiron speaks:*

*I prep<u>a</u>re the altar of your mouth to b<u>ea</u>r the spirits journey through your soul's desp<u>ai</u>r to its release in <u>ai</u>r.*

We move above the moving tree
In light upon the figured leaf
And hear upon the sodden floor
Below, the boarhound and the boar
Pursue their pattern as before
But reconciled among the stars

…

The inner freedom from the practical desire,
The release from action and suffering, release from the inner
And the outer compulsion, yet surrounded
By a grace of sense, a white light still and moving,
*Erhebung** without motion, concentration
Without elimination, both a new world
And the old made explicit, understood
In the completion of its partial ecstacy,
The resolution of its partial horror.
Yet the enchainment of past and future
Woven in the weakness of the changing body,
Protects mankind from heaven and damnation
Which flesh cannot endure.
Time past and time future
Allow but a little consciousness.
To be conscious is not to be in time
But only in time can the moment in the rose garden,
The moment in the arbour where the rain beat,
The moment in the draughty church at smokefall
Be remembered; involved with past and future.
Only through time time is conquered.

*Four Quartets*, 'Burnt Norton', T.S. Eliot

I say that we are wound
With mercy round and round
As if with air: the same
Is Mary, more by name.
She, wild web,
Wondrous robe,
Mantles the guilty globe,

---

* German word meaning 'exultation'.

Since God has let dispense

Her prayers, his providence.

Nay, more than almoner,

The sweet alms' self is her

And men are meant to share

Her life as life does air.

'The Blessed Virgin compared to the Air we Breathe', Gerard Manley Hopkins

In traditional alchemy the processes centrally connected with the airy element or gaseous state were called *evaporatio* and *distillatio*, which move back and forth across the threshold of the watery element or liquid state. When fire was applied to the liquid state in which the grosser elements had been dissolved, these were left behind as dross when that which could be refined, evaporated into air. There, in that airy realm, what takes place cannot be followed by material perception. Only when it reappears, condensed into the drops of rain or dew do we understand that processes beyond our perception or control have worked their magic. In psycho-spiritual alchemy, when the fire of our spirit (the I AM) has done all it can to create the conditions necessary (by actively engaging in the other purifying processes) then the airy stage of transformation can unfold. This takes place in a region, which, as we have said, is like the airy element and not accessible to everyday perception. It exists outside of time and space, until it is distilled into the tears that signify the wisdom that accompanies release and is experienced as grace.

Shakespeare hints at this in Portia's famous courtroom speech from *The Merchant of Venice* when she exhorts Shylock to forgive Antonio, but, in doing so, exposes the racial hatred of the Christians, whose hardened hearts are as much in need of softening as Shylock's.

The quality of mercy is not strained

It droppeth as the gentle rain from heaven

Upon the place beneath.[102]

If there were any doubt that Shakespeare's genius was nurtured in the conscious knowledge of these mysteries we need only look at the ending of his *Cymbeline,* from which we earlier imagined the portrayal of the scene in which Posthumus Leonatus falls asleep, weighed down with the torment of remorse.* There in the world of spirit, the souls of his dead family plead on his behalf that Jupiter show mercy on their struggling son and brother. We saw that Posthumus, so mired in guilt, is not ready yet to understand that the trials he presently endures are to prepare him for the grace that Jupiter informs him will eventually

---

* See final section of Chapter 4: Imagining theatre in the future.

heal his agony. In the meantime Imogen, the wife he had accused unjustly of adultery and whom he sought to punish by ordering her death, has gone through further stages in her own initiation and in the final scene is able to forgive her husband. Now, before the court of Cymbeline, the soothsayer interprets the enigmatic words inscribed on the tablet Jupiter had left with Posthumus as evidence of His divine visitation: the significance of which could not be grasped by his ordinary consciousness when he awoke and which foretold the grace that would enfold him once he had evolved to the level that allowed him to receive it.

> *Soothsayer*: [Reads] 'When as a lion's whelp shall, to himself unknown, without
> seeking find, and be embraced by a piece of tender air; and when from a stately
> cedar shall be lopped branches, which, being dead many years, shall after revive, be
> jointed to the old stock, and freshly grow; then shall Posthumus end his miseries,
> Britain be fortunate and flourish in peace and plenty.'
> Thou, Leonatus, art the lion's whelp;
> The fit and apt construction of thy name,
> Being Leonatus, doth import so much.
> [To Cymbeline]
> The piece of tender air, thy virtuous daughter,
> Which we call 'mollis aer;' and 'mollis aer'
> We term it 'mulier:' which 'mulier' I divine
> Is this most constant wife; who, even now,
> Answering the letter of the oracle,
> Unknown to you, unsought, were clipp'd about
> With this most tender air.

This airy process is expressed in the micro-gesture in our mouth that allows us to experience the state of soul embodied in the pure vowel ä. Its placement only manifests in English usage in its short form /æ/ (m<u>a</u>n) which, like a semitone, marks a stage between the paradisal flow of oneness /ɑː/ (st<u>a</u>r) and the martial energy of /ɛ/ (m<u>e</u>n). The vowel /æ/ arrests the flow, making one conscious of something other than oneself, but does not assert itself more forcefully like /ɛ/ to bring about a separation. To lengthen /æ/, as in ä, we must sustain that placement for as long as we extend our breath, which is difficult. In doing so the tension of that placement spreads throughout the corridor inside the mouth, crossing the threshold at the teeth and we sense that we are moving forward, riding on a cushion of air, up and over the sensation that the placement generates, towards … And as we soar above and over the discomfort of the tension generated by the placement /æ/ (m<u>a</u>n), without being able to get rid of it, we feel ourselves inexorably drawn towards and sometimes even able to achieve the forward placements in the mouth of /ɒ/ (d<u>o</u>t) and /ɔː/

(<u>awe</u>) which intimate our future conscious union. Like the other umlauted vowels, the micro-gesture of the /æ/ embodies the opposing tensions generated when a placement at or from behind the teeth fuses with a placement forward of the teeth.

This helps me understand why, in the Speech and Drama course, Steiner places ä amongst the other vowels ö and ü that lie forward of the centre placement of the teeth [/ɪ/ (<u>si</u>p) and /iː/ (m<u>e</u>)]. Whether we take our starting point from the forward placement of the lips in /ɒ/ (d<u>o</u>t) and /ɔː/ (<u>awe</u>) and then inside the mouth assume the placement /æ/ (m<u>a</u>n) or work back the other way, maintaining the inner structure of the mouth in /æ/ (m<u>a</u>n) while we strive to achieve the outer structure of the lips in /ɒ/ (d<u>o</u>t) and /ɔː/ (<u>awe</u>), or if we simply try to extend the short vowel /æ/ (man) and make it long then we find ourselves inexorably moving forward on that stream of breath, through a vowel corridor encompassing a spectrum of experience that intimates the future. Whichever our approach, to extend the vowel in its longer form we must traverse the threshold of the /ɪ/ (<u>si</u>p) and /iː/ (m<u>e</u>). In doing so we waken to the ego presence which alone can make this crossing between past and future consciously by engaging in the purifying work that is the preparation for that grace. It softens the hardened edges of the /æ/ (m<u>a</u>n) and /ɛ/ (m<u>e</u>n) or the English diphthong /eɪ/ (gr<u>a</u>ce) allowing the vowel to spread its balm and heal the wound of separation. Sensitivity to this deeper wisdom in the sounds allows us to express this softer edge, explore this spectrum of experience when speaking words like 'bless', 'gentle', 'grace' or 'well', as in the closing lines from Eliot's *Four Quartets*, which quote the mystic Julian of Norwich.

And all shall be w<u>e</u>ll
And all manner of thing shall be w<u>e</u>ll.

Of course our everyday relationship to speech requires no such commitment, nor does it reveal such mysteries. We are accustomed to speaking without any conscious presence of the I AM in our soul. Then this vowel or diphthong communicates not the activity that has engaged with time and is now released by grace into the timeless but only the vacuous escape from time to <u>ai</u>ry fantasy.

Something of this vowel corridor, as it manifests in the English language in the diphthong /ɛə/, is embodied in the sequence of eurythmy gestures, showing how the soul initially contracts away from the paradisal open throat of /ɑː/ (st<u>ar</u>), entering the spectrum of the vowels from /æ/ (m<u>a</u>n) to /ɛ/ (m<u>e</u>n), and releasing in the final phoneme of the dipthong /ɛə/. This progression embodies the soul's journey out of primal oneness into separation, which entails both grief and the subsequent release from it. Yet, in that frustrating inability to pin the English diphthong down, the phonetic symbol /ɛə/ also indicates how the soul feels its way even closer to the boundary the lips provide in /ɒ/ (d<u>o</u>t) and /ɔː/ (<u>awe</u> or f<u>all</u>) to reach the neutral vowel or *schwa* which, as we have seen, is the shortened form of /ɜ/ (h<u>ear</u>d).

*Figure 112 Eurythmy gesture for /ɛə/ (air)*

***Planetary being Chiron speaks—ä, English dipthong /ɛə/ (air).***

*I prepare your soul to bear the cross, Beloved, undergo the stations, descend each stair into the nadir of despair and be impaled there, throat aching for the grace of heaven's rain until the 'it is finished' is proclaimed and your spirit is released in gentle everywhere.*

The human soul responds:

*The artist's curse: Like Oedipus, before the citizens of Thebes, tear out my eyes, lay bare my soul, my gaping wounds for all to stare, drag my audience — no chance to look away — into my beyond-repair-defeated lion-lair, force them to sit beside me there, share my agony of shame, heaped up despair, to stare it in the face, scare them with my garish nightmare, reminding them of theirs. Or else invite them to escape, ensnare them in the tinsel glare, the airy fairy nothingness of son et lumière.*

*The artist's gift — the I AM: Through the reality vicarious that I create, share with me, Beloved, your Mary mother of us all, health-bringing power that bears us through the pain until we reach the wellness once again, and save us all.*[103]

Can artists heal who have not known suffering themselves? Yet if our wounds are open and festering, or lurking like tumours spreading unrecognised within our depths, our art will only mirror to an audience their own pathologies. Although this may be a necessary stage along the path to healing, it does not of itself make whole.

One of the most beautiful expressions of the 'wounded healer' archetype is Thornton Wilder's four-minute play, *The Angel that Troubled the Waters*. Based on a story from St John's Gospel, Chapter 5, it depicts a wounded healer (the newcomer) who prays to be healed of the affliction that he feels impairs his ability to carry on his healing work. Amongst the other invalids, he waits at the pool for the angel to stir the waters that bring healing to the first one who enters them. The angel bars his entry to the pool. As the healer pleads in desperation, the moment of alignment for that day has passed. The angel must depart.

> *Angel*: I must make haste. Already the sky is afire with the gathering host, for it is the hour of the new song among us. The earth itself feels the preparation in the skies and attempts its hymn. Children born in this hour spend all their lives in a sharper longing for the perfection that awaits them.

> *The Newcomer*: Oh, in such an hour was I born, and doubly fearful to me is the flaw in my heart. Must I drag my shame, Prince and singer, all my days more bowed than my neighbour?

> *The Angel (stands for a moment in silence)*: Without your wound where would your power be? It is your very remorse that makes your low voice tremble into the hearts of men. The very angels themselves cannot persuade the wretched and blundering children on earth as can one human being broken on the wheels of living. In Love's service only the wounded soldiers can serve. Draw Back!

# Concluding thoughts

The fusion of micro-gestures in the mouth which channels each umlauted vowel involves the marriage either of a vowel placement that lies behind and therefore on the way towards or at the very threshold of the sense of separated self-achieved at /i:/ (m_e_), with a placement that lies in front of it and strains with that very consciousness attained by separation to be united once again. That the strong sensations generated by these vowel placements are identical with the struggle and discomfort of our current 'consciousness' or 'spiritual soul' experience only serves to further validate a central premise underlying all these books. It was explored in Chapter 1 of *The Art of Speech* and Chapter 2 of *Word Made Flesh:* vowel and inner life of soul are facets of the one experience that over time our separated intellect has caused to be detached but whose essential unity can be recovered by such conscious processes as those suggested in these books. It is not surprising then, as we have shown in Chapter 3, in our explorations of the comic style, that the same strong sensations of struggle and discomfort generated by these vowel placements are the means by which our souls progress towards the healing that is the final goal of comedy.

The micro-gestures of the vowels and the CPGs of the planetary beings are means by which the actor of the future can explore and penetrate, sphere by sphere, the consciousness our High Work Masters have bestowed and will continue to bestow on us. Chapters 6 and 7 have suggested that this consciousness has always worked through human beings to inspire the creative processes that constitute our cultural achievements and our lives. However, until now, artists have been largely unaware of their source; often experiencing that they are obsessed or possessed by what drives them to create. Now, since the end of Kali Yuga, we will increasingly be able to collaborate with the macrocosmic beings who bestow their soul capacities upon the human soul.

In these final chapters I have sought to open doors and windows to the chambers in our soul within which we may experience our own creative process consciously. I have done so by suggesting how vowels themselves can be a meditative path for actors/artists that expands to the periphery of our known planetary system and the beings who inhabit it. In *Volume 4* we will expand beyond the vowels and the planetary spheres to the gestures of the consonants that are the portals through which we can investigate the starry beings of the zodiac. They are the macrocosmic artists inspiring human beings to fashion the evolving cycles of our human culture: successive civilisations that are the vessels in which, through time's long ages, maturing human beings may increasingly collaborate with them in the work of art that is ourselves: the Magnum Opus.

# Appendix A

# A phenomenological approach

The stream of thought referred to as phenomenology is being researched currently within a range of disciplines by academics who see that it provides the philosophical foundations for a new paradigm. It is being sought with increasing urgency, as human beings face the extinction of our planet as a consequence of following the paradigm pursued since the Renaissance. In relation to theatre practice, phenomenology is the academic rationale behind the increasing recognition in tertiary level trainings that valid research can be performance led.

Phenomenology contrasts with the rational scientific methodology that has dominated Western consciousness since the Enlightenment. The latter strives for objective knowledge of phenomena — things in themselves — by claiming to exclude the observer's contribution to the nature of reality: which can then be deemed untainted by subjective bias. This approach stems from what phenomenology identifies as a false dichotomy made by the observer's consciousness between itself (which it designates as the subjective element) and the so-called world outside itself (the objective element); false because it fails to acknowledge that the very belief it can exclude the subjective in its attempt to achieve objective knowledge is in itself a subjective standpoint that affects the reality perceived.

Phenomenology is a philosophical position (first articulated as such by the philosophers Husserl and his pupil Heidegger) that seeks to validate the essential contribution to reality made by the participants' direct experience as channelled through their senses. In this view the subject's consciousness is not something separated from the world but arising out of and a part of it. When applied to theatre practice, phenomenology acknowledges the embodied perception of the artist as a no less valid object of investigation than the laws of time and space that govern the Newtonian conception. The following words were written by Ted Toadvine in the context of an exploration of phenomenology as the basis for a new approach to environmental science and ecology.[104] However we cannot fail to recognise their implication for the actor's art.

> My body's struggle to express would then be nothing other than the world's struggle to express itself through me, as if I were an organ of this single massive body named Nature. Human being might be thought of as nature's engine of self-expression, its own coming to consciousness.

Already, two centuries before, Goethe had applied this approach to the world of living form, and described it, in relation to his scientific work, as a 'delicate empiricism'. His term implies the need to approach phenomena with a feminine sensibility that would allow nature to reveal herself to the beholder, rather than the masculine tendency to analyse in order to control. The words 'masculine' and 'feminine' are used in this context to distinguish archetypal qualities that are explored in depth in Chapter 7 and are distinct from gender issues of male and female.

Goethe's approach was articulated further by Steiner who expanded the range of sensory experience beyond what can be channelled only through the traditional five senses. He identified at least twelve senses, including those that enable us to sense within our own body (warmth, life, balance, movement), those that channel our experience of the outer world (sight, taste, smell, touch) and those that channel more subtle or supersensible experience (hearing, word, thought, ego).[*] On this basis, he developed a path of spiritual cognition that progresses through the stages of Imagination, Inspiration and Intuition,[105] which depends for its validity on the seeker's ability to penetrate what they experience with a clarity of thought and judgement no less rigorous than that applied by scientists to material phenomena.

When developed, our ability to sense our own beingness is what Steiner called the twelfth sense or the sense of ego. Through it we become ever more receptive to the beingness within phenomena. Therefore, *detached observer* consciousness, on which the materialistic scientific paradigm depends, will never know the highest level of reality, which is its 'beingness' or 'selfness', since this can only be experienced by the beingness or selfness of another.

---

* See *The Art of Acting,* pages 194–199.

**Appendix B**

# Table of phonetic symbols

*International Phonetic Alphabet (IPA)*
*Standard Received English (SRE)*

Vowels

*Simple or pure vowels*

/ɪ/ (s<u>i</u>p)

/iː/ (m<u>e</u>)

/ɛ/ (m<u>e</u>n)

/æ/ (m<u>a</u>n)

/ʌ/ (c<u>u</u>p)

/ɑː/ (st<u>ar</u>)

/ɒ/ (d<u>o</u>t)

/ɔː/ (<u>awe</u> or f<u>all</u>)

/ʊ/ (t<u>oo</u>k)

/uː/ (sh<u>oe</u>)

/ɜ/ (h<u>er</u>d)

/ə/ (<u>a</u>way) schwa, neutral vowel

Diphthongs

/eɪ/ (d<u>a</u>te)

/oʊ/ (n<u>o</u>)

/aɪ/ (l<u>i</u>fe)

/aʊ/ (<u>ou</u>t)

/ɔɪ/ (j<u>oy</u>)

/ɪə/ (<u>ear</u>)

/ɛə/ (d<u>are</u>)

/ɔə/ (d<u>oor</u>)

/ʊə/ (t<u>our</u>)

/ju/ (imb<u>ue</u> or f<u>ew</u>)

/uɪ/ (sw<u>ee</u>t)

Consonants

/ŋ/ (so<u>ng</u>) ng

/ʍ/ (<u>wh</u>en) wh

/θ/ (<u>th</u>ing) th

/ð/ (<u>th</u>e) th

/ʃ/ (<u>s</u>ugar) sh

/ʒ/ (plea<u>s</u>ure) sh

/tʃ/ (<u>ch</u>ild) ch

/dʒ/ (<u>j</u>udge) j

/ɫ/ (wa<u>ll</u>) ll

/j/ (<u>y</u>ear) y

/r/ (rolled or trilled as in Scottish dialect) r

/ɹ/ (RP—<u>r</u>ing) r

*Please note: phonetic symbols for all other consonants remain as per the usual alphabet.*

# Extra texts for Chapter 6, The stages of life

## 'Nutting'

Among the woods,
And o'er the pathless rocks, I forc'd my way
Until, at length, I came to one dear nook
Unvisited, where not a broken bough
Droop'd with its wither'd leaves, ungracious sign
Of devastation, but the hazels rose
Tall and erect, with milk-white clusters hung.
A virgin scene!—A little while I stood,
Breathing with such suppression of the heart
As joy delights in; and with wise restraint
Voluptuous, fearless of a rival, eyed
The banquet, or beneath the trees I sate
Among the flowers, and with the flowers I play'd;
A temper known to those, who, after long
And weary expectation, have been blessed
With sudden happiness beyond all hope.
Perhaps it was a bower beneath whose leaves
The violets of five seasons re-appear
And fade, unseen by any human eye,
Where fairy water-breaks do murmur on
For ever, and I saw the sparkling foam,
And with my cheek on one of those green stones
That, fleeced with moss, beneath the shady trees,
Lay round me scatter'd like a flock of sheep,
I heard the murmur and the murmuring sound,
In that sweet mood when pleasure loves to pay
Tribute to ease, and, of its joy secure,
The heart luxuriates with indifferent things,
Wasting its kindliness on stocks and stones,
And on the vacant air. Then up I rose,
And dragged to earth both branch and bough, with crash
And merciless ravage; and the shady nook

Of hazels, and the green and mossy bower
Deform'd and sullied, patiently gave up
Their quiet being: and unless I now
Confound my present feelings with the past,
Even then, when from the bower I turn'd away
Exulting, rich beyond the wealth of kings
I felt a sense of pain when I beheld
The silent trees and the intruding sky.—

Then, dearest Maiden!, move along these shades
In gentleness of heart; with gentle hand
Touch—for there is a spirit in the woods.


### 'Skating'

In the frosty season, when the sun
Was set, and, visible for many a mile,
The cottage windows through the twilight blazed,
I heeded not the summons: happy time
It was indeed for all of us; for me
It was a time of rapture. Clear and loud
The village clock tolled six. I wheel'd about,
Proud and exulting, like an untired horse
That cares not for its home. All shod with steel,
We hiss'd along the polish'd ice in games
Confederate, imitative of the chase
And woodland pleasures,—the resounding horn,
The pack loud-bellowing, and the hunted hare.
So through the darkness and the cold we flew,
And not a voice was idle: with the din
Meanwhile the precipices rang aloud;
The leafless trees and every icy crag
Tingled like iron; while the distant hills
Into the tumult sent an alien sound
Of melancholy, not unnoticed, while the stars,
Eastward, were sparkling clear, and in the west
The orange sky of evening died away.

Not seldom from the uproar I retired
Into a silent bay, or sportively
Glanced sideway, leaving the tumultuous throng,

To cut across the image of a star
That gleam'd upon the ice; and oftentimes,
When we had given our bodies to the wind,
And all the shadowy banks on either side
Came sweeping through the darkness, spinning still
The rapid line of motion, then at once
Have I, reclining back upon my heels,
Stopp'd short; yet still the solitary cliffs
Wheel'd by me, even as if the earth had roll'd
With visible motion her diurnal round.
Behind me did they stretch in solemn train,
Feebler and feebler, and I stood and watch'd
Till all was tranquil as a summer sea.

from William Wordsworth's The Prelude

## 'Legend'

The blacksmith's boy went out with a rifle
and a black dog running behind.
Cobwebs snatched at his feet,
rivers hindered him,
thorn branches caught at his eyes to make him blind
and the sky turned into an unlucky opal,
but he didn't mind.
I can break branches, I can swim rivers, I can stare out
any spider I meet,
said he to his dog and his rifle.

The blacksmith's boy went over the paddocks
with his old black hat on his head.
Mountains jumped in his way,
rocks rolled down on him,
and the old crow cried, You'll soon be dead.
And the rain came down like mattocks.
But he only said,
I can climb mountains, I can dodge rocks, I can shoot an old crow any day,
and he went on over the paddocks.

When he came to the end of the day, the sun began falling,
Up came the night ready to swallow him,
like the barrel of a gun,
like an old black hat,
like a black dog hungry to follow him.
Then the pigeon, the magpie and the dove began wailing
and the grass lay down to pillow him.
His rifle broke, his hat blew away and his dog was gone and the sun was falling.

But in front of the night, the rainbow stood on the mountain,
just as his heart foretold.
He ran like a hare,
he climbed like a fox;
he caught it in his hands, the colours and the cold—
like a bar of ice, like the column of a fountain,
like a ring of gold.
The pigeon, the magpie and the dove flew up to stare,
and the grass stood up again on the mountain.

The blacksmith's boy hung the rainbow on his shoulder
instead of his broken gun.
Lizards ran out to see, snakes made way for him,
and the rainbow shone as brightly as the sun.
All the world said, Nobody is braver, nobody is bolder,
nobody else has done
anything equal to it. He went home as easy as could be
with the swinging rainbow on his shoulder.

Judith Wright

# Additional volumes in this series

## Tongues of Flame

*A meta-historical approach to Drama*

*The Actor of the Future 1*

Preface

Introduction

Finding the true names of things: reading the script—poetic and literal consciousness

Chapter 1 — The key to the Mysteries: The founding myth of Western Drama

Chapter 2 — 'It takes so many thousand years to wake': Drama at the threshold

Chapter 3 — When will the lost word be found? Crossing the threshold: why a theatre of the word?

Chapter 4 — 'The fabulous wings unused': towards a drama of the future

Chapter 5 — 'We shall not cease from exploration'

The century of research: experimental theatre practice in the twentieth century

- Pioneering initiatives
- Steiner's contribution
- Steiner' s Mystery Dramas

Epilogue

The crucible of art

Between Earth and Heaven

# Word Made Flesh

*The Actor of the Future 2*

Chapter 1
Building the bridge between gesture, voice and speech

Chapter 2
Sound Experience (1): Expanding the horizon of the Vowels
Ensouling the vowel
Vowel moods from Shakespeare
Mapping a character's inner journey through a progression of the vowels

Chapter 3
Sound Experience (2): Vowels as key to laughing and weeping

Chapter 4
Sound Experience (3): Character-types and vowels
Blood and nerve-sense polarities
From soul type to individual soul
Approaching the planetary beings—vowels as a bridge to higher worlds

Chapter 5
Our High Work Masters (1): Vowels and the planetary beings

Chapter 6
Our High Work Masters (2): Vowels and the planetary beings in Shakespeare's *King Lear*

Chapter 7
Our High Work Masters (3): Consonants and the starry beings of the zodiac

Chapter 8
Our High Work Masters (4): Consonants and the starry beings of the zodiac in Shakespeare's *King Lear*

# One More Time

An actor's journey through humanity's backstory

*The Actor of the Future 4*

(publication planned 2024-5)

Introduction

Chapter 1
The act of creation
Meditations on the zodiacal archetypes and their relationship to the consonants.

Chapter 2
Ancient Indian—the Age of Cancer

Chapter 3
Ancient Persian—the Age of Gemini

Chapter 4
Egyptian/Babylonian—the Age of Taurus

Chapter 5
Greek/Roman/Mediaeval—the Age of Aries

Chapter 6
Renaissance into present times—the Age of Pisces

Chapter 7
Looking to the future—the Age of Aquarius and the Age of Capricorn

Epilogue

# Appendix E

# DVD Series

These DVD presentations complement *The Actor of the Future*, volumes 1-4 demonstrating in a living way, many of the themes and moments they explore. It must be understood that the etheric dimension of the speech technique and Chekhov methodology cannot be recorded by a physical machine.

DVD 1: *Human Being! Know Thyself: The birth of the Greek drama out of the mysteries of Eleusis* — 2 hours

DVD 2: *The Place of the Skull: Initiation in the age of the Consciousness Soul from Shakespeare to Modern Times* — 2 hours

DVD 3: *'The Fabulous Wings Unused': Humanity at the threshold.*

*'Thank God our time is now when wrong comes up to face us everywhere': Recognising what it means for the whole human race to cross the threshold* — 2 hours

Available online at the Rudolf Steiner Book Centre

https://www.rudolfsteinerbookcentre.com.au

# Current trainings

The methodology recorded in these books, systematically explores the integration of Steiner's Creative Speech with Michael Chekhov's psycho-physical technique for actors. It was developed by myself through the many cycles of my own training, the generations of students I have taught, and through years of research in my own artistic practice.

At the **Heartfire Centre for Speech and Drama**, based in Australia, the next generation of teachers and artists who are committed to the principles of this approach continue to evolve it further. They offer full-time trainings as well as shorter courses:

- for those seeking a spiritually based path for the art of speech and acting;
- for teachers of speech and drama in schools;
- for those seeking an embodied and artistic path of self-development.

After graduation, actors dedicated to the ongoing research in this methodology and the artistic demonstration of its fruits have the opportunity to join the **Heartfire Ensemble**.
Full details can be found on the Heartfire website:
www.heartfirecentre.com

**Performing Arts International**, based in the UK features the work of Sarah Kane. Over many years she has developed her own integration of the Steiner speech and Chekhov acting methodologies. Details of her work can be found on the website:
www.performingartsintl.org

# Bibliography


Dante Aligheri, *The Divine Comedy*, translated by Clive James, Picador, UK, 2013.

Gudrun Burkhard, *Biographical Work: The Anthroposophical Basis*, Floris Books, UK, 2007.

Michael Chekhov, *The Actor is the Theatre,* archival collection at the University of Windsor, https://collections.uwindsor.ca/chekhov/page/about

T.S. Eliot, *Four Quartets,* Faber and Faber, London, 1959.

Jane Gilmer, *The Alchemical Actor*, Leiden and Boston, Brill, The Netherlands, 2021.

John Jocelyn, *Meditations on the Signs of the Zodiac*, Steinerbooks, New York, 2006.

Margaret Jonas, *Astronomy and Astrology: finding a relationship to the cosmos.* Compiled and edited from the work of Rudolf Steiner, Rudolf Steiner Press, UK. 2009.

Rudolf Steiner, *Occult Science*, Rudolf Steiner Press, London, 1972, particularly Chapter 4, 'Man and the Evolution of the World'.

Rudolf Steiner, *Speech and Drama*, Rudolf Steiner Anthroposophical Publishing Company, London, 1959.

Rudolf Steiner, *Spiritual Beings in the Heavenly Bodies and the Kingdoms of Nature*: Ten lectures given in Helsinki in 1912, Anthroposophic Press, New York, 1992.

Rudolf Steiner, *Spiritual Hierarchies*: Ten lectures given in Düsseldorf in 1909, Anthroposophic Press, New York, 1931.

Rudolf and Marie Steiner, *Creative Speech*, Rudolf Steiner Press, London, 1978.

Judith Wright, *Collected Poems*, Angus and Robertson, Sydney, 1994.

Jane Ahlquist, *Astrology: History and Purpose,* Unicorn House, 2015.

# Practice texts from plays

In order of appearance
Shakespeare:
*Hamlet, Macbeth, King Lear, Romeo and Juliet, Taming of the Shrew, Coriolanus, Twelfth Night, A Midsummer Night's Dream, The Merchant of Venice, Cymbeline, As you like it, King John*

In order of appearance
Others:
*Equus*, Peter Shaffer
*Four Mystery Plays*, Rudolf Steiner
*The Importance of Being Earnest*, Oscar Wilde
*Androcles and the Lion*, Bernard Shaw
*The Doll's House*, Henrik Ibsen
*The Trojan Women* and *The Bacchae*, Euripides,
*The Bear, The Cherry Orchard, The Three Sisters*, Anton Chekhov,
*The Lady's not for Burning, The Dark is Light Enough*, Christopher Fry
*The One Day of the Year*, Alan Seymour
*The House of Bernarda Alba*, Federico García Lorca
*The Angel that Troubled the Waters*, Thornton Wilder

# Practice texts from poems

In order of appearance
'The Wattle Tree' and 'Legend', Judith Wright
(Thanks to Harpers Collins Publishers Australia Pty Ltd for permission to reprint these poems from *Collected Poems*, Judith Wright)
'Morte d'Arthur' and 'The Lotos-Eaters', Alfred, Lord Tennyson
'Ode to the West Wind', Percy Bysse Shelley
'I would enkindle every human being', and the 'Foundation Stone Meditation', Rudolf Steiner
*Four Quartets*, TS Eliot
'The Prelude' and 'Ode on the Intimations of Immortality', William Wordsworth
'When I was a memory in the egg', author unknown[106]
'I am not yet born', Louis Macneice
'How like an angel', Thomas Traherne
'Fern Hill', Dylan Thomas

'The Scholar Gypsy', Mathew Arnold
'The Shepherd's Hymn', Richard Crashaw
'Song of a man who has come through', DH Lawrence
'As Kingfishers Catch Fire', Gerard Manley Hopkins

# List of Illustrations

## Original artworks

The opening colour plates, *Creative Speech transforms the human larynx into a grail cup* and *Eurythmy integrates the human ether body with the life that sustains the universe*, along with *The planetary beings pour their soul capacities into the human soul* in Chapter 5 are original works created by Raphaela Mazzone for the *Actor of the Future* series.

All other illustrations in *Between Earth and Heaven* are original life-drawings by Raphaela Mazzone based on the Speech Eurythmy of Diane Tatum, and Speech Formation and Chekhov techniques demonstrated by Dawn Langman.

## Other artworks

*Sheela na gig* in Château de Caen, France.
*Sheela na gig* in the Church of St Mary and St David, Kilpeck, Herefordshire.
*Scene from Aristophanes' Birds,* (end of fifth century BCE) in the collection of the J. Paul Getty Museum, Malibu, California.
*Dramatic mask*, Carl Milles, Royal Dramatic Theatre, Stockholm, Sweden.
*Theatre mask of a First Slave in Greek comedy*, second century BCE, National Archaeological Museum of Athens.
*The Representative of Humanity*, Rudolf Steiner, in Goetheanum, Dornach, Switzerland.
*Being of World Humour,* detail of *The Representative of Humanity*, Rudolf Steiner, in Goetheanum, Dornach, Switzerland.
*Samuel Beckett*, drawings by Raphaela Mazzone showing Beckett in two modes inspired by portraits of Samuel Beckett.
*Study of Christ for the Last Supper*, Leonardo da Vinci, in Pinacoteca di Brera, Milano, Italy.
*The Comedy Illuminating Florence*, Domenico di Michelino, in Cathedral of Santa Maria del Fiore, Florence, Italy.
*The Representative of Humanity*, Rudolf Steiner, in Goetheanum, Dornach, Switzerland.
*Figures of Lucifer,* details from *The Representative of Humanity*, Rudolf Steiner, in Goetheanum, Dornach, Switzerland.

*Figures of Ahriman*, study and detail from *The Representative of Humanity*, Rudolf Steiner, in Goetheanum, Dornach, Switzerland.

*The I AM*, detail from *The Representative of Humanity*, Rudolf Steiner, in Goetheanum, Dornach, Switzerland.

*Christ in the centre is surrounded by symbols of the Four Evangelists*, in Church of St Trophime, Arles, France.

*The Ptolemaic view of the universe*, in Petri Apiani cosmographia, per Gemmam Phrysium, apud Louanienses medicum ac mathematicum insignem, restituta : additis de adem re ipsius Gemmae Phry. libellis, ut sequens pagina docet, Vaeneunt Antuerpiae : in pingui gallina Arnoldo Berckmanno, 1539.

*The Empyrean* (highest heaven), Gustave Doré, from the illustrations to *The Divine Comedy*.

*Melencolia I*, Albrecht Dürer, in Art Gallery of New South Wales, Sydney, Australia.

*The voyage of life: childhood*, Thomas Cole, 1842, in National Gallery of Art, Washington D.C, USA.

*The voyage of life: youth*, Thomas Cole, 1842, in National Gallery of Art, Washington D.C, USA.

*The voyage of life: manhood*, Thomas Cole, 1842, in National Gallery of Art, Washington D.C, USA.

*The voyage of life: old age*, Thomas Cole, 1842, in National Gallery of Art, Washington D.C, USA.

*Venus of Willendorf*, in Naturhistorisches Museum in Vienna, Austria.

*Priapus of Ephesus*, in Ephesus Archaeological Museum, Selçuk, Turkey.

*God thinks Adam, God creates Adam*, Chartres Cathedral, Chartres, France.

# Notes

1   In Lecture 11 of the *Speech and Drama Course*.

2   Bibliography or reading list: For a thorough exploration of the relationship between taste and articulation refer to *Healing Sounds: Fundamentals of Chirophonetics* by Alfred Bauer, Rudolf Steiner College Press, 1993.

3   In *Fundamentals of Chirophonetics*, in addition to the tastes of sweet, sour and bitter, Alfred Bauer explores the therapeutic applications of the speech placements connected with the tastes of milk and salt. Till now I have not found a way to explore these last two in relation to artistic expression, hence the suggestion made here. This is an area for further research.

4   From 'The Two Fires' 1955, *Collected Poems*, Judith Wright.

5   There have been many attempts to translate this meditation. Like all attempts each one falls short in some respect even as it manages in others. The version printed here was translated by Cecil Harwood and John Davy. One of its limitations lies in the pre-feminist exclusive use of English masculine nouns and pronouns to render the German 'mensch' which invokes more of the sense of humanity or the human being. I have therefore made some alterations which I hope remove what may otherwise make it more difficult to access for current readers. A second limitation is the reversion to archaic English forms of 'thee', 'thou' etc. However, I have decided that while these expressions may sound outdated and smack of past religious sensibilities they do still invoke a sacred dimension of the self and other of which 'you' and 'your' have been divested. As a text for speakers, the rhythm of this translation flows easily and invites the engagement of the centres and their corresponding placements.

6   Quoted from Michael Chekhov's *To the Actor*, page 138.

7   Refer to the classic reference *The Golden Bough* by Frazer. For an excellent imaginative reconstruction of this ancient consciousness, refer to Mary Renault's novel *The King Must Die*. Edouard Schuré's *The Genesis of Tragedy* and *The Sacred Drama of Eleusis* are excellent attempts to recreate from the known fragments an imaginative vision of the esoteric origins of theatre in the mysteries of Eleusis and its subsequent development. In *Drama Myth and Psyche*, Michele Langman also explores  this metamorphosis from the ritual of blood into a sacrament of consciousness.

8   Aristotle *Poetics 1 with The Tractatus Coislinianus, A Hypothetical Reconstruction of Poetics 2*, translated by Richard Janko, Hackett Publishing Company, Indianapolis/Cambridge, 1987.

9   Lecture 14, *Speech and Drama Course*.

10  'Villein' was the term used in the mediaeval feudal system to denote a peasant, tenant farmer who owed allegiance to the lord of his manor. It is easy to see that this class of human beings were the ones by whom, had they lost the fear of punishment, those in power would have felt most threatened.

11  An English translation of the Anglo-Saxon description of the monster Grendel in *Beowulf*.

12  See disc 1 of DVD series for a performance of this scene. See appendix E for details.

13  These were handed down in oral form for many centuries and only written down sometime in the fifteenth century CE.

14  Old Testament: Deuteronomy 33:27.

15  These further differentiations do not appear in *To the Actor* but can be found in archival material from Chekhov's time at Dartington, edited by Deidre Hurst du Prey. For those wanting further information see the link for the archival collection at the University of Windsor in the Bibliography.

16  For further information about Chekhov's impulse in clowning, contact Marjolein Baars, who has done extensive work in this area. See also endnote 25.

17  Euripides' *The Bacchae* translated by Philip Vellacott. Penguin Classics. 1954.

18  Revelation of St John.

19  This image is taken from St John's apocalyptic vision of the End of Time.

20  See Chekhov's *To the Actor*, Chapter 9: 'Different Types of Performances', page 141 in the original 1953 English edition, Harper and Row Publishers, New York.

21  If you are not familiar with it, descriptions can be accessed online as well as video clips that show it in action.

22  See note 20 above.

23  Puck, *A Midsummer Night's Dream*.

24  *A Midsummer Night's Dream*. Act 2, scene 1.

25  I refer the reader to the work of my Dutch colleague, Marjolein Baars. Based in Amsterdam, she has taught and performed internationally, also developing the application of Chekhov's methodology to clowning in the context of the social arts. She has focused now for many years on the training of practitioners to work with sufferers from dementia. She is the founder of Tiny Hero Productions and has received an EU grant to pursue this research, https://tinyhero.nl/.

26  Quoted from the final chorus of *Oedipus Tyrannus*.

27  The Greeks called her Melpomene.

28  In the comic mantra this vowel appears in its long form in the stressed syllables of 'hurly burly'. However, in such unstressed syllables as 'whispers', the spoken vowel is somewhere between the long vowel /ɜ/ and the schwa or English neutral vowel /ə/ which is the short form arising from the same placement in the mouth.

29  The Greeks called her Thalia.

30  This last expression is one of the famous 'malapropisms' from Sheridan's comedy of manners *The Rivals*.

31  See Oscar Wilde, *The Importance of Being Earnest*. Bunbury is the imaginary friend whose illness can always be invoked as the excuse for a visit that allows one to avoid doing something one doesn't want to do.

32  Deuteronomy 33:27.

33  Steiner's first *Mystery Drama*, scene 6.

34  There will be a more detailed study of Beckett's significance, in the chapter on our modern age in *The Actor of the Future 4: One More Time*.

35  The Globe theatre in London was constructed as an image of this world. The Chorus in Shakespeare's *Henry V* calls it 'this wooden O'.

36  TS Eliot quotes Julian of Norwich at the end of *Four Quartets*.

37  See the Book of Revelation by St John.

38  In another view on the etymology, Athenaeus of Naucratis (2nd–3rd century CE) says that the original form of the word was *trygodia* from *trygos* (grape harvest) and *ode* (song), because tragedies were first performed during grape harvest.

39  The gates having been burst asunder when Christ, as his first deed following the crucifixion, descended into Hell to lead those who were willing to salvation.

40  Coleridge, *Biographia Literaria*.

41  Shakespeare, *Hamlet*.

42  Shakespeare, *A Midsummer Night's Dream*.

43  It was for this reason that initiation in the ancient mysteries demanded neophytes to undergo rigorous preparation for each stage of enlightenment.

44  A list of additional Steiner works that provide detailed insights into the following:
- Elemental Spirits: *Man as Symphony of the Creative Word*, Rudolf Steiner Press, Sussex, England, 1991.
- Greek Gods: *Wonders of the World, Ordeals of the Soul and Revelations of the Spirit*, Rudolf Steiner Press, London, 1963.
- Hierarchical beings; angels, archangels etc: *Spiritual Beings in the Heavenly Bodies and in the Kingdom of Nature*, Anthroposophic Press, NY, 1992.
- Souls of the dead, ranging from ghosts who are still bound in regions of the lower astral world to those who have progressed further: *Between Death and Rebirth. Theosophy* for a detailed description of the stages of Kama Loka and beyond.
- The working of karma and reincarnation into human character: *Karmic Relationships: Esoteric Studies* vols 1-8, Rudolf Steiner Press, London, 1955–1972.

45  *A Midsummer Night's Dream*: Act 3, scene 1.

46  Refer to Steiner's *Occult Science*, lecture cycles such as *The Fifth Gospel*, *The Incarnation of Ahriman*, *The Fall of the Spirits of Darkness*.

47  Steiner, fourth *Mystery Drama*.

48  See Blake, 'Night'.

49  TS Eliot, *Four Quartets*.

50  It is important to realise that the spirit presences inhabiting the realms of the *Commedia* are not symbols or images constructed by Dante in accordance with poetic convention. He is describing his experience of the ongoing participation of these spirits in his consciousness. As Virgil was to Dante, so has Shakespeare been to me and many others. In the same way I too can sense the ongoing presence of those who have been my guiding spirits while they lived on earth and since their deaths; whether intimate or distant, in the body still or not, whether related to me personally or through their influence on the age in which I live, or ages long since passed. Whatever the circumstances and challenges, resolved or unresolved, these beings compose the supersensible material through which my soul and spirit must continually sift in order to extract the lessons I am here to learn. And in doing so, I sense that my sustained relationship with them and engagement with their journeys, in turn, contributes to their further evolution; as Dante's does to Virgil's and the other characters with whom he interacts.

51  See Gospel of John 14:2.

52  From T.S. Eliot, *Four Quartets*: 'The  Dry Salvages'.

53  To have this experience we must first be guided to experience these gestures by a teacher of eurythmy. By eurythmic consciousness I mean 1. that we begin to sense our own life/etheric body and how it weaves within the cosmic life/etheric and 2. that our soul experience belongs to a vaster tapestry of feeling and perception than the range of our everyday sensations and emotions.

54  Quoted from Wordsworth, 'Tintern Abbey'.

55  From Dante Aligheri, 'Purgatorio', canto 30, translation by Clive James.

56  From the first of T.S. Eliot's *Four Quartets*: 'Burnt Norton'.

57  I have chosen to focus on the diphthong /aɪ/ (l<u>i</u>fe) as it manifests in SRP (standard received pronunciation of the English language).  As discussed in *The Art of Speech* the English language manifests a very flexible relationship to all the vowels, and each of the pure placements can transform into a range of diphthongs. In the German language there is a form of this diphthong that is closer to the SRP diphthong English speakers would identify as /eɪ/ (d<u>a</u>te) as well as the more open form of /aɪ/ (l<u>i</u>fe). Within the context of this exploration there is a rich field for research to be followed up that looks at the implications for our experience

within this Moon sphere of the diphthong that arises as a result of the planetary beings of Mars handing over their activity to the planetary beings of Mercury compared with the handing over of activity from the Venus beings to those of Mercury.  Far more important than any dogmatic idea of right or wrong designation or pronunciation is the realisation that the range of vowels in practice can be as infinitely nuanced as our soul experience which continues to evolve in ever more complexity.  Most importantly, through this kind of exploration we can recognise that these evolving nuances are no more arbitrary than the vowel shifts. However unconsciously they may occur in the human beings who speak them, they are the gift of the planetary beings whose own more complex interactions in our souls make possible these more complex nuances within our souls.

58  Not the same Romeo of Shakespeare's play.

59  From the opening line of Milton's 'Paradise Lost'.

60  St Paul adopted the Greek word *agape* to denote the love that does not stem from blood and family or from sexual attraction or any natural sympathy, but the unconditional love that God has for all aspects of creation and that human beings can evolve towards. It is a love that devotes itself to serve the further evolution of the other.

61  I was intrigued to find that the Clive James translation of the question differs from the other three I have consulted and which all reverse the question as below.

> *Laurence Binyon:*
> How a sweet seed bitter fruit may bear.
> *Dorothy Sayers:*
> How from sweet seed sour harvest can be had.
> *Longfellow:*
> How from sweet seed can bitter issue forth.

It was beyond me to find out if this was a typo or a conscious choice by James to re-interpret Dante differently. This caused me to consider that if it were the latter the conflicted understandings of the text might indeed arise from the very nature of the problem, in which each version of the question must imply the other.

62  The phrase 'corporeal or vegetative eye' was William Blake's way of distinguishing the means of 'seeing reality' afforded by the physical organ of sight and the imaginative vision that could penetrate the physical to see the reality beyond. 'I question not my Corporeal or Vegetative Eye any more than I would Question a Window concerning a Sight: I look thro it & not with it." William Blake from *The Last Judgement*.

63  In the Old Testament.

64  For our everyday perception, the pathway of the sun as it moves across the sky appears to rise each day in the east and move towards the west. However, in the yearly cycle of the sun that gives rise to the cycle of the seasons the sun appears to move on its ecliptic from the west towards the east.

65  Referring to the story of the widow's mite in The Gospel of St Luke, 21:1-4. Though the offering the widow makes to God is financially a pittance compared to the offerings of the rich, Christ says that her offering has far more value because she has given all she has.

66  In fact Dante is already exiled when he writes the poem but within the context of the poem he portrays his exile as something that still lies ahead.

67  In his *Philosophy of Freedom,* Steiner called this 'ethical individualism'.

68  King David from the Old Testament is one of the souls that Dante encounters in the sphere of Jupiter.

69  The asteroidal belt orbiting the sun, is situated roughly in between the orbits of Mars and Jupiter

[70] Shakespeare, *The Tempest*.

[71] Thinking of the planets in this way, by now we should be aware that when shame combines with violence towards the self it is the interaction in our souls of the Mars forces with those of Jupiter.

[72] A phrase referring to God the Father from the Book of Daniel in the Old Testament which was the inspiration for one of William Blake's most famous paintings.

[73] In the Ptolemaic system, the region of the Primum Mobile was the last of the concentric spheres that still appeared to move around the earth before the beyond-space-time Empyrean. As the last sphere of the physical universe, it is moved directly by God, and all the spheres that it encloses are caused to move by its motion.

[74] The 'midnight hour' is the name Steiner gives to that moment when, after death, each human spirit has completed its ascent through the planetary spheres and in the realm of Saturn, with the help of the highest hierarchies, turns its gaze towards the earth again and begins preparing its descent into its next incarnation.

[75] The Christian virtue hope has been explored in the Mercury sphere through the character of Romeo who, though he lost his temporal status, retained his hope in things eternal. It is interesting that the text that inspired Tallis's composition was taken from the Old Testament Book of Judith:

> '*Spem in alium nunquam habui*
> *Praeter in te, Deus Israel …*
> I have never placed my hope
> In any other than you, God of Israel …'

and that Dante places Judith in the Empyrean, among the souls who dwell in the mystic rose, the abode of God.

[76] This poem dedicated to Maisie Jones was found amongst her papers after her death. Efforts to find the author proved unsuccessful. Any information regarding the author would be welcomed.

[77] William Ricketts: a remarkable sculptor who created a sanctuary in the Dandenong Ranges outside of Melbourne. One of the first white Australians to recognise what Western consciousness could learn from the Indigenous/First Nation peoples, his sculptures celebrate their relationship to an earth of living spirit.

[78] A detailed exploration of the planetary qualities in relation to child development has been undertaken by Susan Laing and can be found in her website.
https://www.creativelivingwithchildren.com/the-profiles/background-information-to-the-development-profiles/
Although her explorations focus on child development, the qualities and behaviours described also illuminate the manifestation of planetary qualities in adults.

[79] Based on the image provided in *The Human Life* by George and Gisela O'Neill and Florin Lowndes. Published by Mercury Press 1990 USA.

[80] Shakespeare, *King Lear*.

[81] Dylan Thomas, 'Do not go gently into that good night'.

[82] Vincent van Gogh wrote a letter to his brother Theo on 10 July 1888, in which he wondered: 'Why, I say to myself, should the spots of light in the firmament be less accessible to us than the black spots on the map of France. Just as we take the train to go to Tarascon or Rouen, we take death to go to a star. What's certainly true in this argument is that while *alive*, we *cannot* go to a star, any more than once dead we'd be able to take the train. So it seems to me not impossible that cholera, the stone, consumption, cancer are celestial means of locomotion, just as steam-

boats, omnibuses and the railway are terrestrial ones. To die peacefully of old age would be to go there on foot.'

83 Mamilius in *The Winter's Tale*; Macduff's children in *Macbeth*.

84 The author is aware that even this division is a complex issue with many variations and degrees of variation. Nevertheless, at the time of writing, broadly speaking most human beings still identify with a male or female body, the form of which expresses the masculine or feminine tendencies.

85 Geoff is based in East Grinstead, Sussex and is one of the significant second-generation pioneers of Speech Formation in the English language. He has toured internationally as an actor, speaker and director in drama and eurythmy projects. He works also as a freelance teacher and trainer of Speech Formation.

86 See also *The Spear Thrower*, Peter Bridgemont.

87 Apollo was one name given by the Ancient Greeks to the god or being of the sun. Therefore connecting the Apollonian polarity of form, with the Spirits of Wisdom, whose activity is centred in the sphere of Jupiter, seems to contradict Steiner's insight that the sun sphere is the centre of activity of the Exusiai or Spirits of Form.

So long as such ideas are only abstract concepts it is easy to dogmatically attach the exclusive connection of one specific function to one specific hierarchy. However, our phenomenological approach to vowels and diphthongs allows us to explore ideas like these experientially. In this way we begin to sense how the planetary spheres are not discreet but interpenetrating regions of activity. Eurythmy and Creative Speech allow us to experience how each hierarchy works together with the others, in different and ever-changing combinations, to make their soul capacities available to human beings. The full-bodied gestures and the micro-gestures in the mouth of the diphthong /aʊ/ (out) [ sun sphere] and vowel /ɔː/ (awe) [Jupiter sphere] reveal just such cooperation. We can gain some sense of this if we explore the mantric syllable revered in sacred rituals of the East sometimes spoken as the AUM, sometimes OM (see page 85, *The Art of Speech*).

Explored from this perspective we can recognise how AUM and OM reveal the intimate co-operation of the spirits of form (sun sphere) and spirits of wisdom (Jupiter sphere). When we speak both syllables we can experience how each contains the other. The /ɔː/ (awe) placement in the  mouth holds the centre through which the gesture of the diphthong passes as it makes its journey from the furthest back beginning of the /ɑː/ (st*a*r), 'crossing sky and earth', to reach its destination in the furthest forward placement of the /uː/ (tr*ue*). If we experience this movement in the mouth with our whole body of sensation then we feel how the forming power of Jupiter's embrace is what draws the Sun to make the journey of the diphthong possible; encompassing the future in the past, the end in the beginning. Their cooperation teaches us that whatever tries to form, must be penetrated by the wisdom that knows and values all aspects of the life it seeks to form, including the processes that must unfold in time. Without such wisdom form will impose itself and crush that life.

88 There are several anecdotes recounting how Michelangelo, frustrated that he could not achieve the perfection he demanded of himself, would smash his sculptures. One of the most famous examples was the report by his students of how they had to drag him away from the statue now known as *The Deposition* to prevent its further destruction.

89 Quoted from 'Dejection: An Ode', Coleridge.

90 We are still working with the classical conception of the solar system.

91 Steiner called this current age in which we are presently evolving the age of the 'consciousness' or 'spiritual soul'. It manifested first in the cultural changes that led to the Renaissance

and will continue to evolve for the next two thousand years or so. A detailed exploration of this theme of evolution in our culture will be central to the final volume in this series: *The Actor of the Future 4: One More Time*.

92  Throughout these books I have drawn attention many times to the fact that this methodology is not a fixed technique based on a fixed set of conclusions. It is a research methodology that allows us to investigate artistic questions knowing the understanding of our answers will continue to evolve as our experience expands and deepens.

93  We must wait for *The Actor of the Future 4: One More Time* to consider how the advent of these newer planetary influences, reflected in the shift in impulse that can be easily discerned in what has taken place in Western culture since the Renaissance, might in turn be related to the greater cosmic cycles of activity connected to the starry beings of the zodiac. According to this cosmic view of history, the responsibility to inspire the culture epoch that would develop from circa 1413 CE, was transferred from the starry beings of the constellation Aries, whose task it had been to guide the epoch that had been unfolding since circa 800 BCE, to the guiding powers of the constellation Pisces. Under their guidance, human consciousness will continue to evolve for the next approximately two millennia.

94  I use the term to distinguish the sensational, predictive, more fatalistic level of astrology, as promulgated in popular weekly magazines, from the work of such astrologers as Robert Powell, Liz Greene, Jane Ahlquist, Richard Tarnas, Robert Hand, and Paul Platt, who encourage our capacities to take responsibility for our maturing souls in cooperation with the cosmic influences.

95  Jane Gilmer, *The Alchemical Actor,* Leiden and Boston, Brill, 2021.

96  The word 'alembic' is an alchemical term for one of the vessels (very often made of glass) in which alchemists subjected substances to purifying processes.

97  Such a complex cyclic interaction is revealed for example in TS Eliot's *Four Quartets*. This is a meditation that moves intentionally through each element in turn. Yet even as one element provides the focus and fundamental ethos of each meditation, all four elements and transformation processes are constantly in conversation with and weaving through each other.

98  It is significant that in the decades that immediately followed the discovery of Uranus in 1781, a number of the great Romantic artists explored the story of Prometheus. It is as though this being sought to orbit close again in order to engage with human consciousness. The most well-known works created at this time within his field of energy were Goethe's 1774 poem, 'Prometheus', Beethoven's 1801 music for the ballet 'Creatures of Prometheus' (of which the overture is most well-known), Schubert's 1819 art song 'Prometheus' based on Goethe's poem, Mary Shelley's 1816-18 *Frankenstein* (which she subtitled 'The Modern Prometheus') and Shelley's *Prometheus Unbound* begun in 1818 and published in 1820.

99  Scientists are still debating.

100  It is well established now that when we suppress our pain, we also suppress our capacity to feel our other feelings.

101  There are many variations in the details of the different versions of the myth that tells the story of the centaur Chiron. But the central thread that weaves through all of them is that after conception he had been abandoned by his father, the God Cronus (or Saturn from the generation of the Titans), who had taken the form of a stallion in order to impregnate the nymph who had turned herself into a horse in order to escape his pursuit. At Chiron's birth he was rejected also by his mother who was horrified that she had given birth to a creature that was part horse and part human being. However, the child was fostered by the god Apollo who taught him the arts and in particular the art of healing, which enabled him to transform the animal aspect of his

nature so that he could teach and heal his fellow creatures. At some point while Chiron was instructing Hercules in the use of poison-dipped arrows, Hercules was forced to fight a battle in which he shot many of these arrows. Inadvertently one of them pierced Chiron's thigh. Although he pulled out the arrow and treated his wound with healing herbs and all his skills, he could not heal it. The wound could never heal but because he was immortal Chiron could never die. Then Zeus agreed to accept that Chiron would replace Prometheus and free him from his suffering in Tartarus. Chiron, by agreeing to sacrifice his immortality, can eventually die and thus be freed from suffering.

[102] I suggest that the artistic freedom to colour the characteristically more sharp edged vowel /ɛ/ (gentle) and diphthong /eɪ/ (rain) in this passage with the more spacious and therefore softer surface area of /ɛə/ (air) will convey Shakespeare's intention movingly. This is a clear example of how we can move beyond a pedantic adherence to the vowel, as it presents itself in written form, to sense how a certain vowel experience can be used artistically to colour other vowels.

[103] Reference to Gerard Manley Hopkins, 'The Blessed Virgin Mary Compared to the Air We Breathe'.

[104] Ted Toadvine, *Singing the World in a New Key: Merleau-Ponty and the Ontology of Science*, published by Janus Head, 2004. Ted Toadvine is Professor of Philosophy and Environmental Studies and a Participating Faculty member of the Comparative Literature Department at the University of Oregon. He served as Head of the Department of Philosophy in 2011–2014.

[105] The capitals are used to distinguish Steiner's application of these terms from their common use.

[106] See note 76.